CATHERINE OF ARAGON AND HER FRIENDS

by

JOHN E. PAUL

FORDHAM UNIVERSITY PRESS
NEW YORK

FORDHAM UNIVERSITY PRESS

BRONX, NEW YORK 10458

First published 1966

CATHERINE OF ARAGON
Portrait by Miguel Sittow, probably painted soon after
Catherine came to England.

TO
MY MOTHER

Contents

Illustrations

Foreword

THE following pages tell the story of Catherine of Aragon and her friends, and the story commences almost from the moment of her arrival in this country. In telling it, the term "friend" has been used in a wide sense: it applies, for example, to Catherine's personal friends, to prominent members of her suite at different times over the years, to some of the great humanists, to her counsellors at the divorce trial, and, apart from those counsellors, who were all clerics, to certain important secular priests and members of religious orders. In stating this classification here, there is inevitably some overlapping. On the other hand, the figures actually introduced in the book do not constitute an exhaustive list: to have written, for instance, about all the members of Catherine's suite at various times, even if their names were always known, would have resulted in nothing much more than a short catalogue, since they played no significant part in the story.

Although the book is in no sense a life of Queen Catherine, sufficient of the background of her life has been described, so that there may be a valid appreciation of the activities of her friends in relation to Catherine herself. In particular, a chapter on the Divorce and the chief effects of it on her existence has been included. For practically all the important information about Catherine and Princess Mary original authorities have been consulted, including some Spanish material, but two modern works which have been useful should be mentioned: the late Dr Garrett Mattingly's *Catherine of Aragon*, which is a sympathetic study of the Queen, and Miss H. F. M. Prescott's splendid and scholarly *Mary Tudor*.

I have felt it essential to have chapters on Fisher and More, not because there is anything very new to say about these great figures, but because to have made only passing references to them would have created an unforgivable gap, since they were two of the greatest of Catherine's friends. But I have tried to give no more than a short account of their relationship to the Queen and her cause.

It remains to be stated, what indeed is obvious and generally acknowledged, that probably no queen in English history needed friends, or deserved them, to the same extent as did Catherine of Aragon in the grim fate that overtook her.

I am deeply grateful to Dr J. J. Scarisbrick for giving me the idea of writing about the members of Queen Catherine's suite—an idea which I was able to expand into the subject now reflected in the title—and for his kindness in reading the typescript. I also wish to thank all those who have in any way shown their interest and given me encouragement. I am especially grateful to Captain Jack Buchanan-Tinker, M.C., Professor Paul Skwarczynski, Abbot Aelred Sillem of Quarr Abbey and my other friends there, the Rev. Francis Edwards, S.J., Mr E. E. Reynolds and Mr and Mrs Carpenter Turner. Lastly, but no no means least, I am much indebted to Mrs B. E. Downs for so efficiently preparing the typescript.

J.E.P.

Part I

THE EARLIER YEARS

CHAPTER 1

Catherine of Aragon Arrives: London and the Welsh Marches

I

IN OCTOBER 1501 a young Spanish princess reached the shores of the pleasant land of Devon. She was Catherine of Aragon and had come to England for her marriage to Prince Arthur of Wales. Her arrival was a momentous event.

Catherine, now nearly sixteen years of age, was the youngest child of Ferdinand of Aragon and Isabella of Castile, and Arthur, the eldest son of Henry VII and Elizabeth of York, was little more than fifteen. The arrival was the consummation of a long train of negotiations which had commenced in 1488 and which had for their object a marriage alliance, in an age prodigal of royal marriage alliances, between England and one of the greatest of European powers. Spain had become a nation of the first rank, and had achieved its strong, centralized power, involving the union of the kingdoms of Aragon and Castile, by the tenacity and courage of its two rulers and by reforms just and unjust, and sometimes unscrupulously carried out. It had driven the Moors from their mountain strongholds, the intrepid Queen Isabella capturing their capital, Granada; it had sent its ships across the seas in search of great new wealth; it had created and made durable its large, formidable armies.

The new marriage alliance was important to both Spain and England, since it provided for Spain an ally against its ambitious rival, France, and for England a strong friend among the growing sovereign European states, thus helping to maintain and increase the stability of the new Tudor dynasty, and to put an end, it was hoped, to the machinations of pretenders. The first Tudor, who

3

was in many ways the last of the English mediaeval monarchs rather than the first of modern kings, had accomplished a considerable task: he had fortified the English kingship from the essential qualities of mediaeval kingship, and after the turmoil of so much of the second part of the fifteenth century, he had ensured what most Englishmen wanted—the restoration and maintenance of order and justice and an abiding internal peace. He had, also, by the time of Catherine's arrival, accumulated a vast fortune as a firm basis of his power. In short, he was now able to face on almost equal terms the strong united monarchy of Ferdinand and Isabella; and the alliance of England with Spain, despite many anxious moments before its conclusion and royal perfidies afterwards, was to endure for nearly forty years, and to be of paramount importance in the direction of England's foreign policy.

Catherine had had a disturbed journey to this country. Her departure had been delayed, first by an attack of fever and then by a sudden, though local, Moorish rising which her father, Ferdinand, had been obliged to put down, so that he could not accompany her to the coast. Nor could Queen Isabella be with her all the way. The journey through Spain began in May and continued across much flat, arid land and sometimes hilly or mountainous country, often in blistering heat. Then, after the embarkation at Corunna, there had been such fierce hurricanes from the turbulent Bay of Biscay that the Princess's sea captains had been compelled to put back to Spain. They embarked again in September, this time from Laredo; but even then their troubles were not over, for, off Brittany, shattering storms arose, so that great fear came upon Catherine and the whole of her retinue. She eventually reached Plymouth on the afternoon of 2 October 1501.

Ample preparations to receive Catherine had been made not only in Plymouth but also in all the towns and villages through which she passed. The way across south-west and southern England to London was made by easy stages, and she was able to note with her vigilant, intelligent eyes the nature of the new land which, for the next thirty-five years—more than half the span of a long life for those times—was to be her home till her death. It was a fair land, now mellowed by the breath of autumn, and differing markedly from much of her own country, with its infertile plateaux and the bare, mountainous nature of other parts, differing, also, on the other hand, from the southern parts of Spain, with their olive groves and palms and vines, and cool gardens with their fountains and bright, heavily-scented flowers, and overhead, in summer, the deep blue of the sky. This new land had many rivers and shining streams and great areas of forest and woods. Around small towns and villages, which were generally dominated by exquisite parish churches and sometimes by massive castles, were the open fields and common pastures. The houses of the poor were mostly of wood, often with sills bearing rosemary, sage and other herbs, which served a useful as well as a decorative purpose. But the manor-houses of the nobles and greater gentry were luxurious residences made of timber or stone, and galleried, with pleasant oriel windows; great parks and enclosures surrounded them. Abbeys were numerous and, as Robert Aske was to say in the days of the religious troubles, were one of the beauties of the realm.

It was the English people at large, the folk she was to know and, as Queen, to see often, whom Catherine would have noted with an appraising eye as she passed through village after village on her slow progress. She must have observed the general fairness of their colouring which was in marked contrast to the dark hair and eyes of so many of her countrymen. They were for the most part goodly to look upon, well-proportioned and dressed becomingly in bright colours, simple folk in modest gowns, but also important people in luxuriant attire, despite the restrictions which sumptuary laws imposed, laws that were frequently ignored. The court dress of men often consisted of long robes of green velvet or red brocade and black velvet caps, decorated with one or more brooches or jewels, or else it consisted of tunics of red cloth, thickly padded, extending half-way down the leg, and they wore long hose and piked shoes. Gentlewomen had long trailing skirts of coloured velvet or cloth of gold, and over their hair, which was not generally seen, they wore caps, often of white linen, the hair being drawn together under kerchiefs.

They were a good-humoured race, these English people, but

B

they were insular and reserved, and their self-confidence was considerable. "They are great lovers of themselves", said an Italian visitor to this country a few years before Catherine came, "and of everything belonging to them; they think there are no other men than themselves, and no other world but England; and whenever they see a handsome foreigner, they say he looks like an Englishman." They were intelligent and quick at things to which they set their minds. They did not take easily to foreigners, these self-sufficient rather proud people, but from the first they loved this simple, dignified, fair young Spanish princess, and the affection she evoked from the country people now, and later from the people of London when she reached the capital, she retained to the end: they were her friends in anxious days.

Catherine met many of the gentry from the west country soon after her landing, and thenceforward the principal inhabitants of the towns and villages came, no doubt, to meet her on her leisurely journey to London. Before she reached the capital King Henry was making preparations to see her, and on 4 November, in bad weather, with heavy mists rising from the swollen Thames, he set out from his palace of Richmond and arrived at the village of Easthamsted. There Prince Arthur joined him. But a difficult situation faced them immediately, for the protonotary of Spain came from Catherine's entourage to explain that, by the strict command of the King's Most Catholic Majesty, the Princess was not to have any communication with Prince Arthur until the day of the marriage ceremony. This was an affront. Was not Henry King of England and was not Catherine Arthur's affianced bride? Henry consulted his council. They answered unequivocally: the marriage agreements were complete; the Princess was on English soil, and the commandment of her was in the power and at the disposition of the King of England.

Henry reached the village of Dogmersfield where Catherine was staying, surrounded by many nobles and ladies of Spain and by gentlemen and ladies of the district. Her council told the King that the Princess was resting. That was nothing. He would not be withstood. He would see the Princess, he said, even if she were in her bed. And so, after a short interval, the King and Catherine met, and goodly words were spoken in the native language of each—a strange proceeding enough, for, though Henry knew no Spanish and Catherine as yet no English, they both knew Latin; Catherine knew it well and Henry at least sufficiently. They were soon joined by Prince Arthur, and there were more speeches which, this time, were translated into Latin by a bishop, so that everyone understood what was spoken. After supper the Prince paid a social call of great courtesy to the Princess, who called for her minstrels, and all "solaced themselves with the disports of dancing".

We see in this episode an exemplification of the rigid etiquette governing the lives of well-bred, unmarried Spanish women which had long held sway. Nor is it difficult to see at work the severe, directing mind of the Princess's high-bred duenna, Doña Elvira Manuel, who, in the cramped and miserable atmosphere of Catherine's life at Durham House in London from 1502 onwards, was to be her vigilant guardian and, by force of circumstances, her only possible friend of any consequence. Catherine's enlightened mother bestowed on all her four daughters the benefits of Renaissance learning, and Vives, the great humanist and her countryman, was to break through and disperse that mist of mediaeval ignorance which had so long burdened women's minds. But the long and time-honoured Spanish tradition of protecting a young girl with almost claustral restrictions was not changed by even so enlightened an educationist as Vives, nor did he wish to change it; and Doña Elvira was in an unique position to make this centuries-old tradition almost undisturbedly observed.

The Princess's entry into London was triumphant. She came from Chertsey and Kingston to Lambeth and then to Southwark and London Bridge. At Kingston she had met the magnificent Duke of Buckingham, the richest and noblest lord in England, who came with three or four hundred of his retainers in the ducal livery of black and red.

London, with its inner suburbs, was a very beautiful city at this time, and Catherine with her eager glance would have noted the marked features of its outward charm. To William Dunbar, the Scottish poet, it had been, and it still was, "the flower of all cities, the seemliest in sight, a paradise of pleasure that held the throne of beauty". There were the imposing royal residences, the Tower, Whitehall and also Baynard's Castle, which Henry VII had rebuilt, and which was close to the great priory of the Black Friars, with the King's Wardrobe near by. There were the splendid houses of the bishops and merchants, some built of stone and others of timber, and often gilt and gabled; the important religious houses clustered in and around the city, with their thick orchards and cultivated gardens; the many steepled churches of the city, all dominated by the great church of St Paul's; whilst much to the west, in the distance, could be discerned the majestic mass of Westminster. In the city of London itself was the tangible evidence of mercantile prosperity, a prosperity as great as that of Venice: the splendid halls of the goldsmiths, haberdashers and vintners, and, in the busy precincts of St Martin-le-Grand, were the master goldsmiths, shoemakers and pouchmakers. There were the elegant, small, timbered dwellings of less important citizens, dwellings with painted black and white façades, the upper stories often leaning towards one another above narrow passages. There was the surpassing beauty of London Bridge, bearing the burden of its many elegant houses, whilst the Thames itself, the great highway of Engand, was a sea of masts and alive with traffic— large vessels from Venice and the Levant, laden with carpets and spices and wines, and gilded and coloured barges, and many wherries, moving awkwardly like gigantic beetles, and on its waters there was also a great, white, slowly-moving carpet of the King's swans.

At the Princess's coming to London Bridge she was entertained by a costly "pageant of corvin [Cordovan leather] work" and two maidens representing St Catherine and St Ursula came forth to deliver graceful speeches. She was richly apparelled, after the manner of her country. She wore a little hat of carnation colour, fashioned like a contemporary cardinal's hat and trimmed with gold lace. Her hair, which was fair auburn in colour, hung down on to her shoulders, and was held in a coif. Her hat was so fastened to her head that her hair from the middle of the head downwards could be seen.

Catherine had already met many of the great people of the realm and was to meet many more: it would take time to fix in her mind their real identity. Some would be Court figures when she became Queen and never much more than acquaintances; some would be her friends. Some whom she had met or would shortly meet would die before the coming of great trouble; others would desert her. One person whom she was not for a long time to meet had come specially to see her, leaving for the occasion a neighbouring monastery where he was learning Greek. He was a young man with keen, observant, humorous eyes, and he watched intently the procession into the city of the young Princess and her numerous attendants. Soon afterwards he made a record of what he saw: "You would have burst out laughing", he said of Catherine's Spanish escort, "if you had seen them, for they looked so ridiculous, tattered, barefooted, pigmy Ethiopians, like devils out of Hell". But as for Catherine, "everyone is singing her praises. There is nothing wanting in her that the most beautiful girl should have. May this most famous marriage be fortunate and of good omen for England." This young observer was to be a famous Englishman who never ceased to be devoted to Catherine. His name was Thomas More.

Catherine was married to Prince Arthur at St Paul's on 14 November 1501 by Archbishop Warham, before Henry VII and Queen Elizabeth and a great assembly of the bishops and abbots, and of nobles and gentlemen and their ladies. Among those ladies was a woman of royal blood, who was to be the greatest of all Catherine's friends. She was Lady Margaret Pole, whose husband, Sir Richard Pole, a prominent royal servant, had much to do with the marriage preparations in St Paul's, arranging, among other things, for the construction of a "hault place" in the nave, close to the consistory, and ensuring that the Archbishop was conveyed to it shortly before the coming of the Princess.

The entertainments after the marriage ceremony must have cost the careful Henry VII a moderate fortune, but he was never parsimonious where his royal importance could outwardly be enhanced and where he felt it necessary to impress the representatives of foreign courts. He had therefore ensured that those members of Catherine's suite returning to Spain would carry back a glowing account of all that had happened. There were ten consecutive days of entertainments of every kind—banquets, "disguisings", music, dancing, cards, dice, archery, pageants and tournaments. One magnificent banquet, "exceeding the price of any used in great seasons", lasted from seven in the evening till two in the morning. At the jousts the most resplendent figure was the Duke of Buckingham, who came in his great pavilion of white and green, borne by many of his servants dressed in the Buckingham livery of black and red. And Catherine met the royal children: Henry, Duke of York, then a fine boy of eleven, dancing with his elder sister Margaret. He danced in so goodly and pleasant a manner, we are told, that it gave the King and Queen singular delight. It was on this occasion, too, that Catherine met Mary, the youngest and most handsome of Henry VII's children, who was to become a close friend and whom she was to see frequently at Court in later days.

II

Catherine, now married to Prince Arthur, went to the Marches of Wales in December 1501. There had been a difference of opinion between the King and his council concerning the advisability of sending Catherine with the Prince, and the King had been undetermined about the matter for some days, but in the end he decided that she should go. She went with her large staff of Spanish attendants and servants, all under the surveillance of the Princess's duenna. Catherine was the undoubted wife of Arthur, but he was, even now, only fifteen years of age and not robust. The question therefore arose whether they should, for a time, not enter fully into the marriage state. Doña Elvira and her husband, Don Pedro Manrique, doubtless leading others of the Spanish retinue, believed that Ferdinand and Isabella preferred them not to do so at once, in view of Arthur's tender age, but Catherine's chaplain, Alessandro, with the approval of de Puebla, the Spanish ambassador, advised that they should. The definitive measures were taken by King Henry, who arranged that the youthful pair should not be separated nor have separate households.

Considerable preparations were made to receive the Prince of Wales and his young wife, though Arthur was not a stranger to the Marches and must have known something of their history. That history begins several centuries before the time of Henry VII. William the Conqueror and his Norman successors never succeeded in subduing Wales, which was a mountainous country and difficult to hold even if conquered. Instead of subjugating it, a long line of castles was placed along the country's borders as an insurance against invasion, and the castles were in the charge of the marcher lords, who were tenants-in-chief of the English crown, having many duties and ill-defined privileges. In this setting, an ambitious, unscrupulous marcher lord, necessarily far removed from the central government and difficult to control, could make an English king apprehensive.

To deal with the administration of the Marches a Council was actually inaugurated by Edward IV, but it was not made a permanent institution till the time of Henry VII. Edward IV created the council for his son, Edward, and a little later another council of considerable size and with wide powers was established. But it was Henry VII, a Welshman, anxious to improve the administration of Wales, who has the credit of definitely setting up the Council of the Marches, and it is possible that long before Arthur's marriage a council had been appointed for him as Prince of Wales, though complete proof of this is absent. In any case, he seems to have frequently visited Shrewsbury, one of the chief March towns, and to have been entertained there. When he actually went to the Welsh Marches with his young bride he had a council of ten, under the presidency of Dr William Smith, Bishop of Lincoln. Sir Richard Pole was an important member of the Council.

Pole, one of those typical administrators upon whom Henry VII constantly relied for stable rule, was a steady supporter of the new dynasty, of a rather middling order in the society of that day, loyal, efficient, hard-working. His family cannot be traced back

further than three generations, but it had the significant ramifica-
tion that Sir Richard himself, through his father's marriage, was
related to the King's mother, Margaret Beaufort, his own
mother's half-sister. Sir Richard's union with Margaret Pole,
daughter of George, Duke of Clarence, the brother of Edward IV,
and an undoubted Plantagenet, was not therefore so ill-assorted
a match as his comparatively unimportant origin, at least on the
paternal side, might imply; and we see here a particular instance
of the kind of marriage which would help to weld Lancastrian
and Yorkist interests in fortifying the Tudor dynasty. The
example of this, *par excellence*, was Henry VII's own union with
Elizabeth, the daughter of Edward IV, and Margaret Pole's first
cousin.

Soon after Henry VII's accession, Sir Richard Pole, no more
than a landed gentleman of small property in Buckinghamshire,
became an Esquire of the Body, probably in recognition of his
assistance to Henry in obtaining the crown at Bosworth. A little
later he was granted for life the office of Constable of the Castle
of Harlech and then made Sheriff of Merioneth. But the most
important office of all, and one which concerns us most, was that
of chamberlain to Prince Arthur, a post which he held at least
from 1493.

Margaret Pole, a tall, elegant woman of great dignity, and even
in old age still handsome, with eyes of singular beauty, was
married to Sir Richard Pole, probably in 1494. By that time Pole
was already the Prince's chamberlain, and his own and his wife's
association with the royal house thus began long before Catherine
of Aragon's arrival in England. When Catherine came, Margaret
Pole was almost a middle-aged woman by the measure of Tudor
days, for she was born two years before the commencement of
the last quarter of the fifteenth century and a few years after the
Wars of the Roses had so far exhausted themselves as to give her
uncle, Edward IV, the opportunity to achieve that degree of
security of the Crown which was an essential condition of more
resolute government. Her father's attainder had caused her
brother, Edward, the young Earl of Warwick, who was slightly
older than herself, to be dispossessed of all the properties to which

he was entitled; but he was brought up with Edward IV's children in the royal palace of Sheen, and it is reasonable to assume that Margaret was with them. After Edward IV's death, the boy earl received honourable treatment from Anne Neville, Richard III's queen and the sister of his own mother, but when she died in March 1485, he was confined to Sheriff Hutton, a Yorkist castle, and it is not improbable that his sister was there also. Henry VII treated him severely. The victor of Bosworth, always in fear of a potential, valid claimant to the throne, kept him in the Tower until an opportunity occurred to dispose of him by judicial murder in 1499. Margaret was of less political consequence to the first Tudor and we lose sight of her in official records until we hear of her marriage to Sir Richard Pole.

Margaret Pole, although the spouse of an experienced local royal servant, was not yet the distinguished noblewoman, court figure and wealthy landowner that she became in her widowhood many years later, with the restoration of vast estates. Sir Richard was, however, an important officer of Arthur's household, and it was at the royal residences of Ludlow and Bewdley—but chiefly at the former—that the Poles came into close contact with the young Tudor prince, and at one or other of those residences that probably their younger children were born—Geoffrey and Ursula, their only daughter, who was to marry Henry Stafford, the Duke of Buckingham's son and heir.

Ludlow, now shorn of its former splendour, was a magnificent castle of Norman origin, with an expansive Norman keep and strong, resistant Norman arches. It was built on a steep rock and gave full protection against marauding parties, except on that side where it unites with the town, from which it seems once to have been cut off by a wide ditch. Towards the north a picturesque view still opens out, a view of the winding of the Teme and of the Clee Hills and the hills near Stretton. It was here that Richard Plantagenet, Duke of York, Margaret Pole's great-uncle, had mostly lived, and it was Ludlow, the capital of Wales, but with an atmosphere essentially English, that Richard's son, Edward, Earl of March, afterwards Edward IV, regarded as his own town. Of all the strongly-fortified March towns, none gave stronger support to the Yorkist cause. Henry VII followed Edward IV's example in sending his son Arthur to Ludlow as Prince of Wales, and it was here that Arthur's small court was formed and here that his father came to see him during the rest of his short life.

We can only imagine something of the business events and social scenes of those long cold days during Catherine's sojourn at Ludlow in the winter of 1501-2, for there are few surviving records about them. She would have become acquainted with some of the Welsh worthies upon whose loyalty Henry VII had depended, and still depended, especially people like Rhys ap Thomas, "Father Rhys", now over fifty, a great landowner of south-west Wales, who had assisted Henry to the Crown. These Welsh chieftains and officials would have come often with the Poles and members of the Princess's council to Arthur and Catherine in Ludlow's Great Hall—a hall hung, no doubt, with much arras and the Tudor arms and the arms of the Spanish royal house, and with trophies and the arms of the Welsh chiefs; and there Catherine with her Spanish attendants would have heard, in wonderment but not understanding, the telling of some of those great legends of which the Welsh were so proud: *The Weird Witch of the Wood and Grimalkin her Cat*; or *The Mountain Bard*, who did not mix with people in the busy world but dwelt alone in the high mountains of Snowdon and sang melodiously; or the *Legend of Merioneth*, where Sir Richard Pole was sheriff; or the *Sighs of Ulla*, which was a legend of Cadwallader.

But that winter was to close for Catherine in early sorrow, for in April 1502 Prince Arthur died at Ludlow, possibly of some form of consumption. His body was taken to Ludlow parish church in great procession, with Sir Richard Pole as chamberlain and other gentlemen going before it. The Prince's own arms were borne by Sir Griffiths ap Rhys, and eighty men carried torches. There were requiems and many ceremonies in the church. The body rested at Bewdley on its way from Ludlow for burial at Worcester, the way being made difficult by the ill conditions of the primitive roads—roads that were mere lanes of deep mud into which the long cortège of litters and carts and wagons plunged perilously. "On St. Mark's Day the procession went from Ludlow to

Bewdley. It was the foulest, cold, windy and rainy day and the worst way I have seen: yea, and in some places they were fain to taken oxen to draw the chair (car or chariot), so ill was the way."

Sir Richard Pole and some other members of the Prince's council wrote to the royal councillors at Greenwich, telling them of Arthur's death. The news was broken to the King in London by his confessor, a Franciscan Observant. And Lady Pole, we can scarcely doubt, gave all possible consolation to the bereaved young Princess.

CHAPTER 2

Doña Elvira and Fray Diego

I

THE DEATH of Prince Arthur was to make the greatest difference to Catherine's mode of existence, and her new life, with rare, short intervals spent at Court, was to last until the end of Henry VII's reign. It was, in any case, now imperative to remove Catherine from Ludlow, which was regarded by the Spanish monarchs as too unhealthy a place for their daughter. She returned to the English Court, but within a short time was compelled to live an increasingly unhappy life within the inhospitable walls of Durham House in the Strand. In the end she became deprived of almost the bare necessaries of life, and the egregiously mean diplomatic policies of Henry and Ferdinand—policies that were full of suspicion, often tortuous and sometimes malevolent—did nothing to relieve a desperate situation. Moreover, it is curious to note that Catherine, a highly intelligent person, was unable to speak English for years—at least, she informed King Ferdinand as late as April 1506 that she was unable to do so. She became immured in London with a reduced household of Spanish attendants and servants and with little contact with the outside world. And the measure of this lack of social intercourse is her protracted ignorance of English, an ignorance which must have constantly handicapped her, especially at Court, where she was probably obliged to converse in Latin. She does not appear at this time to have spoken much French, of which language King Henry, on the other hand, had a good knowledge.

The control of her household was in the competent, exacting hands of her duenna, Doña Elvira Manuel, descended from one of the most illustrious Castilian families. On her, Catherine implicitly relied for years, until she was found out and there was a fearful day of reckoning. Her authority was complete, for shortly after Catherine's return to London, Queen Isabella told the Spanish ambassador that he should protect Doña Elvira as being the Spanish monarch's deputy. He must countenance her in everything she desired to do, so that everyone might obey her. She should not be forced to give up one small part of the charge which she and her husband, Don Pedro Manrique, Catherine's major-domo, held. Catherine, too, her royal parents said at a later date, was to do all that the duenna advised.

We should give much to possess a portrait of Doña Elvira, for her significance was real during the short period she was in this country, but nothing survives to indicate what she was like. We can only visualize the lineaments of her highly-bred face, perhaps a shrewish face, long, dark-complexioned, with a rather extensive, "aggressive" nose, and black eyes, holding an uncompromising, dominating glance, the eyes of a martinet and an intriguer. Was she one of the Princess's attendants whom the mischievous eyes of Thomas More observed carefully at their entry into London, those attendants who looked so much like devils escaped from Hell?

Doña Elvira plays a prominent part after the return to London in a matter which is most vital in the whole story of Catherine of Aragon. But two other figures are concerned in it, de Puebla, the Spanish ambassador, and Alessandro, her chaplain, who had come to England with Catherine like Doña Elvira herself. Of these two, much the better-known figure—for Alessandro was soon to return to Spain—was de Puebla, who had been in England for years.

Doctor Roderigo de Puebla was not an attractive character. A Jewish convert to Christianity, he was intelligent and a doctor of both civil and common law. There his merits seem chiefly to end. Apart from his Jewish origin, which was not a recommendation in an age intolerant of non-Christians and suspicious of the sincerity of converts, his deficiencies, when they did not condemn him, made him pitiable. He was unpersonable, vain, and a rather faithless envoy; he was jealous of rivals and not very truthful. Catherine came to loathe him, but she was not always fair in her judgement. On the whole, it is surprising that the Spanish monarchs allowed him to remain in England so long, but they probably did not wish to employ him elsewhere and he had acquired a facile mode of approach to Henry which was sometimes useful. The English king, with his singular shrewdness, knew how to use de Puebla for his own shifty purposes, and de Puebla generally served the interests of Henry rather than those of Spain. He was distrusted by the Spanish monarchs, and another representative in England was always sent to conduct important negotiations. On the other hand, Ferdinand, in particular, kept him very short of money and the aristocratic ambassadors sent from Spain, mainly to displace him, treated him disdainfully. Perhaps de Puebla, thus shabbily treated and possessing little real roots in Spain, obtained his revenge by tacitly serving the interests of the English king and by constantly trying to outmanoeuvre the schemes of his arrogant colleagues.

Not long after Prince Arthur's death proposals were being commenced for Catherine's marriage with Prince Henry, the King's only surviving son, and it was a second Spanish ambassador, Estrada, not de Puebla, who mainly conducted the negotiations for it. Such a marriage would continue the Anglo-Spanish alliance which, advantageous to England, was even more beneficial to Spain, whose designs in Italy were opposed by France. Nevertheless, Henry's eagerness for Spanish friendship was such that he even contemplated marriage with Catherine himself, a design which filled Isabella with so much repugnance that she instructed Doña Elvira to prepare for Catherine's immediate return to Spain. The proposal fortunately died an early death and Estrada began negotiations for the betrothal of Prince Henry and Catherine. There were here two important factors: first was the question of the payment of Catherine's dowry, a question which was to figure prominently in the foreign policies of Henry and Ferdinand till the end of the reign; the second concerned the more important matter of obtaining a dispensation from the Roman Curia for the conclusion of the marriage, on account of Catherine's previous union with Arthur. This involved, as subsequent events were to show, the question of the consummation of the former marriage. Doña Elvira's contribution here was vital.

Ferdinand and Isabella had seen a letter which Alessandro the chaplain had written to de Puebla, and they sent Estrada in England a copy of it. We do not know precisely what the chaplain had said, for neither the original letter nor the copy survives, but it seems clear that the two had been talking dangerously, and that the chaplain had discussed with de Puebla, the canon and civil lawyer, some aspect of Arthur's marriage which was of critical importance in procuring from the Pope the essential Bull of dispensation for the new union. Estrada is commanded to be on his guard, so that the two busybodies may do no harm when the affair of the marriage is concluded. So potentially damaging, indeed, were the things that Alessandro must have mentioned that the Spanish monarchs thought he should not remain in England, and Estrada was to arrange for his immediate departure for Spain. But Alessandro was not to know of what Ferdinand and Isabella were aware, and the ambassador was to consult Doña Elvira about the best course to be taken.

Two days later the Spanish monarchs disclosed to Estrada the main source of their anxiety, for he was to get at the truth as to whether the Prince and Princess of Wales had consummated their marriage, since nobody had told them about it. He was to use all practical means to prevent any concealment of the truth. And it was Doña Elvira, the person, *par excellence*, among the household staff in a position to know the facts, who gave the vital information to Ferdinand and Isabella: "our daughter", they wrote a month later, "remains as she was here [that is, *virgo intacta*], *for so Doña Elvira has written to us*".

The treaty of marriage between Prince Henry and Catherine was concluded on 23 June 1503, and two days later the royal pair were betrothed. Their marriage was to be solemnized as soon as Prince Henry completed his fourteenth year. There was to be a marriage portion of two hundred thousand crowns, but as a hundred thousand crowns had been paid to Henry VII at the conclusion of the marriage of Arthur and Catherine, it was agreed that half of the marriage portion might be paid in plate and ornaments as well as coins. With regard to the sum already paid, the Spanish monarchs renounced all right to repayment: they had previously pressed strenuously for it. A dispensation for the marriage was to be sought from the Pope and this was in due course obtained.

The new espousal made little difference to the mode of Catherine's existence and she continued to live an uncongenial life in London in a household strictly controlled by Doña Elvira and her satellite husband, Don Pedro. There were rigid rules and observances and a monotonous secluded life. Even when Catherine stayed at the palace of Westminster she led the same sort of existence, in accordance with the express desires of Doña Elvira. King Henry entirely approved of this proceeding, possibly for the reason that the Princess was once again a daughter-in-law; and though some people thought that she should have greater freedom, this she could not get and there was nothing for her to do but submit. The wishes of the Spanish monarchs and of King Henry coincided in this matter and it was all, said the English king, for her honour and dignity. Catherine was, it is true, becoming very restive, but what could she do? It was all very well to talk of honour and dignity, but she was a Spaniard in a land wholly dissimilar from her native country, and she had practically no outside intercourse, except for occasional visits to the Court where her manner of life did not materially alter. She was young, she wanted relaxation from the strictness of royal etiquette, she wanted sparkling recreation, but was constrained to find what consolation and friendship she could among the members of her own household, especially among her maids of honour, such as Doña Maria de Rojas, whom she wished to retain about her person after a marriage which had been proposed for her. But above all there was the watchful Doña Elvira Manuel, the woman she had known in far-off Spain and the trusted deputy of her parents.

Durham House in the Strand, which was Catherine's home, was actually the mediaeval town house of the Bishops of Durham. There were long seasons when the bishops were not in residence and the house, or rather mansion, was then used by royal and other guests, but Catherine seems to have used at least part of it till the end of the first Tudor's reign. Wolsey lived there for two years after Catherine became Queen, and generations later Raleigh used to look out from a little turret of the house towards the Thames and delight in as pleasant a prospect as could be found in London. The hall was described by Norden in 1590 as stately and high and supported with lofty marble pillars; there were long gardens to the river.

Bickerings and quarrels in Catherine's household seem to have been frequent and these were so affecting her health towards the summer of 1504 that she summoned up sufficient courage to write to King Henry about them. Could he do anything to restore peace? He was cautious and correct. He was sorry, he replied, that the few servants she had could not live in amity, but he was unable to help her. If they were English it would be an easy matter, but as they were Spaniards and sent by her parents they were not within his jurisdiction. She should write to Spain about her distress, or, since Estrada, the Spanish ambassador, would shortly be returning there, he could place the whole problem before her parents. The real root of the trouble was the household's penuriousness.

Within the next month or two something was done, for the King ordered £300 to be paid to her, and de Puebla helped in re-organizing the household. All expenditure had to be accounted for to Doña Elvira, and de Puebla, in an unwonted paean of praise, told the Spanish monarchs how right they were in feeling no moment of anxiety so long as the Princess had such a person as Doña Elvira about her. As far as he could, he would increase the duenna's authority; and, as a first step, he took her a head-dress as a present from King Henry, a "St Peter in gold", which was an unusual gift, for, normally, anything of that kind was given only to royal persons. Nor was it presented to Doña Elvira in secret but before the Princess and her ladies, in order that her authority might openly be seen to be enhanced. And would de Puebla's own illustrious sovereigns, on their part, to mark their appreciation of her worth, do something equally magnanimous? For instance, it would be a gracious act if the Order of Santiago were conferred on her son, Don Iñigo Manrique, the Princess's equerry: he was an excellent fellow, honourable and fully deserving of such favour.

C

For the moment all seemed well. There was more order in Catherine's household, and perhaps more serenity, whilst the ambassador had surpassed himself in being agreeable to Doña Elvira. Nevertheless, he had always to regard her as in some sense a rival. But how long would this new state of things last? It did not, in fact, endure more than a few months, for early next spring Catherine was found asking King Henry for further help. Her accumulating debts, she said, were not indeed the result of buying luxuries. She had actually been obliged to borrow, otherwise she would have starved. Her father threw the onus of meeting all her obligations on to the English king and not a penny was he willing to contribute.

Doña Elvira had made a complete captive of de Puebla, although that was neither a particularly meritorious nor a necessary victory, and now more than ever she had tightened her control of the Princess's household. But two things were to be her undoing in the second half of 1505. First, originating probably in an inherent taste for intrigue and in a certain recklessness in which the strength of her personal position probably made her feel secure, she became involved in an act of disloyalty to her sovereigns and also to Catherine. Secondly, she seemed blind to the fact that Catherine, although she had always implicitly obeyed her parents, King Henry and Doña Elvira herself, was now a woman and had been made only too well aware during the last few years of the failings and foibles of human nature as exhibited by members of her household. It was a matter of perhaps only a short time before she would assert herself and break the bondage to her imperious duenna.

The real knave in the episode of 1505 is Doña Elvira's brother, Don Juan Manuel, King Ferdinand's ambassador at the Court of Maximilian, who, restless, bold and cunning, had ingratiated himself with the Archduke Philip, Maximilian's son. Don Juan became particularly important after the death of Isabella of Castile in November 1504, for, though King Ferdinand was by Isabella's final settlement made Regent of Castile, the settlement was uncongenial to many disaffected Castilian nobles, who had invited Philip to assume the government by right of his wife,

Joanna, Isabella's eldest surviving daughter, to the crown of Castile. Philip's claim to govern arose because he was the guardian of Joanna, alleged to be mentally unstable. Don Juan Manuel was persistently intriguing on behalf of the archduke against Ferdinand. But the duenna was also a schemer, and was in the habit of communicating to her brother all the secrets of the English court which she learnt from Catherine, who, quite unsuspectingly, could thus cause damage to her father's interests.

Influenced by her brother, Doña Elvira won over Catherine to a proposal for an interview at Calais between Philip and his wife and King Henry, and there were comings and goings by the envoy from Flanders. Catherine hoped to go to Calais and her enthusiasm for the visit is easily understood: she would see the sister for whom she had always had great affection and she was probably only too conscious of the relief which it would give from the drab monotony of existence at Durham House. Doña Elvira persuaded Catherine to write to the archduke suggesting the interview, and suspiciously quick answers came that it was desired wholeheartedly. Catherine with the greatest excitement showed the letters to de Puebla: she would, she said, write to King Henry immediately, beseeching him to make the necessary arrangements. So much for Catherine's enthusiasm: the duenna's zeal was of another kind, and her motives were neither so simple nor so pure. The Spanish ambassador, indeed, shrewdly perceived that what Philip was intending was an alliance with Henry against Ferdinand.

Catherine's letter to Henry, with the letters from Philip and Joanna, was to be conveyed by her master of the hall, Don Alonzo de Esquivel, who had horses saddled and was ready to start. Poor de Puebla, in his isolation, was alarmed. By all means Henry must know of the sinuous motives in the air and it was de Puebla's duty to tell him. He mentioned to Catherine that since he was himself going to the King he could very well deliver all the missives. If she did not allow him to do so, she would be neglecting her father's instructions. He was Ferdinand's accredited representative. But she was so much in the thraldom of the duenna, that she would not let him take the letters to King Henry. All that

Catherine would allow was a short delay until he had spoken to Doña Elvira.

And so he braved the fierce duenna. She would grievously offend him, he told her, if any other person but himself went to the King. He reminded her of the favours he had obtained for her. His honour as an ambassador was at stake and he was obliged, so he wrote to Ferdinand, to put an end to her brother's treacherous schemes. Doña Elvira, obstinate at first, finally promised, because of the apparently cogent reasons he gave, to stop the Princess from despatching the letters. De Puebla went back to his house and, evidently satisfied, sat down to his dinner. But it gave Doña Elvira the opportunity she wanted, and Don Alonzo galloped off to the Court.

As soon as the news reached him, de Puebla became saturated with wrath and a sense of humiliating defeat. With unchecked emotion, tears streaming down his lined cheeks, he sought out Catherine and attempted to banish her illusions and to warn her of the intrigue afoot: how Doña Elvira was working on behalf of her brother, how she had been passing information to him, and how the proposed interview was only to advance the schemes of the archduke against her father. The full strength of Catherine's family loyalty was now evoked and at de Puebla's dictation, and temporarily conquering her dislike of him, she wrote another letter to King Henry, urging him to value her father's interests above those of any other prince in Christendom. Had she known what the ambassador had told her, and under oath to keep it secret, she would never have thought of sending the first letter by her master of the hall. She was despatching the present letter by a special messenger in great haste, in order to overtake the first. It was unnecessary to write at length, for the ambassador would follow immediately to explain everything. And so little de Puebla, ageing and gouty, was hurried on by his indignation and injured pride.

Thus had Catherine been made aware of the duplicity of her duenna, the woman of great family whom her mother had entrusted with the guardianship of herself and the surveillance of her household, and of whom she had made a friend and confidant.

Catherine disliked grave dissimulation in a person whom she had fully trusted more than any other fault of character, except lack of moral or physical courage. But the young Princess would now be mistress in her own household, such as it was, and never again be dominated by another woman. In short, Catherine had, in one sense, at least, grown up.

There is little or no record of the relations between her and Doña Elvira during the next few months, but Catherine could not have dismissed from her mind the grim episode that had occurred. And then the silence in the records is broken, for in December 1505 we find her writing to her father from the Court at Richmond. She said Doña Elvira had asked, a few days previously, for leave to go to a physician in Flanders, in order to be treated for a disease which had caused the loss of one of her eyes. She went, but she did not return. Catherine never referred to all that had happened in that late summer of 1505.

We get a clue to what must have caused the duenna's departure by something which was said by the master of the hall himself long afterwards. Something must have occurred to raise a great storm of southern passion in that rambling house in the Strand, the noise of high, angry voices sounding through the gaunt rooms. Thereafter Doña Elvira was despatched. Don Alonzo said she went away in a "horrible" hour, and that the telling of such a thing was more suitable for conversation than for letters. Even he seemed to have incurred Catherine's displeasure, for, though evidently still in the Princess's household, he had seen her only three times since Doña Elvira had left, more than eighteen months previously.

The archduke did indeed see King Henry in January of the next year, 1506. He had set sail from Zealand for his kingdom of Castile with some fifty sail, but in the Channel they were all assailed by a great tempest and forced to take shelter on the Dorset coast. Henry and the archduke met in London, offering mutual protestations of good will and concluding a treaty of alliance. Both were extravagant in courteous conduct and the English king was lavish in his entertainment. Catherine must, however, have been grievously disappointed, for precautions were taken against any private talk with Joanna, whom she saw in the company of others for only a short time. Finally, Ferdinand and his son-in-law met in Spain with outward signs of amity, but Philip's vicarious rule of Castile was brief, for he died in September of the same year, 1506.

II

After Doña Elvira departed, Catherine must have felt herself to be in almost complete isolation. For more than two years she seems to have been without any person in her household or else-where to whom she felt she could confidently appeal for advice or moral support. Perhaps, at times, she missed the presence even of her domineering duenna. Nothing occurred to enable her to remove her distrust of de Puebla, and constantly in her correspondence with Ferdinand this is emphasized. He had from the beginning done a thousand dishonourable things against her father. He had caused her so much trouble that she had had severe attacks of tertian fever. She did not want "this doctor" to remain in England and asked for an ambassador who would be Ferdinand's true servant. Much later, she spoke again of de Puebla's duplicity: she still wanted another kind of ambassador, but said that de Puebla was trying to prevent Ferdinand from sending one. De Puebla was a mere vassal of the King of England and her father must believe only what she herself wrote about her affairs.

In addition to the failings of the ambassador, there was the distress which lack of money constantly caused Catherine. She was a mere pawn in the shabby political game being played between Henry and Ferdinand. Henry was now almost patho-logically avaricious, whilst Ferdinand meanly put off again and again the payment of the 100,000 crowns due as the remainder of Catherine's dowry. Many times she wrote to her father asking for help in her extreme need, but never had an answer: she wanted help not for extravagant things, she said, but for food. Henry told her that he was not obliged to give her anything, because Ferdinand had not kept his promise about the payment of the marriage portion. She was in the greatest anguish and her people were ready to beg for alms. She was without suitable clothing and had sold some bracelets in order to buy a dress of black velvet. Since coming to England she had had only two new dresses, for those which she brought from Spain had lasted all the time. She was ill, but it was worry that caused her ill-health, something for which medical skill could not provide a remedy. She wanted a confessor, a Franciscan Observant friar who was also a man of letters, and she asked Ferdinand to send one as a matter of urgency. What perhaps caused Catherine the greatest worry was an affected disinclination on Henry's part to proceed with the solemnizing of her marriage to Prince Henry, and his talk of other marriage projects for him. Henry was not very serious in all this, but he used these projects as weapons to force Ferdinand to meet his wishes. Catherine was in despair.

A confessor was not sent from Spain as Catherine had asked, for in the spring of 1507 she found a "very competent" one herself, Fray Diego Fernandez. In her manifold anxieties Fray Diego was the one person to whom she now turned for advice and consolation; and from the beginning he seems to have influenced her considerably, largely, it would seem, by the appeal which he made to her inherently pious nature and by the pledge of obedience which he exacted, in virtue of his priestly position. Imprudent she may have been at times in acting on his advice and he himself unscrupulous in giving it, but Catherine in her youth and comparative inexperience gave him her entire confidence. She never fluctuated in her sincere attachment, not even when calumnious tongues were busy, or at the end, after he was faced with a grave charge.

In the same spring of 1507 Catherine asked Ferdinand for a new ambassador. She preferred to have Don Pedro de Ayala, for he was clever and knew England perfectly, or Gutierre Gomez de Fuensalida, Knight Commander of the Order of Membrilla. But whoever was sent should be a person of great experience and knowledge, for England was so isolated from the rest of the world that negotiations with Englishmen required particular circumspection. It was Fuensalida who was sent early in 1508, and it was a mistake.

Perhaps Ferdinand's intention was to have an envoy in England who would not only look after his own and Catherine's interests, but who would also be able to make dignified representations to the English Court, in contrast to the slovenly and unsatisfactory demeanour of de Puebla. Certainly, Fuensalida had dignity, but his dignity seems to have been little removed from arrogance. He was of distinguished descent and had given loyal service to his country in wars, in embassies and in other special spheres. He had two important tasks to perform in England: he was to conclude as soon as possible the marriage of Catherine to Prince Henry and also to finish the hazardous business of the marriage portion. With all that we know of Henry and Ferdinand, these tasks would have been difficult of accomplishment for an ambassador of pre-eminent qualities, and Fuensalida was not that. Henry must have contrasted him with the easy-going, pliable de Puebla, and have found it hard to establish satisfactory relations with a Spanish grandee who was rigid, humourless and tactless. Henry, sometimes for a long period, refused to see him and Catherine came to dislike him as much as she disliked de Puebla, but for quite different reasons.

Fray Diego had been Catherine's confessor for a year when Fuensalida arrived in England, and in the virulent struggle which developed between them had already been able to win the Princess's trust. But the ambassador, according to what he told Ferdinand, and which perhaps was true enough, had worked well on behalf of Catherine, who showed, until late into the year 1508, how satisfied she was with all that he had done. He laboured hard, he said, to put things right, for the ill-treatment of the Princess was such that even a captive of the Moors never suffered so much. But Fray Diego became envious and disgruntled, for he expected to be the centre of Catherine's affairs and he acted in such a way as to bring the ambassador into discredit. According to Fuensalida's *ex parte* statement the friar's conduct was scandalous: he went about London not with a suitable companion but with three or four persons armed with swords and bucklers. Even the courtiers complained about him, said the ambassador, and some Castilian and Genoese merchants had heard of his licentiousness spoken of many times. And what was he doing going from inn to inn and from silversmith to silversmith selling his mistress's plate? That was not the function of a confessor to the Princess.

Catherine was very angry with the ambassador and strongly defended the friar: his moral character was unexceptionable and he was discreet and honourable. If he sold her plate, she had asked him to do so and she knew he would do it well. On another occasion, when Fuensalida asked her to discharge Fray Diego and take another confessor of virtue and experience, she replied by turning her shoulder on the ambassador. She did not wish to see him again.

At last, Ferdinand arranged for payment of the marriage portion, though he said that Henry was not fulfilling his part of the contract in refusing to take jewels and plate as part of the payment. Ferdinand, however, had agreed to pay the sum of 100,000 crowns in coin and had sent the necessary instructions to an Italian banker, Francesco Grimaldi. If Catherine's marriage fell through, the money must be returned to Spain. It was vital to make that condition, because Ferdinand was dealing with people of no honour.

Grimaldi becomes a figure in the troublesome story of the household drama, on account of his marriage to one of Catherine's ladies, Francesca de Caceres, a marriage which Catherine regarded as highly injudicious because of Grimaldi's close association with the ambassador in financial matters. Fray Diego had advised Catherine in the business and Fuensalida became enraged because of the interference in the affairs of his embassy. In the event, Catherine turned Francesca out of her house and the marriage took place from the ambassador's quarters. It would take reams of paper, wrote Catherine to her father, to repeat all that the ambassador said about her household, because of the affection which he felt for Francesca, and she begged Ferdinand not to believe what he said.

The close of this episode was, however, near at hand, but before it happened the Spanish king, no doubt as weary of the whole business as Catherine certainly was, wanted to recall both Fuensalida and Fray Diego. He had actually named a confessor to replace the friar. But Fray Diego stayed on, apparently through Catherine's influence, whilst Fuensalida left England, his mission accomplished, after Catherine had married King Henry VIII in June 1509 and had been crowned Queen. Francesca de Caceres never seems entirely to have lost her sense of attachment to Catherine and Fuensalida's successor, Luis Caroz, could speak of Francesca's devotion to her; but the friar felt marked antipathy towards Francesca, forbidding her to enter the palace or see the Queen. Catherine does not seem to have wanted her back and she eventually entered the service of Princess Mary, the King's sister.

Fray Diego remained as Catherine's confessor and became her chancellor; but he eventually got into unsavoury trouble, and perhaps Fuensalida was right when he spoke of the friar's licentiousness. It is difficult to be sure: both Fuensalida and his successor, Luis Caroz, had a motive in accumulating charges against the friar, and a royal court was notoriously a centre for detracting gossip. On the other hand, Fuensalida, not possessed of outstanding qualities, had a thankless mission to fulfil in difficult circumstances and found himself frequently thwarted by Fray Diego, who, in any case, always had the ear of Catherine.

Some years after the commencement of the new reign, the friar was charged with having committed fornication and for that reason was relieved of his post with the Queen. But he swore to King Ferdinand "by the holy gospels" that he was not guilty; that the charge was brought against him by people who hated him; that he was condemned before he had any opportunity to answer the charge; and that, indeed, he was never given such opportunity. The jealousy of him displayed by the Spanish ambassador—he was speaking of Luis Caroz, but it was equally true of Fuensalida—was well-known. That may really be the crux of the matter.

Catherine did not forget him and remained grateful. He returned to Spain more than six years after her accession and the Queen wrote commending him to her father for his services: he had, she said, served her faithfully all the time he was in England and much better than certain persons pretended.

CHAPTER 3

The Court: Mary of France

I

FEW REIGNS have begun with such brilliance and expectation of glory as the reign of Henry VIII. Henry was just under eighteen years of age at his accession in 1509 and Catherine, when she married him in June of that year, was some five years his senior. The new king had been left a vast fortune by his father, and young, enterprising and replete with newly-born martial ambition he seemed determined on spending it. People spoke of him almost ecstatically as the country's great hope, and William Blount, Lord Mountjoy, the intimate companion of his earlier years, who was soon to be Queen Catherine's chamberlain, voiced exuberantly in well-known words the sentiments of most. "If you could see", he wrote to Erasmus, "how the world is rejoicing in the possession of so great a prince. . . . Avarice is expelled the country. Liberality scatters wealth with bounteous hand. Our king does not desire gold or gems or precious metals, but virtue, glory, immortality."

Certainly, the young Henry had excellent qualities. He was the handsomest monarch the Venetian ambassador had ever seen, tall, of athletic figure, with the Tudor fair complexion and auburn hair combed straight in the French fashion. Besides his own language, he spoke Latin, French and a little Italian, and knew enough Spanish to converse with Catherine when she chose to speak in her native tongue. He observed more than a minimum practice in religion, for he is said to have heard several Masses a day, besides attending Vespers and Compline in the Queen's chamber. He had three special interests: he had considerable taste for both music and theology, whilst his passion for ships and the sea was such that he may almost be claimed to be the founder, in any real sense, of England's navy. Deriving his talent for music from his Welsh ancestry, he played well on the harpsichord and the lute, and was able, like most gentlemen of the Tudor period, to sing from music at sight. As much as any of his other interests, music and dancing were those which he could constantly, and did, indulge. His early rather "clerkly" education had given him a taste for theology, and his answer in 1521, *Assertio Septem Sacramentorum*, to Luther's attack on the Church, was a competent, though unremarkable, exercise in divinity.

Henry had a genuine appreciation of scholarship generally and revelled in the company of learned men. But as he was big, robust and hearty, he also delighted in outdoor activities. He was an admirable tennis-player; the Venetian ambassador said, "it was the prettiest thing in the world to see his play"; he was fond of hawking and hunting, always having eight or ten horses stationed beforehand along the country route he intended to take. He wrestled, he jousted often and he was excellent at the long bow, as good as the most efficient of his men-at-arms. He was affable and gracious when there was no danger of opposition to his will in a serious matter, and on occasions he displayed un-doubted charm. Thomas More once wrote to Fisher that the King had a way of making every man feel that he was enjoying his special favour, "just as the London wives pray before the image of Our Lady by the Tower till each of them believes it is smiling upon her".

But he was voluptuous and reckless in spending, like his Yorkist maternal grandfather, Edward IV, and his sensuality and other grave defects of character would reveal themselves more intensely as the years advanced. He was not, however, more sensual than some other monarchs of his day.

Historians are sometimes inclined to emphasize Queen Catherine's piety to the obscuring of other aspects of her charac-ter. She was not merely a "grave and gentle lady", for, at least in the earlier years of the reign, she was frequently light-hearted, as befitted her Latin origin: it was said, for instance, that she was

of a lively disposition and that she always had a smile on her face.
But she could be serious and forthright in speech where strong
principles were involved or her deep sense of loyalty impugned.
She was notably pious, and her ardent religious character helped
to influence and discipline a court whose general moral tone
would otherwise have been considerably lower. She attended
Matins at midnight in the chapel of the Observant Franciscan
Friars at Greenwich, received the sacraments and fasted frequently,
and wore the habit of the Third Order of St Francis beneath her
royal robes.

Catherine did not inherit the great beauty of her mother,
Isabella, but in youth her face and person were attractive, and her
appearance had agreeably impressed the critical eye of Thomas
More. Her colouring was fair, and, in particular, she had, like
her young royal husband, an exquisite complexion. In later years,
with the bloom of youth gone, her rather short figure became
increasingly squat, but she never lost her dignified bearing.

Possessing prudence, she had little vanity, and show or praise
did not appeal to her, for like many other royal persons she
quickly assessed at its true value a courtier's affectation or flattery.
If she insisted on ceremony it was because it was due to her royal
rank and not because she was vain. She could be tenacious of will,
if occasion demanded it, and though sometimes she could be very
candid in her utterances, generally her demeanour was marked by
great grace and courtesy. Like her mother, where she gave her
confidence she gave it wholeheartedly, but she detested serious
forms of deceit. Considerably courageous herself, she admired
courage in others, and she was truthful in a court which was not
conspicuous, as the years passed, for veracity. Hardship did not
deprive her of the power of sympathy with the trials of others
and she never lost the affection of the common people.

Long before the great crisis of her life Catherine was able to
demonstrate both her capacity for rule and the independence of
her views in important matters of policy. For example, she acted
capably as Regent in England when the King went to France in
1513, whilst at the time of the Field of Cloth of Gold in 1520 she
tried, summoning all her strong feeling against the possible

loosening of Anglo-Spanish bonds, to prevent an interview between Henry and Francis I. She called her own council and gave such good reasons against Henry's going to France as "one would not have supposed", said the Spanish ambassador, "she would have dared to do or even imagine". On this account "she is held in greater esteem by the King and his council than ever she was".

Catherine had a love of music like her royal spouse and relished the company of men of learning. Besides knowing her native tongue and English, she had been well-grounded in Latin, in which language she was completely at home, and she came to acquire a knowledge of French.

Both Henry and Catherine were the dominating figures of a magnificent court, a court with which no other, said Erasmus, could compare. Here Catherine, with the narrow atmosphere and crippling misery of her days as Princess of Wales almost forgotten, savoured the fruits of luxurious living and the benisons of culture; and she moved, a small person of regal dignity, among a great company of resplendent figures. And here were her particular friends, among them the Poles: Margaret Pole, from 1513 Countess of Salisbury, her eldest son, Henry, Lord Montague, and Ursula, her only daughter, who was to be Henry Stafford's wife; faithful Maria de Salinas, a Spanish lady-in-waiting, who married Lord Willoughby d'Eresby; the Marquis of Exeter and his wife, Gertrude, Lord Mountjoy's elder daughter, who at a time of great trouble was to render Catherine indirect but sterling service; the Duchess of Norfolk, eldest daughter of Buckingham; the Abergavennies. But above all there was, in these earlier years, Mary Tudor, the King's favourite sister, Catherine's closest companion in so many events of the court.

Mary, the youngest of Henry VII's daughters, was born about 1496. She was universally acknowledged to be very handsome and was known at the time of her French marriage as "La Reine Blanche". She was good-natured and had a lively disposition. She was of great courtesy and of high courage, and was loyal to her friends. She was pious after a conventional pattern. She was, indeed, the great friend of Catherine, who always took in her a

maternal interest which evoked marked gratitude. But Mary
did not share the Queen's intellectual tastes nor apparently her
deep devotional and spiritual interests.

As usual with royal children, great care was taken with Mary's
education, and John Palsgrave, who taught her French, wrote
the first French grammar in the English language. She did full
credit to his teaching, for we learn that when she left England for
her marriage to Louis XII in 1514 she spoke in French to some
merchants who had come specially to wish her farewell, and she
delighted everybody. The whole court was then speaking French
and English as in the time of Henry VII. She was also taught
Latin and music, like all the royal family, and she was efficient
at embroidery, that great stand-by of all well-bred women of
the day.

The earliest glimpse we have of Mary is during the first stay
of Erasmus in England in 1499, and the great scholar has left us a
well-known, vivid account of a visit which he paid to the
children of Henry VII at Eltham in company with Thomas More.
Erasmus had come to England with Lord Mountjoy, his pupil,
who, although still a minor, had married Elizabeth, daughter of
Sir William Say. On his return, Mountjoy stayed with his
father-in-law, probably at his home in Hertfordshire, bringing
with him Erasmus. But the latter moved on and shortly afterwards met Thomas More.

More, says Erasmus, came over to see him one day at Greenwich and took him for a walk as far as Eltham, the next village,
where all the royal children, except Prince Arthur, were being
educated. When the two came to the Great Hall at Eltham (this
is still standing with its fine timber roof), the royal attendants
and some of Mountjoy's servants assembled, "and there in the
midst stood Prince Henry, then nine years old, having something
of royalty in his demeanour ... combined with singular courtesy".
On his right was Margaret (the future wife of James IV of
Scotland), eleven years old, and on his left played Mary, a child
of four. Edmund was an infant in arms. More paid his respects
to the boy Henry and presented him with some writing. "For
my part", adds Erasmus, "not having anything of the sort, I had

nothing to offer, but promised on another occasion I would in some way declare my duty towards him, especially as the boy sent me a little note while we were at dinner, to challenge something from my pen. I went home and in the Muses' spirit, from which I had been so long divorced, finished the poem in three days." This poem was an elegant Latin ode, praising Henry VII, his children and the kingdom.

Catherine used to see Mary when she stayed at the royal palaces during her father-in-law's reign on those rare visits which helped to relieve the barrenness of her normal life before she became Queen; and in 1506 she was present at Court when the Archduke Philip and Joanna, his wife, Catherine's sister, came on their unexpected, accidental visit to Henry VII. During the elaborate entertainments arranged for the royal visitors at Windsor there was, as usual, much dancing, and King Henry, after Mass and dinner on the Sunday, invited Philip "to see the ladies dance for pastime". Henry received him in the Great Chamber and they both went to an inner room where were "my Lady Princess (Catherine) and my Lady Mary, the King's daughter", and they brought the royal princesses to the festivities. Catherine danced with a Spanish lady "in Spanish array", but although she invited Philip to dance with her he preferred to talk with Henry, and probably they talked politics. Mary danced a little, then sat by Catherine on the carpet under the great cloth of state, close to where King Henry and Philip stood, and later played on the lute and the clavichord. She played very well, we are told, and was greatly praised by everyone, because, although she was so young (she was not more than ten years of age), she bore herself so courteously. Then, led by the King and Archbishop Warham, all went to Evensong.

In 1508, Mary, in pursuance of the Anglo-Spanish alliance, now of many years' standing, was solemnly espoused to Charles of Castile, the son of Philip and Joanna, and Catherine's nephew. A sickly, grave child, and solemn beyond his years, he was one day to become the Emperor Charles V. Mary was to marry him when he was fourteen years old, but the espousal was never destined to end in actual marriage, for Ferdinand in 1514 performed another of his numerous acts of perfidy. He conceived considerable jealousy of the proposed marriage and began plotting with France. Henry VIII was furiously indignant and Mary solemnly and publicly renounced the marriage contract on 30 July.

There was, however, more than adequate diplomatic compensations for the failure to marry Prince Charles, as, by a notable coup, the English king suddenly brought about Mary's betrothal to Louis XII of France. It was an astute measure, though it meant a large personal sacrifice by Mary, who was young, handsome and elegant, whilst Louis was gouty, pocky and physically worn-out. A dilapidated man of fifty-two, although he happened to be King of France, was hardly compensation for even a rather delicate, sedate and melancholy boy of sixteen, who might one day, if he lived, have a great part of Europe at his feet; but Mary married King Louis by proxy in August 1514 with elaborate ceremony in a noble chamber at the palace of Greenwich, the walls of which were specially covered with great quantities of arras of cloth of gold. A considerable company of lords and ladies in colourful attire assembled for the occasion. Then, at length, came King Henry followed immediately by Queen Catherine with Mary by her side.

The event of the betrothal to a French king seems a marked anti-climax in the plane of international affairs to the rather fleeting glories of the previous year, when Henry had invaded the soil of France, had won the Battle of the Spurs and had secured the surrender of Thérouanne and Tournay. But Mary had doubtless noted these events with as much appreciation as everyone else had done, as well as the competent regency of Catherine while Henry was in France, a regency during which occurred the victory of Flodden Field. Flodden was more devastating a battle than any that had been fought abroad, for it saw the slaying of the Scottish king, James IV, and the flower of Scottish chivalry. Mary did not go with Catherine on her journey towards the north in the days before the battle, but probably made banners and ensigns for the army, in company with other ladies of the Court.

D

Henry and Catherine both went to see Princess Mary off for France from Dover Castle for her marriage to the French King. Her sea journey was made in the foulest weather and it was with the greatest difficulty that the Princess's party reached the French coast. Mary married Louis in the autumn of 1514 and was crowned Queen of France in the monastery of St Denis before entering Paris. At one of the series of entertainments that now followed, the new Queen stood up, "so that all men might see her and wonder at her beauty", but the French king "was feeble and lay on a couch for weakness". Peter Martyr, the Italian humanist, had written previously from Valladolid to Furtado de Mendoza with some venom and accurate prognostication that King Louis was at Abbeville, "waiting for his new bride, who will be his death"; and six weeks later he again wrote that if Louis lived to smell the flowers of spring "you may promise yourself five hundred autumns". The marriage which was intended to inaugurate perpetual peace lasted just eighty-two days. On New Year's Day 1515 King Louis was dead.

Before Mary's marriage Henry had promised that, in the event of the French king's death, she was free to marry whom she wished. She had already, in fact, been attracted by Charles Brandon, a younger son of Sir William Brandon, Henry VII's standard-bearer at Bosworth. Charles Brandon was practically a "new man", for little is known of his forebears beyond his grandfather, but handsome, bluff and hearty, and excellent at hunting and jousts, he became a great favourite and boon companion of Henry VIII. He took part in the invasion of France, was created Duke of Suffolk and became Ambassador to Louis XII. Brandon was thus close at hand on the French king's death, and precipitately, largely, it would seem by her importunity, he married Mary secretly in France. But they were both now faced with the anger of Henry. Suffolk's guilt was clear, because he had promised the King that he would not marry Mary without his consent, and Mary herself became filled with anxiety.

The event caused some stir. Henry exhibited great wrath, real or feigned, for secretly he did not look without favour on the match; but there was little doubt about the feeling of some of the

King's council, particularly of those who were members of the old nobility and who were jealous of an upstart's possible increase of power; other people felt that the country had been deprived of a strong diplomatic asset. According to the Venetian ambassador, the uproar in the country about the new marriage was very great and some members of the Lords and Commons almost came to blows. There was danger, indeed, that Suffolk would lose his head.

Letters asking for condonation poured from Mary to Henry and for intercession from Suffolk to Wolsey, who had the ear of the King. Even the new French king, Francis I, intervened on their behalf with Henry. In the end, the matter was resolved, chiefly through the aid of Wolsey, now riding swiftly to further power, but it may reasonably be assumed that Queen Catherine, Mary's friend, must also have been an eloquent advocate. At any rate, Mary and Suffolk were now publicly married at Greenwich in May 1515 in the presence of both Henry and Catherine, but general rejoicing was absent, owing to the momentary unpopularity of the union. To the end of her life Mary was always known as "the French Queen" or the "Dowager Queen of France". Henry obliged his sister and her husband to pay great sums for many years as the price of his forgiveness.

For a time after their marriage Suffolk and his royal wife seem judiciously to have kept away from London, spending their days quietly on their estates in Suffolk. Their chief seat, Westhorpe, was a handsome residence with battlements and much ornamental carving and splendid chimney-pieces. The whole summer of 1515 was spent there, but Mary came to London later in the year to see the King's great new galley, a ship of many guns and capable of holding a large number of fighting men. Henry was very proud of it and his admiration illustrates his marked interest in the English navy. Dressed in a sailor's coat and trousers made of cloth of gold, he acted as pilot of the new vessel at its launching. A gold chain, bearing the inscription, "Dieu et mon Droit", dangled from his coat and suspended from it was a whistle on which he blew as loudly as a trumpet. Queen Catherine named the galley, "the Princess Mary", in honour of the King's sister.

Mary spent much of the summer of the next year in Suffolk, though she had come to London earlier. In March she gave birth to a son, Henry, named after the King. In the March of 1517, Catherine, on her way to the great shrine of Walsingham, visited Mary in Suffolk. Mary was then known to be with child, and in July her daughter Frances was born, the child who was to become a strong Protestant and the mother of the ill-fated Lady Jane Grey. Queen Catherine and her own infant daughter, Princess Mary, born in February 1516, were by deputy the child's godmothers.

But before the birth of Frances, Mary the French Queen had been at Court and during her stay there Evil May Day occurred, an episode in which the aid of Wolsey and Thomas More among others was invoked at an early stage in an attempt to prevent an ugly development of an unfortunate beginning. In the final stage Queen Catherine made a dramatic appeal to the King to show compassion on a multitude of prisoners and persuaded Queen Margaret of Scotland and the French Queen to join her: it can almost be called the "Drama of the Three Queens".

The genesis of the Evil May Day riots must be sought in an earlier economic background. Previous to 1517 the general problem of unemployment had reached such dimensions as to attract the notice of Parliament. In London, in particular, artisans and traders contended that strangers in their midst were allowed to exercise their crafts and sell their wares to the grave detriment of Englishmen, even causing Englishmen to starve by taking away their work. That may, of course, have been true, but the English government was obliged to take cognisance of international factors. Nevertheless, it is perhaps understandable that desperate, ignorant men should have thought merely of their sectional interests and have been unable to realize the wider implications of government policy, especially in its relationship to foreign countries and their merchants and craftsmen, who came to this country to offer their wares or to practise their special skills.

The trouble which exploded in 1517 originated in the irresponsible initiative of one John Lincoln, a broker in the city of London, who induced a cleric, Dr Bele, to make use of the pulpit, the chief and powerful instrument of mass communication in an age without newspapers or radio, to inveigh against the foreign merchants and traders of London. He subtly moved the people to rebel against them. "From Bele's sermon many a light person took courage and openly spoke against the strangers." There was some violence. As May Day approached, a rumour arose, no one knew how, that on that day the city would rise and slay all aliens. This news reached the King's council, and Wolsey, after consulting the mayor and aldermen, made an order that every man in the city should repair to his own house and not stir out of it from nine o'clock in the evening till seven o'clock on May Day. Each alderman was to be held responsible for the observance of the order in his ward.

The May Day Riots of 1517 had a simple and, it would seem, an innocent origin. An alderman, Sir John Mondy, came from his ward and found two youths in Cheap playing "buckerels", a street game of Henry VIII's time. A large number of young men were looking on, because "the commandment of the King's council was then scarce known, for then it was but nine of the clock". Mondy bade them all leave and one youth asked, "Why?" " 'Thou shalt know', said Mondy, and took him by the arm to have him to the counter [the counter prison]. Then all the young men resisted the alderman and took him from Master Mondy, and cried 'Prentices and Clubs'."

Out of every door now came apprentices and craftsmen, brandishing clubs and other weapons. More and more people poured forth and soon there were hundreds in a general mêlée. A general proclamation in the King's name was made, but no one obeyed it. Thomas More and his assistants appeared at St Martin's Gate and had almost brought the disturbance to a standstill when people in the ward of St Martin began throwing stones and bricks at divers persons, who were attempting to persuade the rioters to return home. The riot spread rapidly and few houses, we are told, were left unspoiled.

Order was by degrees restored, but prisoners were made to the number of several hundred; some were men and some mere boys of thirteen or fourteen. These, tied with ropes, were brought through the streets. Some were arraigned and sentenced for treason, and ten pairs of gallows in various places in the city were set up, the gallows being placed on wheels and moved from street to street and from door to door. A number of the prisoners were brought forth and executed, including the original ring-leader, John Lincoln, who suffered in Cheap. Others, with ropes still about their necks, waited to be despatched, but a sudden command came from the King to stay their execution. They were sent back to prison.

What had happened to cause this royal order? The reason is unknown, but it is possible that Wolsey had been in conference with the King, and had pleaded for clemency. The King himself, not yet after only eight years on the throne possessed of that inexorable power and strong hold on his people which were characteristic features of the second half of his reign, was faced with the possibility of executing hundreds of his subjects and, as a result, of reaping a good measure of unpopularity. That may have given him reason to pause now. About 12 May a great assembly was commanded, and the chroniclers and the Venetian ambassador tell us of the drama of that day.

The scene was Westminster Hall, its walls hung with much rich tapestry of gold. Present there was Wolsey, his strong, bulky form enveloped in crimson silk, and the eyes of his fleshy, powerful, quelling face missing nothing of all that went on; and there were other members of the King's council, among them, no doubt, Buckingham and Norfolk and the Earl of Shrewsbury and the Earl of Surrey, who had come to the city to help to restore order on the fatal day. Many other lords were there and a large number of citizens, all assembled by royal command. There was a great canopy of brocade, beneath which sat the lusty, dominating figure of the King. Prisoners to the number of more than four hundred had been ordered to be sent from the city; and, unkempt and haggard after days of huddled confinement, and with halters round their necks, as if their execution were imminent, they paraded before the King. He spoke to them severely, and doubt-less long, in rebuke of their manifest treason. And it was after that, we are told, that "our most serene and compassionate

Queen with tears in her eyes and on bended knee", and "by her means" Mary, the French Queen, and Margaret, the widowed Queen of Scots, kneeling also, begged the King for mercy. Wolsey pleaded, too. The King was at length pleased to grant his royal pardon which, being ceremoniously announced, the prisoners filled the place with a great shout and then cast their halters to the roof of the Hall.

II

Many of the sumptuous social events at Court in which Henry and Catherine, Mary and her husband, Suffolk, acted as the leading figures were the reflections of the foreign political manoeuvres of Wolsey, the man whose rise to power and his maintenance in it were some of the most significant happenings of the long reign. There were visits to this country by foreign potentates or special receptions of ambassadors or particular acts of thanksgiving or congratulation. Events of this kind generally called for elaborate banquets with music and dancing, hunting expeditions and hawking, tournaments and other entertainments. The genial folly of masking was a great pastime with the young, exuberant King.

But it was music, with its frequent concomitant, dancing, which vivified so much of the court life, and the leading devotee of the Muse was the King himself. Even most of the great noblemen's houses with their huge staffs and their constant need to offer hospitality to royal visitors took care that there was an adequate provision of musicianship. And among these great households were those of Queen Catherine's special friends. The Marchioness of Exeter, in particular, ensured that her staff were musically well-equipped. There was Anne Browne, for example, a young unmarried woman, who was not only good with the needle, but could also play well upon the virginals and the lute. Some of the men servants were even more musically capable. There was Hugh Brown (perhaps a kinsman of Anne Browne), who seems to be an excellent example of the person who can teach, although his executive powers are not more than mediocre. He could "play somewhat on divers instruments", we are told, but "his knowledge is to teach men to do things in music which he himself cannot express nor utter, and yet he can perfectly teach it, wherefore he was master of the musicians". There was also Thomas Wright, who could play well on the harp, and could sing and juggle and "make other conceits and pastimes"; and Thomas Harrys, who "luteth and singeth well", and he played cunningly upon the viols and divers other instruments.

It was, however, the King himself who set the fashion for the keen love of music in England. His enthusiasm was shared by the Queen, by Mary, the King's sister, and the rest of the Queen's friends and associates, and, indeed, by all members of the Court. It was ubiquitous. When, for instance, the King went on his war to France in 1513, he sang and played on the flute, the lute and the cornet in the presence of Margaret, Archduchess of Austria, in the castle of Lille. He had taken in his great retinue his lutenist, Peter Camelianus. He delighted in both instrumental and vocal music, and in his earlier years sometimes practised on the organ and the lute day and night. With his pronounced predilection for dancing he preferred light, simple and merry music—the jig, hornpipe, galliard and pavane—which was less complicated and had greater general appeal than music with contrapuntal characteristics, and so was particularly suitable for amateurs.

The King was assisted in his love of music by Dionysius Memo, a Crutched friar, who was sent to him from Venice. Master Memo had been the organist at St Mark's and brought with him to England an excellent organ at great expense. Soon after his arrival he was commanded to play before the King and Queen and the rest of the Court, and so pleased everybody that the King made him the chief of his musicians and promised to make him a royal chaplain. Even when the appalling sweating sickness was raging in the country during the late autumn of 1517, the King, moving from place to place to avoid it and dismissing his whole Court, kept with him Dionysius Memo and only "three favourite gentlemen".

Henry composed songs, not only the well-known "Pastyme

with good companye", but lesser-known ballads like "Grene growth the holy [holly]":

"Grene growth the holy, so doth the ivé,
Thow winter's blastys blow never so hye,
As the holy growith grene and never changyth hew,
So I am, ever hath bene, unto my lady trew".

And in the royal chapels the King maintained a high standard of male singing, with the aid of William Cornish, Gentleman of the Chapel to both Henry VII and his son. Cornish was an excellent choirmaster and the Venetian ambassador, Giustinian, paid tribute to the singing: "High Mass", he says of one occasion, "was sung by His Majesty's choristers whose voices are really rather divine than human; they did not chant but sang like angels, and as for the counter-bass voices I don't think they have their equal in the world".

Due to her rank as a Dowager Queen, Mary was always close to the King and Queen at all the musical events, and at the stately banquets and ceremonies of the Court. At a great feast given in July 1517 in honour of the Imperial ambassador, the King sat between Catherine and Mary, with Wolsey beyond on the right and the ambassador on the left. Feasting lasted for more than three hours, and then came music and dancing. A stage was set in the middle of the hall, and boys sang and played flutes, rebecks and harpsichords, "making the sweetest melody". Dancing went on after this for two hours, the King "doing marvellous things both in dancing and jumping, proving himself, as he in truth is, indefatigable". He was still only 26.

After the High Mass for the general peace proclaimed at St Paul's in 1518 there was luxurious entertainment, followed in the evening by a great supper and much dancing "in the richest and most sumptuous array possible, being all dressed alike". In this the King and Mary the French Queen were the leaders. But a few days later there was a more solemn affair, the betrothal of the infant Princess Mary, Queen Catherine's daughter, to the infant Dauphin. At this ceremony the King stood in front of the throne, and at the side of it were Catherine and the French Queen, with the small Princess in front of them, dressed in cloth of gold and wearing a cap of black velvet adorned with many costly jewels. She was under three years of age and the Dauphin was even younger.

The Emperor Charles V came to England in May 1520 and Henry and Catherine received him in Archbishop Warham's Palace. At High Mass Mary was seated next to Catherine and at all the social events which followed she was, as usual, her constant companion. One of these events was a rather hilarious feast. The tables, loaded with rich things, were surrounded by "enamoured youths" ("giovani innamorati", says the Venetian ambassador) who stood behind the ladies. Certain of the Spaniards "played the lovers' parts" bravely and "nothing could have been better". One of them, the Count of Capra, "made love so heartily that he had a fainting fit . . . and was carried out by the hands and feet".

The entertainments of the Field of Cloth of Gold in June of the same year were some of the most costly of the century. We get glimpses from the Venetian ambassador's despatches of the magnificent scenes and displays: the temporary palaces with the exquisiteness of their decoration and furniture; the great assemblies of the hundreds of richly-attired English and French nobles and of the cardinals and other prelates; the elaborate banquets and the tilting and the music and the dancing and the masques. The first dance of all was led by Mary and a French nobleman. But Mary was never far away from the company of Queen Catherine.

The French Queen's visits to the Court became rarer after 1521 and she appears to have spent much more time at Westhorpe, looking after her children and managing her household, which was very large and compatible with her own and her husband's rank. Moreover, the continuance of the war with France prevented the payment of any French revenue due to her, and in 1526 both Mary and Suffolk still seem to have been heavily in debt to the King. Financial restrictions, apart from other reasons, made any long visits to the Court difficult for Mary.

Nevertheless, she emerged from her comparative seclusion on important occasions and in 1523 she helped Henry and Catherine to welcome King Christian II of Denmark and his wife, Isabella,

Catherine's niece, to the Court. Wolsey had met the royal
visitors at the waterside at Greenwich and they were afterwards
received by Henry and Catherine with lavish courtesy in the
Great Hall of the Palace. At dinner Catherine displayed much tact
by placing Mary below herself at table, but above the Queen of
Denmark, "which I found", says the Spanish Ambassador, a little
put out, "very strange, since the Lady Mary is now married to
the Duke of Suffolk".

CHAPTER 4

Margaret Pole and Master Fetherston

I

AFTER CATHERINE'S departure from Ludlow in 1502 until she married Henry VIII and was crowned Queen in 1509, she was to see little of Lady Margaret Pole. The death of Prince Arthur ended Sir Richard Pole's appointment as Chamberlain, but he continued those activities in Wales that were involved in the Constableship of Harlech and the sheriffalty of Merioneth, for he had been given these posts for life. In addition, he served on commissions of gaol delivery in the Welsh border towns and in places farther afield. But Sir Richard Pole died in 1505 and Margaret Pole was left with children to rear and educate. To a person of her high descent and social standing, life must now have presented many difficulties, for she could have had few financial resources of her own, whilst her husband had possessed only modest estates in Buckinghamshire. Moreover, Henry VII was not the sort of king to make generous grants of money or land to his courtiers or their kinsfolk, not even to the relict of one who had rendered long and loyal service.

But Margaret Pole's circumstances were considerably changed soon after Henry VIII's accession, and we seem to see at once clear evidence of the renewal of her friendship with Catherine, and perhaps the demonstration of her influence in Lady Margaret's favour. Within a month or two of Catherine's coronation, at which Margaret Pole had, of course, been present, an annuity of a hundred pounds was granted to her by the King, who was beginning to take a strong interest in the education of his cousin, Margaret's promising son, Reginald, the future cardinal. Reginald Pole, now somewhat over thirteen years of age, had probably in his earliest years been educated at home under the supervision of his mother. He subsequently spent five years with the Carthusians at Sheen and the King made a grant towards his maintenance at school. He matriculated as a nobleman at Magdalen College, Oxford, and to pay for his stay there, Henry commanded the Prior of St Frideswide's to provide a pension until a benefice could be found for him. But the full tide of good fortune was seen in 1513 when Margaret Pole was created Countess of Salisbury and restored to all the lands of the earldom of Salisbury. It was some measure of justice for the judicial murder of her brother, Edward, Earl of Warwick, who had been innocently inveigled into a plot devised by Perkin Warbeck to escape from the Tower in 1499 while they were both imprisoned there. The plot failed, and its failure provided Henry VII with an opportunity to get rid of them both, especially of the one who was an undoubted Plantagenet and had inherently strong claims to the throne.

The statute which restored the Salisbury estates to Margaret Pole said that Edward, Earl of Warwick, had been restrained from his liberty in the Tower and other places from the age of eight, having no experience or knowledge of the world "by policies or of laws of the realm", so that if he had committed any offence it was rather by innocence than by malicious intent. His long imprisonment, indeed, more especially his confinement within the grim, forbidding Tower, seems to have adversely affected his mind, for it was said he was unable to discern a goose from a capon.

Many years after these events Cardinal Pole said that the great trials which Queen Catherine subsequently underwent were a divine visitation for the guilt of her father, Ferdinand, in desiring the earl's death and for the guilt of Henry VII in committing the deed of which he so greatly repented on his death-bed. Pole maintains that Ferdinand, when negotiating Catherine's marriage with Prince Arthur, was averse from giving her to one who would not be secure in his own kingdom. But Pole is writing nearly fifty years after the marriage took place and it is clear that a decision about the marriage contract had been made before Warwick's execution. Henry, indeed, had given full proof of the security of his throne. He must, however, have been conscious of some guilt, and the cardinal speaks of Henry's desire for pardon and for the restoration of the Salisbury estates on condition of Margaret Pole's forgiveness. His mother, he says, was called before Henry VIII and his council to hear the condition which his father had made.

With the restoration of the Salisbury property Margaret Pole was now a great landowner and a considerable personage in her own right. Her estates were spread over many counties, as far north as Yorkshire where the Yorkist interests had been extensive, and there were properties in the Marches of Wales. The most valuable in point of income were Stokenham in Devonshire, the manor and burgh of Christchurch in Hampshire and the manor of Ware in Hertfordshire. Her real home, however, was at Warblington in Hampshire, and here would have come her son Reginald at intervals during the course of his humanist studies at Oxford. But she also seems to have been much interested in the property at Christchurch, where the Austin Canons had a large priory dating from the eleventh century, with additions down the centuries till the early part of the sixteenth century. The priory is still in an excellent state of preservation, for, unlike most of the monastic churches, it did not suffer destruction at the Dissolution, but continued to serve as a parish church. Margaret Pole built in the north part of the choir the fine Salisbury Chantry made of Caen stone which was probably the work of Torrigiano, whose sculpture adorns the tombs of Henry VII and his Queen in Westminster Abbey. The fan vaulting of the Chantry is, in particular, of delicate beauty.

Warblington, like her other restored property, came to Margaret Pole through her maternal grandfather, Warwick the Kingmaker, and then through his daughter, Isabel Neville, Margaret's mother. It was dominated in the early part of the sixteenth century by a castle, probably built by Margaret Pole herself, soon after the property was restored to her. A high octagonal turret of stone and red brick which formed part of a gateway is all that remains of a splendid building. There is an early seventeenth-century description of Warblington Castle as it was long before its almost complete destruction in the Great

Rebellion, and much as it must have been in Margaret Pole's days. This account says that it occupied some two hundred square feet and had "a fair green court within, and buildings round, the said court; with a fair gallery, divers chambers of great count; and two towers covered with lead; a very great and spacious hall, parlour and great chamber, with a chapel and all other offices; a fair green court . . . before the gate, and a spacious garden with pleasant walks adjoining . . .; two orchards and two little meadows . . .; and near the said place a fair fish pond, with a gate for wood [sic], and two barns, stables and other outhouses". There seem to have been four storeys and, judging by the remains, there were apparently mullioned windows with arched heads to the lights. The castle was, in all, a fitting place to receive royal visitors.

A noble and ancient parish church lies immediately to the south of the castle's remaining tower, and a short distance away there is a small coastal inlet and farther south the open sea, with the waters of Spithead a little to the south-west. The country round is not wanting in picturesqueness and it evokes historic memories. Some distance to the east, off the coastal plain that continues for many miles, is the old harbour of Bosham, whence Harold departed on his famous visit to Duke William of Normandy; and a few miles further along that same coastal land could have been seen from the castle's upper chambers the elegant fabric of the Cathedral of Chichester, where was the famous shrine of St Richard. Inland, in the royal county of Sussex, might have been discerned the small but beautiful Benedictine priory of Boxgrove, lying in a plain a few miles from Chichester and still standing almost till the end of Margaret Pole's days at Warblington, and Halnaker with its old mill, and Slindon, where Stephen Langton died, and much in the distance, the Arun running through its gap at Arundel, where is still the majestic castle built on a height, and, stretching wide, a line of the reposeful Downs. To the west of Warblington, after a few miles along the coastal road, commenced the long hill of Portsdown, overlooking the wide expanse of plain extending to Portsea, whence the ships and armies of Margaret Pole's royal ancestor, Edward III, sailed to the wars in

France. And it must have been along Portsdown, having avoided Stansted and Southwick beyond the hill, because those places were stricken by the plague, that Henry VIII came on a brief visit to Warblington in 1526.

Margaret Pole, as Countess of Salisbury and possessing extensive and valuable properties, was now high in the hierarchy of the nobility, and it is worth noting what, in the context of Tudor times, her considerable position meant. Aristocratic principles were then still strong and the ownership of great estates involved both responsibility and an awareness of social rank; and it seemed to be a condition of survival for great nobles that, even if most of the old power of feudal magnates had gone, there should be much outward show—the trappings of chivalry and jousts and tournaments—and also the provision of considerable hospitality. In that way a competitive social hierarchy advertised to the world the fact of its survival and maintenance: it was not a good proposition for a nobility to appear to be mean or shabby or in decay, any more than it would be now for great industrialists or important politicians. Moreover, as a general rule, order and degree and meticulous rules of etiquette were stringently observed in the society of Tudor times. It is also to be noted that the Court of Henry VIII was luxurious, and noble houses felt obliged to make attempts to approach its standards, especially in the matter of providing for the costly favour of royal visits.

But Margaret Pole, although she maintained an establishment appropriate to her rank, was not able, nor was it necessary, to entertain so lavishly as did her grandfather, the Kingmaker, or his brother, the Archbishop of York, who once gave a banquet at which a vast number of guests were present, including dukes and duchesses, earls and countesses, bishops and abbots, and for which the kitchen made use among many other items of some two thousand geese and two thousand pigs. Even the magnificent Duke of Buckingham, Shakespeare's "Bounteous Buckingham, the mirror of all courtesy", who was to be the father-in-law of Ursula Pole, celebrated Twelfth Night in 1509 with a feast for over five hundred at dinner and four hundred at supper at his chief manor of Thornbury in Gloucestershire. Nor did the

1. HENRY VIII
After Holbein.

2. THREE CHILDREN OF HENRY VII AND ELIZABETH THE QUEEN
Engraving after Maubeugius, 1496.

3. MARY QUEEN OF FRANCE AND CHARLES BRANDON
Artist unknown. Probably painted soon after their nuptials, 1516.

Countess of Salisbury find it necessary to keep a standing household like that of her father, George, Duke of Clarence, who was politically and socially a more considerable figure. He had a permanent household of just on three hundred servants and travelled with a staff of nearly two hundred.

II

The birth of Catherine's daughter, Mary, on 18 February 1516 at the Palace of Greenwich was to make significant changes in Margaret Pole's life and to bring her into even closer association with the Queen. That a daughter had been born instead of a son was a disappointment for both the King and Queen, who much desired a male heir, but, said Henry: "We are both young; if it is a girl this time, by the grace of God the boys will follow". The new Princess was christened with much solemnity and ceremonial observance two days after her birth. A great assembly was expected and all the area from the gate of the palace to the door of the Observant Friars' church was railed off and well-gravelled and strewn with rushes. Near the church "was set a house, well-framed of timber [and] covered with arras, where her godfather and godmother abode". The royal child was borne to the font by the Countess of Surrey and received the name of Mary, out of compliment, perhaps, to the King's sister. The Countess of Salisbury was the sponsor at the confirmation.

After a few years it became necessary to appoint a governess for the royal child and the first holder of the appointment was Lady Margaret Bryan, wife of Sir Thomas Bryan. But in May 1520 there is evidence that Margaret Pole was the royal governess, a post which she was to retain, with a short interval, for some thirteen years. This appointment is an incontestable proof of Catherine's close friendship and of the confidence which both she and the King reposed in her. That Margaret Pole, royal, pious, courageous, intelligent, religiously enlightened, held this important post for such a long period and during the most impressionable years of Mary's life is a measure of some of the responsibility which she

E

bears for the essential formation of the Princess's mind and character. Master Richard Fetherston, Princess Mary's schoolmaster for eight years, was to share that responsibility, though to a smaller extent. He, too, was to be an unswerving friend and supporter of Queen Catherine and one day was to die for his religious faith.

In the summer of 1520 we hear of the progress which the royal child is making. Some lords of the council visited her at Richmond in July and wrote to Henry, who had gone to the Field of Cloth of Gold, telling him of Mary's good health and how she was increasing in wit and virtue. They found her in the Presence Chamber with the Countess of Salisbury and her gentlewomen and with the Duchess of Norfolk and her daughter. Then came the French envoys, and Mary, so the councillors tell us, welcomed them "with most goodly countenance, proper communication and pleasant pastime in playing at the virginals that they greatly marvelled and rejoiced the same, her young and tender age considered". She was four years of age.

But in 1521 Margaret Pole caught something of the recoil from the business of the treason of the Duke of Buckingham. Her eldest son, Henry, Lord Montague, a friend of the Duke's and his considerable dicing partner, came under suspicion for having been associated with him and was actually sent to the Tower, though later he was released. Arthur, another son, was expelled from the Court, but nothing for the moment was decided about Margaret Pole herself "on account of her noble birth and her virtues". It is clear, however, that she was under a cloud, for Wolsey sounded old Lady Oxford about assuming the post of governess, if only for a season. In the end it was Sir Philip Calthrop and his wife who were chosen to serve the Princess. Yet Margaret Pole does not seem to have been long held in suspicion since we find that Mary journeyed in February 1522 from Greenwich to Richmond, and a boatman was paid for taking her there, "by order of the Countess of Sarum".

There are glimpses during this year of 1522 of the Princess's peripatetic existence, with the Countess of Salisbury doubtless in constant attendance. In early March she was at Richmond, where the Spanish ambassador was paying a visit; Queen Catherine would not let him leave without his seeing her. She danced a slow dance, he says, "and twirled so prettily that no woman could do better". At Catherine's command "she danced a galliarde and acquitted herself marvellously well". She played two or three songs on the spinet and "showed unbelievable grace and skill and self-command, such as a woman of twenty might envy". She was "pretty and very tall for her age, just turned seven". Mary was still at Richmond for Easter and later in the same month visited the convent of the Bridgettines at Syon where she made an offering of twelvepence. Then in June she was at Greenwich where the King received her cousin, the Emperor Charles V. And so during the next few months to Hanworth and Windsor and Chertsey and Esher. In August Lord Abergavenny, a kinsman of the Poles, sent Mary a present of a horse which she seemed anxious to test, for John Wylde, a forester of Windsor, was paid five shillings for bread and ale for attending on her in Windsor Forest.

These were calm, pleasant days for Princess Mary and her household, but by 1523 there were signs of discontent in the country about taxation and further discontent two years later was to affect Mary's life considerably. Wolsey, the man to whom the King had delegated so much administrative control, was running into a storm of difficulties. The vast fortune which the King had inherited from his father had been mostly spent on his ambitious wars in France, and, latterly, demands for subsidies to finance them had provoked many strong complaints, reaching their maximum in 1523, when Parliament agreed upon a sum much less than that which Wolsey wanted. In 1525 there was much passive resistance to the benevolence known as the Amicable Loan; and it became clear that only by comprehensive reform could expenditure be reduced, and the extraordinary financial demands and the discontent which inevitably flowed from them be avoided.

Reform began by the establishment of a council for Henry's natural son, the Duke of Richmond, to administer the affairs of the North, and a similar council was instituted for Mary, as Princess of Wales, in the Marches of Wales. This reform did not of itself reduce expenditure, but by leading, it was hoped, to increased efficiency, overall financial economy would result. These developments also seem to have been largely forced upon Wolsey because of the impossibility of managing personally the vast amount of business which now came to hand; in other words, he was forced by necessity rather than desire to delegate a great bulk of his work. In any case, it was high time for stricter control in both the North and the Marches of Wales, for, since the beginning of the reign, six hundred complaints of robberies had been received in the diocese of Durham, whilst in the Marches there were even more serious complaints.

Elaborate preparations were made for Mary's journey to the west and a large household travelled there in the August of 1525 under the competent supervision of the Countess of Salisbury. History was largely repeating itself, for Margaret Pole would be going to the region where her long association with Queen Catherine had begun, and she would be renewing her acquaintance with all those picturesque border towns which she had known more than a quarter of a century ago—Tewkesbury and Bewdley, Hereford and Ludlow, Worcester and Shrewsbury and Chester. Princess Mary's first place of residence was Thornbury, but afterwards she seems to have divided her time between that place and towns in the Marches. Thornbury, formerly the seat of the Duke of Buckingham, had been forfeited to the Crown by his attainder four years previously. It was well suited to be a royal residence, with its inner court and exquisite oriels and turrets and its clustered chimneys, and its great gardens and galleries, all an attractive combination of castle and hall.

Careful provision had been made for Mary's staff and we read of cloth being delivered to her councillors and servants, and especially to five of the lady governess's servants, who were to be dressed in the Princess's livery of blue and green, each for the purpose to have three yards of cloth at four shillings the yard; and cloth at three shillings and fourpence a yard was delivered to twelve ladies and to two of Master Fetherston's servants, and to the chaplains, clerk of the closet, four gentlemen ushers and four cupbearers. There was furniture for the high altar and for three other altars, and there were vestments, Mass books, corporasses with their cases, two cushions of cloth of gold and two of crimson velvet, and cloth, curtains and carpets for "the wardrobe of beds". The King's pleasure was that everything should be sent speedily to the Princess's council "with such carts as shall come from Bristol and Thornbury and the parts thereabouts".

Reparations were made to the castle of Ludlow by Wattere Roggers at the commandment of Master Sydnore, Surveyor-General to the Princess. These were some of the items: making a key for the wicket of the great gate; sawing wood and felling timber at the Fryth, at fourpence a day; soldering over my Lady's (Lady Salisbury's) chamber, fourpence; to carpenters for working, sixpence a day; for the wardrobe and great chamber, fourteenpence; and, most important, "a potation for the whole workmen, tenpence".

Princess Mary had a total staff of over three hundred persons. The fifteen gentlewomen, all to be dressed in black velvet, who were to attend on her, were to have as their head the Lady Salisbury. And there was also Master Fetherston, the school-master. Elaborate regulations were drawn up for the governance and education of the royal heiress, and we realize how important were the functions primarily of the lady governess and then of Richard Fetherston.

We are told that above all things the Countess of Salisbury shall, "according to the singular confidence that the King's Highness hath in her, give most tender regard to all such things as concern the person of the said princess, her honourable education and training in all virtuous demeanour". At "seasons convenient" she was "to use moderate exercise for taking the open air in gardens, sweet and wholesome places and walks, which may confer upon her health, solace and comfort, as by the said lady governess may be thought convenient. And likewise to pass her time most seasons at her virginals, or other instruments musical, so that the same be not too much, and without fatigation or weariness to intend to her learning of Latin tongue and French. At other seasons, to dance, and amongst the residue to have good respect unto her diet, which is meet to be pure, well-prepared, dressed and served, with comfortable, joyous and merry communication in all honourable and virtuous manner; everything about her [was to] be pure, sweet, clean and wholesome, and as to so great a princess doth appertain, and all corruptions, evil airs and things noisome and displeasant to be forborne and eschewed." Those gentlewomen and maidens attendant upon her were "to use themselves sadly [seriously], honourably, virtuously and discreetly in words, countenance . . . and deed with humility, reverence . . . so as of them proceed no manner of evil or unfitting manners or conditions, but rather all goodly and godly behaviour". And all such attendance was to be as thought suitable by the lady governess.

Such were the royal instructions for Margaret Pole. All seemed of good portent, for about this time the Venetian ambassador wrote of Mary: "The Princess went to her principality of Wales with a suitable and honourable escort. She is a rare person, and singularly accomplished, most particularly in music." And in order that there should be no set-back to her progress her council was commanded to meet once a month, or when required, to ensure that the instructions about her health and education were carried out. At these meetings Lady Salisbury was to be present, and the Princess also, if Lady Salisbury and the council thought it well. Princess Mary's health was carefully watched, for in 1528 when the sweating sickness was prevalent in the country, Margaret Pole and the council considered it necessary that those councillors occupied with the business of the many suitors daily thronging to the Court should not come into the Princess's presence.

Master Fetherston, who taught Princess Mary her lessons, possessed good academic qualifications and had been at Cambridge. A year or two after his appointment he is always mentioned in Government documents as "Doctor", though there is no evidence that either of the English universities gave him that title. We know that he taught excellently and that Princess Mary made great progress.

It was Luis Vives who probably helped Catherine to select Richard Fetherston. This famous countryman of Queen Catherine's, her friend and adviser, came to England in 1523, and for the next year or two seems to have resided at Corpus Christi College, Oxford. He wrote from Oxford to Catherine in the year of his arrival giving her some written advice for which she had asked and which Princess Mary's tutor could act upon in teaching her. "And because", he says, "you have chosen a man who, in particular, is learned and honest (as was only right), I have been content merely to sketch the matter lightly [for] he will explain the rest. Those things, nevertheless, which I think either obscurely related or neglected by writers of the art of grammar, I have somewhat indicated in more words." He then adds a short guide for a pupil in studying Latin.

Vives wrote specially for Mary the *Satellitium* or *Symbola*, a book of more than two hundred maxims which were intended to safeguard a child's mind from dangerous intrusions. He dedicated it to Queen Catherine, who has often, he says, asked him to produce something of the kind for Princess Mary to preserve her "more securely and safely than any spearman or bowman whatever". Linacre also composed a work for the Princess, *Rudimenta Grammatices*, and received an appointment both as Latin tutor and as supervisor of her health generally, but the appointment does not seem to have been anything more than a sinecure.

When exactly Master Fetherston began to teach Mary is uncertain, but it was probably at the time of her going to the Marches, for Catherine wrote to her daughter in 1525, mentioning both him and the Countess of Salisbury; but this fact does not rule out the possibility of his assisting in Mary's education in some way before that date. Catherine is well, she writes, in answer to Mary's enquiry about her health, and she is glad that Mary is well also. "As for your writing in Latin, I am glad that ye shall change from me to Master Fetherston, for that shall do you much good, to learn by him to write right. But yet sometimes I would be glad when ye do write to Master Fetherston of your own inditing, when he hath read it, that I may see it. For it shall be a great comfort to me to see you keep your Latin and fair writing and all. And so I pray you to recommend me to my Lady of Salisbury."

Mary proved to be an intelligent, industrious pupil and though she did not have the quick and penetrating intelligence of her stepsister, Elizabeth, she became competent in languages and was more than an ordinary amateur in music. She was able to write a Latin letter before she was ten; to the French ambassador she spoke in 1527 in French and Latin; and long afterwards, when she was Queen, the invariably well-informed Venetian ambassador could write of her more than moderate knowledge of Latin literature, of her speaking Latin, French and Spanish, of her understanding Italian perfectly, though she did not speak it, and of her good grounding in Greek.

As Princess Mary, like Queen Catherine, visited the convent of Syon, so she would also stay at those religious houses which were in or near the Welsh Marches. Thus, in 1526 she came with Margaret Pole to the cathedral priory of Worcester and remained for five weeks. Some careful reparations to the apartments were made before their arrival: "sewing of the hangings in the court chamber"; and to Colsull the glazier was paid 2/6 for "glazing of a hole in the entry next to the chapel" and a larger sum "for glazing of the window at the stair head of the stone chamber".

Mary went on to Battenhall, but in Holy Week she was back in Worcester, departing after Low Sunday. Her servants were in pocket at her leaving by the considerable sum of £17.13.4, paid by the priory. In August she returned and in her entourage was "the King's joguler". She spent the Feast of the Assumption there, and then the prior accompanied her to Evesham and Cropthorne.

Before the last sojourn at Worcester it would seem that Margaret Pole's sons visited the priory, for there is an item in the prior's journal for wine "to my Lady Salisbury's sons", and "expenses for my Lord Montague" are mentioned.

But as well as learning and piety there was fun at seasons for Mary, especially during the long winter in the Marches, and for her first Christmas there were careful preparations, because a great number of visitors were expected. Her council asked Wolsey whether spice plates could be provided and a "ship of silver for the alms dish requisite for her high estate", and could trumpets and a rebeck be sent? Was a lord of misrule to be appointed? This "lord", "the master of merry disports", was important in all great households and provided amusements during the long Christmas season—"fine and subtle disguisings, masks and mummeries, with playing at cards, more for pastimes than for gain".

There was entertainment, too, when Mary went to court and in May 1527 at a great banquet given to the French ambassadors, an elaborate mummery was performed for their benefit. The ambassadors had come to ask for the hand of Mary either for Francis I or his second son, the Duke of Orleans, and as the occasion was important, she doubtless received good coaching by the Countess of Salisbury for her part in the entertainments. Eight damsels, we are told, as beautiful as goddesses, came forth from a cave, all richly dressed in cloth of gold, "their hair gathered into a net, with a richly-jewelled garland, surmounted by a velvet cap, the hanging sleeves of their surcoats being so long that they well nigh touched the ground, and so well and richly wrought as to be no slight ornament to their beauty". They came down gracefully from the cave to the sound of trumpets, the first to descend being the Princess, hand-in-hand with Queen Catherine's friend, the Marchioness of Exeter. Her beauty in this array produced such an effect on everybody that all the other marvellous sights previously witnessed were forgotten.

But troublesome currents were ahead. The winter of 1528 was hard and there was a dearth of corn in the country. The Princess's household at Ludlow was as much affected as other great establishments, and money was very short. To effect economy, certain gentlemen and yeomen of the household were allowed to go to their homes. Some servants were discharged, but, since they were poor and nobody knew what would happen if provision were not made for them, various abbots and priors were asked to give assistance.

CHAPTER 5

The Humanists:
Vives, More and Whytford

SOON AFTER the accession of Henry VIII, the Court, with the King and, perhaps more realistically, Queen Catherine, at its head, became the centre not only of manifold social pleasures, but also of diverse intellectual interests. The royal Court, said Erasmus—the greatest name of all in this age of the new humanism—was resplendent indeed: it was the seat and citadel of the best studies; and he congratulated the King's Latin secretary, Richard Pace, upon having such a sovereign. The King, before coming to the throne, wrote in his own hand to Erasmus in Italy and now always welcomed him to Court affectionately, whilst the Queen wanted him as a teacher. She had knowledge to a degree, said Erasmus, uncommon to her sex, and erudition and prudence were the surest recommendation to both the King and the Queen.

But if a sympathetic English Court attracted scholars at home and from abroad, Spain itself had been famous for learning and for royal encouragement of learned men from a much earlier date. Scholarship developed there rapidly in the fifteenth century, and Spanish humanists are found visiting Italy, spending years at the Spanish college of Bologna before returning to their own country. Already there was a marked Italian influence on Spanish poets, and the Sicilian Siculo was appointed as Professor of Latin Eloquence and Poetry at Salamanca, where the Milanese, Peter Martyr, also lectured. Two Italian humanist brothers, Antonio and Alessandro Giraldino, became tutors to Isabella's daughters, and Alessandro, the younger brother, came to England in the entourage of Catherine in 1501. In the sixteenth century, the intensity of humanistic studies became even more marked, and during the first half of the century Spain is said to have produced ten humanist scholars to one in England. The Greek text of the Alcalá Bible was in existence in 1514, two years before the Greek Testament of Erasmus. Moreover, love of learning was found among the nobility, a circumstance in marked contrast to what was happening in this country.

All this indicates the importance of Catherine's Spanish cultural background and helps us to understand the reality of the intellectual atmosphere of the English Court after she became Queen. Catherine was not likely to forget that the Court of Ferdinand and Isabella had been the most celebrated in Europe, and she was naturally disposed to look with favour upon scholarly men, especially upon the aspirations of any Spanish humanists, and to increase their influence. It is noteworthy that Luis Vives spent long periods in England in the halcyon days of the reign.

Almost all the notable English humanists, Linacre, Fisher, More, Archbishop Warham, Mountjoy, Bishop Fox of Winchester, Richard Whytford and Richard Reynolds of Syon, Cuthbert Tunstall, Richard Pace, Thomas Starkey, Reginald Pole and the rest were figures in a strong chain of acquaintanceship or friendship with one another. That chain was reinforced by foreign names like those of Erasmus and Luis Vives. Some of the figures, such as Fisher and More and Richard Whytford, were Catherine's particular friends. Others, like Warham and Tunstall, were to be her counsellors in the time of trouble: Warham to be an ageing "supporter", normally with little steel in his character, but to show, before his death, something of commendable determination in his attitude to the King's claims, whilst Tunstall, of whose mind and character everyone spoke highly, was to end up upon the King's side after some unexpected opposition. But it was Luis Vives who was to have perhaps the closest intellectual association with Queen Catherine.

Before Vives first came to England in May 1523, he had been in communication with both Henry and Catherine, and had been hoping for an appointment at the English Court to enable him to devote himself to scholarship rather than to teaching, an occupation which he disliked. For some years he had been working on an edition of St Augustine's *The City of God*, and when he finished it he dedicated it to King Henry. In the dedication he refers among other matters to Henry's love of learning and, in particular, he praises his work on the seven sacraments and the defence of the papal primacy, the *Assertio Septem Sacramentorum*. Nothing, he says with something of the sycophancy common to penurious, expectant scholars of the time, could be more elegant, purer or more religious: "the reputation of your mind's goodness was much more confirmed, if more it might be". Henry in his reply thanks him fulsomely and adds that "our favour and good will shall never fail in your affairs".

This was the beginning of good things for Vives, who followed the work up by dedicating to Catherine his treatise, *The Instruction of a Christian Woman*, a treatise full of pregnant ideas on the proper education of women in the context of the new times. This work and the precise dedication have some relevance to the scheme of education which Vives had drawn up for Princess Mary. "Your dearest daughter Mary", he addresses the Queen, "shall read these instructions of mine and follow them in living, which she must needs do if she order herself after the example that she hath at home, with your virtue and wisdom". It was probably during the Christmas of 1523, when Vives was staying at the Court by royal invitation, that Catherine had confidential talks with him about her small daughter's education.

Vives' ideas for the education of women are based on what he regards as a fundamental principle that girls are naturally more inclined to piety than boys, and are to be nurtured by a diligent reading of the Early Fathers and a daily study of the New Testament. Catherine must have given close attention to his advice, for long afterwards, in 1533, she sent Mary "two books in Latin: one, *De Vita Christi*, with the declaration of the Gospels, and the other, the *Epistles of Hierome* [*Jerome*], that he did write to Paula and Eustochium". Christian poets Vives would allow to be read by both boys and girls, and girls could read even certain pagan poets, like Lucan, Seneca and some Horace.

In one sense the Spanish educationist was reformist, in another sense conservative. He attacked the time-honoured association of ignorance with piety in the education of women: piety was to be enlightened by sweeping away the cobwebs of mediaeval narrowness, by entering the new world of learning, and by praying in the vernacular, but it was also to be protected by conventional safeguards. In this respect Vives was rigorous, and even puritanical, emphasizing the necessity of strict obedience of wives to husbands and of women to their superiors or elders, an insistence on simplicity in dress and food, and an avoidance of public places and of the reading of romances.

In the details of learning he advocated that a girl should be taught in the vernacular instead of Latin, the language of teaching in the Middle Ages. He encouraged girls to make their own textbooks as they went along and to incorporate in them those examples of classical usage which they found in their reading. They should write down whatever had impressed them, for by doing this they would remember better; and they should also exercise and strengthen their memories every day by reciting carefully a few times before retiring to bed what they wished to recall. There should be an adequate training in all housecraft, in the preparation of medicines and medicaments, and in the way to treat injuries. Margaret Pole seems to have had a training of this kind, like most other women of the day, and she was thus able to impart her medical knowledge to her royal charge, Princess Mary. Once Thomas More thanked her son, Reginald, for a medical prescription which he had obtained from his mother and which More had had made up.

It was natural and indeed inevitable that Vives and More should be friends. Some years before Vives came to this country the great Englishman had been delighted with some writings of the Spanish scholar, and had met him in Flanders. When he paid his first visit to England, More was already Under-Treasurer and living in the celebrated house at Chelsea with its library and gallery and long gardens extending to the river. In 1525 Vives stayed a month there and had ample opportunity to confirm, if that were necessary, the praise of More's qualities of which he had already written: his superb intelligence, his learning, his genial disposition. And it was Vives' association with More as well as with Erasmus which paved the way for his introduction to the English Court.

More and Vives had much in common: they were united in their views on the education of children, and particularly of girls; they held the firm necessity of associating education with piety, a view which Erasmus also held; their religion was unimpugnedly orthodox; and they were united in devotion to Queen Catherine. It was the religious orthodoxy of Vives which must have made a particular appeal to the Queen, for, like all the Spanish humanists, like all the Spanish students who went to study in Italy, like all the humanist members of Isabella's Court, he was never guilty of any deviation from orthodoxy in religion. His definitive religious attitude is summarized in his statement that he submitted himself to the judgment of the Church, even if it appeared to him to be opposed to the strongest ground of reason, "for I may be in error, but the Church never can be mistaken on matters of belief". During the course of his second stay in England Vives supplied an interesting commentary on the religious orthodoxy of the King himself. He was then a daily visitor to the Court and on one occasion showed Henry the book which Erasmus had written against Luther, the *De Libero Arbitrio*. The King, after reading a few passages, seemed pleased and said he would read the book through. He pointed out to Vives a particular passage in which Erasmus would deter men from immoderate curiosity about divine mysteries. That, he said, delighted him. The Queen also expressed her pleasure and desired Vives to thank Erasmus for having treated the subject with such moderation.

If Vives was paying daily visits to the Court, Thomas More was now a favourite courtier, a firm friend of the King and Queen, and advancing to fame and fortune. He must often have met the Spanish scholar at Court or have accompanied him to the manor-house at Chelsea. Yet More never wished to be a courtier. He held that elaborate formalities and ceremonies did not become men of sense and for that reason he kept away from the Court as long as possible. Eventually, when avoidance seemed no longer possible, he almost had to be dragged there; all courts, he said, were full of intrigue, though there was less of it in England, whose King had no affectations; but when once he became a courtier Henry valued his companionship highly. Not only was his friendship esteemed but also the support of his intelligence in discussing affairs of state: the King would read despatches from abroad to the Queen in More's presence, and Catherine used often to tell Henry that of all his counsellors More alone was worthy of the position and the name.

More's household at Chelsea was like a school and it was said that a visitor to it would have thought himself to have been in some well-ordered Christian academy rather than in a layman's house. His four children, with Margaret Gigs, his adopted daughter, were taught by carefully-selected tutors, the eager, intelligent pupils receiving every possible encouragement from their famous father. They studied Greek and Latin literature, the Christian Fathers, logic, philosophy, mathematics, astronomy, and they made exercises in Latin every day. There was no strife or useless debate or foolish talk, and idleness was regarded as "the very pestiferous, poisoned bane of youth", and therefore was rigorously excluded. To William Gunnell, one of the tutors to his children, More wrote that if a woman to eminent virtue should add "an outwork of even moderate skill in literature, I think she will have more real profit than if she had obtained the riches of Croesus". But Margaret, the eldest of More's daughters, who married the lawyer, William Roper, had much more than moderate skill in literature and became distinguished for her learning. When some of her Latin compositions were shown to Reginald Pole and Veysey, Bishop of Exeter, who was President of Princess Mary's council in the Marches, they were both astonished that she should have produced them without any help. Yet it was not all academic learning in the famous home, for More delighted in music and saw that his household were skilled in the playing of musical instruments. He even succeeded in teaching his rather shrewish second wife, Dame Alice, to sing, but he failed in teaching her other things.

The King greatly appreciated More's company and used to visit him at Chelsea, sitting down unceremoniously at table with the family, or spending a day or two with him in the country. On leaving him, the King would say that, as he had kept More apart from his family, he could add two days to his holiday, "for I should not like to think that my presence had in any way interfered with your domestic pleasures". At other times Henry would discuss with him problems of astronomy, divinity and similar subjects, and sometimes worldly affairs. The King would lead him up to the roof of the palace and there consider with him the diversities, courses, motions of the stars and planets. Sometimes Catherine was with Henry when More came on social visits, for as he "was of a pleasant disposition, the King and Queen after the council had supped, at the time of their supper . . . [would] commonly call for him to be merry with them".

We do not seem to find any mention of visits paid by Queen Catherine to the house at Chelsea, but it is inconceivable that she did not go there sometimes, either with the King or with Vives. Nothing would have given her greater pleasure when in London than to travel down the short distance from one of the palaces to the celebrated home, drawing from talks with Thomas More and his family inspiration for the education of her own daughter Mary (and perhaps, one day, it was hoped, of a larger family).

One place we know had a special attraction for Catherine—the celebrated convent of Syon, "The Monastery of St Saviour and St Bridget of Syon, of the Order of St Augustine", situated on one of the pleasanter reaches of the lower Thames, within the manor of Isleworth, and conveniently near the royal palace of Richmond. It was the only convent of the Bridgettine order in England, a house of religion for both men and women which had a tradition of strict religious observance, enlightened piety and scholarship. The foundation statutes provided for a community of sixty nuns and twenty-five brethren, seventeen of whom were to be in orders. The women came from leading families in the land, whilst the brethren were theologians and scholars and writers of devotional books, and those who were priests acted as spiritual directors and confessors to influential persons outside the monastery. At least six Fellows of Cambridge Colleges joined the monastery during the last thirty years of its existence, and we find

4. MARGARET POLE
Artist unknown.

5. THE PALACE OF RICHMOND
Drawing by Anthony van den Wyngaerde, 1562.

6. OLD ST PAUL'S, 1551

Richard Pace, the humanist, and formerly one of the King's Latin Secretaries, staying at Syon in 1527 for some special purpose. The Venetian ambassador says that Pace was there, wearing "clerical habits", and "leading a blessed life in that beautiful place . . . [and] surrounded by such a quantity of books that for my part I never saw so many in one mass". He had become, we are told, an excellent Hebrew scholar and had commenced editing the Old Testament. The library was famous, no other religious house in England possessing so many printed books from every part of Europe.

We can understand why Queen Catherine liked Syon. It was not merely that it was near the palace of Richmond, that it was a royal foundation, that it had associations with English dynastic royal houses—for the neighbouring Carthusians at Sheen also had old royal connections—nor was it even that she would meet there kinsfolk of members of the royal Court, like the Prioress, Margaret Windsor, who was related to her own chamberlain, Lord Mountjoy. It was mainly because she found at this great religious house the fulfilment of some of her precise tastes.

Catherine also ensured that her daughter Mary was introduced to the convent. As early as 1520 we find a payment of two shillings being made to My Lady of Oxford's servant for conveying the Princess by water from the palace at Richmond to Syon and back, whilst three shillings and fourpence was paid to My Lady of Syon's servant for quails and rabbits.

Vives used to accompany Catherine on some of her visits to Syon, discussing as they went by boat on the fair stretch of stream such matters as philosophic sentiments or the qualities she looked for in giving preferment to a man: she would, she once said to Vives, rather have a moderate kind of fortune than a very hard or a very mild one; but, if she were forced to choose, she would elect for the saddest lot in life, for in unhappiness consolation is not wanting, whilst in the most fortunate state the mind fails in support when the need arises. (She was being wiser and more relevant than she realized.) As for the qualities deserving of preferment, she looked not only for a piety which was natural in a person, but also for real virtue and merit.

F

There were two priests, in particular, whom Queen Catherine and Vives would have sought at Syon. One was Richard Reynolds, a Fellow of Corpus Christi College, Cambridge, distinguished for his Latin, Greek, and Hebrew scholarship, for his very considerable and orthodox theological learning—as a theologian he was second only to Fisher—for the spiritual depth of his character and for his courage. In due course he was to support the validity of Catherine's marriage to Henry and to be a martyr in 1535 for his maintenance of the papal supremacy.

The other priest was Richard Whytford, of a substantial Flintshire family and an early friend of both Erasmus and Lord Mountjoy. He had been a Fellow of Queen's College, Cambridge, and was a secular priest before he went to Syon. A link in the chain of his friendship with the Queen is provided by Whytford's own friendship with Mountjoy, her chamberlain. While still at Cambridge, Whytford accompanied Mountjoy abroad as his chaplain and confessor. There he met Erasmus, Mountjoy's tutor, and the three became close friends. To Erasmus, Whytford was his "dearest Richard".

Another man of genius whom Richard Whytford may in later days have met was Ignatius Loyola, the founder of the Society of Jesus, who came to London in 1530. At this time Ignatius was only a poor student at the University of Paris and his greatest work lay before him. He came to England with the precise object of asking for alms in his poverty, and he seems to have met with such a generous response here that there was no further need to beg. That he may have visited Whytford, an older man and an experienced, scholarly religious, with whom he would have had spiritual affinities and the value of whose devotional writings he would have readily appreciated, can be a matter of surmise only, but it was a very probable event. He may also have been armed with an introduction to Queen Catherine, for she had not yet been removed from all association with the King; and as she was renowned for her works of charity, it is unlikely that she would have left a deserving, fellow-Spaniard in need, if any appeal had been made to her.

A constant stream of devotional books poured from Whytford's pen from his earliest days at Syon. Any desire for fame would have been completely foreign to his spiritual temperament, and we perceive evidence of his quality of self-effacement, and his desire to guard against possible pride, in the manner in which he usually signed his books: he is either "the old wretched brother of Syon" or "the wretch of Syon".

In his books written for private devotion Whytford was able to envisage the difficulties of the average lay Christian, his many distractions and the cares of his home life, the responsibility of managing his children and his household servants, the problems met in his outside business. Whilst, therefore, he insisted that prayer necessarily required time, training and practice, his approach to the needs of the religious, but especially to those of the layman, was simple, direct and practical, even homely. Perhaps it was his wide experience of life before he entered Syon which enabled him to understand readily the needs of the ordinary man when he came to prayer. There is a welcome simplicity and common sense in the analogies and examples he uses, and these qualities are clearly seen in *The Pipe or Tun of the Life of Perfection*, a copy of which he gave to the King and Queen. Whytford says that the work is a defence of the three vows of religion against the attacks made by the Lutherans on the religious life. He explains that the life of perfection is much like a pleasant, precious and wholesome wine contained and preserved in a tun or pipe, but that when it flows out, that is, when it is no longer contained, the wine perishes. The work is mainly Whitford's own, but included in it is his translation of St Bernard's, *Of Commandment and Dispensation (De Precepto et Dispensatione)*.

Whytford's English style is at its best in his superb rendering of the *Imitation of Christ*, which he calls *The Following of Christ*. The *Imitation* was probably the most popular book of devotion in the fifteenth and sixteenth centuries, and it was Henry VIII's grandmother, Margaret Beaufort, who greatly increased its popularity in England by translating into English from the French version the fourth book, that on the Eucharist. Very soon after this William Atkinson, by command of Margaret Beaufort, translated the first three books, so that there now existed a complete English version. That version and Richard Whytford's must have been well known to the English Court. Whytford's is a completely new translation from the Latin original; it is fairly free, for, though he has kept the sense of the Latin, he has made his own work a piece of exquisite literature. Its simplicity and lucidity, its balance and rhythm, its general charm, are not surpassed even by the admirable collects of Cranmer. It has been claimed that it must have been well known to numerous people during the period between its first publication and the publication of the Authorized Version of the Bible in 1611, and that it may even have had some influence on the translators of the Bible themselves. Queen Catherine must have known it well. Was it not tranquillity as well as scholarship that she sought at Syon?

"First put thyself in peace and then mayest thou the better pacify others. A peaceful and patient man profiteth more to himself, and others also, than a learned man who is unpeaceful. A man that is passionate turneth oftentimes good into evil, and lightly believeth the worst part; but a good peaceful man turneth all things to the best, and hath suspicion of no man. He that is not content is oft troubled with many suspicions, and neither is he quiet himself, nor yet suffereth he others to be quiet. He speaketh oftentimes that he should not speak, and he omitteth to speak that which it were more expedient to be spoken. He considereth greatly what others be bound to do, but to do that whereunto he himself is bounden, he is full negligent. Have therefore first a zeal and a respect to thyself and to thine own soul, and then mayest thou the more righteously, and with the more due order of charity, have zeal unto thy neighbours".

Part II

DIVORCE AND AFTER

CHAPTER 6

The King's Great Matter:
Phelippes, Abell and Shorton

I

IT WAS known in Court circles that after 1525, the year in which Princess Mary went to the Marches of Wales, Queen Catherine would bear no more children. This circumstance meant that her daughter would in normal course succeed to the throne of England. It was one factor of vital significance in the long and complicated sequence of events which would soon engage the minds of the nation. The possible accession of a woman was a matter of acute anxiety and fraught with innumerable dangers; and there was always the example of Queen Matilda to point the moral. Nor could a woman, so it might be argued, remain single. If Mary married a foreign prince—as, in fact, she eventually did—the patriotic spirit of Englishmen would be evoked, for a foreign prince might want to rule, and England's independence, a heritage precious to all Englishmen, might be threatened. If, on the other hand, she married an Englishman, it might arouse the jealousy of her countrymen and there might be civil war. One important aspect of Henry's marital problem was the lack of a male heir; the tragedy of Catherine was that she had been unable to provide a son that survived.

This lack of a son was often, no doubt, in Henry's mind. The Tudor dynasty was still comparatively young, and it was imperative in his eyes that it should be continued. He must sometimes have thought of the insecure thread by which it had hung in his father's days, when both his brothers Arthur and Edmund had died and he was the sole surviving son. His words at the birth of his daughter Mary echoed his need and his hope: "It is a girl this time, but by God's grace the boys will follow". Nor was Catherine's own hope less fervent.

But there was another important factor in the crisis shortly to arise—the passion which the King had begun to feel for Anne Boleyn, one of the Queen's ladies-in-waiting, young, gay, of bright wit and flashing eyes. Various dates have been assigned for the commencement of this attraction, but the most probable date is the latter part of 1526 or early in 1527. At any rate, it was in the spring of the latter year that the King was possessed of scruples about the validity of his marriage to Catherine and considered that his marriage should be annulled and a dispensation granted to enable him to marry again. In the summer Henry told Catherine of the necessity for the dissolution of their marriage, because, he said, they had been living in mortal sin all the time. The Queen had been profoundly distressed, but, to console her, the King gave an assurance that all would be done for the best. He begged her to keep the matter a secret, a request which was fatuously superfluous, for the King's intentions were as well-known as if they had been trumpeted forth from every housetop in the capital. In the autumn of the next year Henry, in an address to the notables of London, amplified the nature of his doubts and referred to the passage in Leviticus which seemed to imply serious and even terrifying strictures if a man married his brother's wife.

Did the King's scruples about his marriage emanate, in fact, from a true or from a false conscience? Did they blaze into consciousness soon after his passionate attraction to Anne Boleyn had commenced—and eighteen years after his marriage to Catherine; and was the whole affair, in the event, a process of rationalization, an "adjustment" of conscience, on the plane of his new impelling desires? And was his determination to obtain the dissolution of his marriage stimulated by Anne's steady refusal to yield immediately to his passion, because, with cool, calculating pertinacity, she was firmly holding in her mind the idea of the possible destiny of a Queen's throne?

In the summer of 1527 Wolsey on his way to France gave

Bishop Fisher, when he sought him out at Rochester on directions from the King, a rather different origin of the King's Matter. He told him in secrecy that in connection with the proposed marriage of Mary to the Duke of Orleans doubts had been raised about her legitimacy. What had, asked the Bishop of Tarbes in London, so Wolsey alleged, been provided "for taking away the impediment of that marriage whereof my Lady Princess cometh"?

Before this interview Henry and Wolsey had been losing no time, and on 17th May a collusive suit had been arranged by the cardinal as Papal Legate and by Warham as Archbishop of Canterbury. The King was cited as a defendant to appear before them. He was required to answer a charge of having lived in incestuous relationship with his brother Arthur's widow for a period of eighteen years. The proceedings were held in secret and Henry appeared personally and answered in his own defence. But the two prelates would take no responsibility for a decision and the question was referred to a number of theologians and lawyers.

While the collusive suit was proceeding, the Imperial ambassador in London wrote in haste to the Emperor Charles V, Catherine's favourite nephew, telling him that Wolsey, "as the finishing stroke to all his iniquities had been scheming to bring about the Queen's divorce". The problem was growing in complexity. On 6th May the Emperor's armies in Italy had captured Rome, sacked the city and massacred a great number of its citizens. In addition, the Pope was made a prisoner of the Imperialists and so was to remain for the next seven months. This did not make matters any easier for Henry and the cardinal, since, in any negotiations with the Papacy, Catherine could ostensibly rely on the support of her nephew, who now had a defenceless Pope more or less in his power.

The Queen was later to blame Wolsey for the origin of all her troubles, but this is a simplification which has no foundation in fact, and at the divorce trial Henry was to acquit him of that offence. What seems to have led her to that conclusion was the cardinal's close co-operation with his master in promoting the royal object. That Wolsey was in favour of the divorce as soon as he was consulted about the project is undoubted; and, deeply involved in it as he became, his prestige, his whole career was, as he was soon to realize and admit, pledged on a successful issue.

In the course of the cardinal's conversation at Rochester in the summer of 1527 he learnt that Catherine had told Fisher of her suspicions about the King's intentions and had asked for his advice. Fisher's reply to the Queen had been that he was willing to give her counsel in anything which concerned her, but that in matters concerning the King he would do nothing. It is clear, nevertheless, he had already made up his mind that the royal union was a valid one. But Fisher's temporary inactiveness had been secured. The seeking of the interview indicates the respect, and perhaps the fear, with which both Henry and Wolsey regarded Fisher, the greatest theologian among the bishops, and it also indicates the confidence which the Queen herself reposed in one who was to be her undeviating friend and supporter till the end.

Henceforth, till the fall of Wolsey, the story of the divorce is full of complex factors. There is the defensive dilatoriness of the Pope, Clement VII, who, after the King's problem was referred to him, was almost always content to temporize in a delicate situation. Though clever, cultured and shrewd in many ways, he was temperamentally ill-equipped to deal, even in a mediocre way, with a combination of problems which, it must be said, would have daunted a Sovereign Pontiff of consummate genius. As it was, he seems to have felt that a policy of constant delay was the only practicable one.

But there was, on the other hand, the egocentricity of the King, who assumed that whatever the Pope finally decided would be in his favour: it never seemed to enter his head that a decision would run counter to his wishes, which were, he considered, so eminently reasonable and just. Campeggio later said that the King always presupposed the invalidity of his marriage, "and I believe", he added, "that an angel descending from Heaven would be unable to persuade him otherwise".

Eventually, a commission was issued to Wolsey and Campeggio, Cardinal-Protector of England and Bishop of Salisbury, and an eminent canon lawyer, to hear the case in England in open court and to declare, if necessary, the nullity of the marriage. Then, after great pressure by the English envoys in Rome and hesitation on Clement VII's part, a secret decretal commission was issued to Campeggio which met all the royal wishes: it assumed a foreordained judgement in the King's favour and founded on an examination of only particular items of evidence. It was a serious proceeding and because it was so serious the commission was to be shown only to the King and Wolsey, and then immediately destroyed. Campeggio was, nevertheless, to do all that was possible to make Henry weaken in his set intentions and, if that failed, he was to try to persuade Catherine to become a nun. If all this were unsuccessful the trial was to be held.

Catherine, after a long pause, became notably active in defence. She certainly had no intention of taking vows of religion, a course which would have nullified the whole of her case. She appealed to Rome. A notarial document was presented to the Pope in which she mentions that she has heard of the proposal to send Campeggio to England in order to determine the King's "pretended suit". She asked the Pope to forbid the trial and impose silence. The cause should not be decided except at Rome. In the Papal Curia she would obtain justice.

In other ways Catherine had been active. The archives in Spain had been searched and a second papal dispensation had been found which fully met, it was alleged, the objections made by Henry and his advisers to the original bull of dispensation. This second dispensation was in the form of a Brief. It caused the King some surprise and perplexity; but the fact that he pronounced the Brief a forgery, and that he made determined attempts to secure it, is a measure of his perplexity. Catherine obtained a copy and kept it for production at the right moment.

Campeggio arrived in England in the autumn of 1528 after a journey from Rome which took three months to accomplish owing to his gouty condition, of which he had made the most out of Clement's express desire for procrastination. The new Legate interviewed the Queen. He used every means of persuasion to induce her to become a nun, but it was quite unavailing.

She intended to live and die, she said, in the state of matrimony into which God had called her. She would never alter that intention. No punishment, although she might be torn from limb to limb, would compel her to change. In sacramental confession she told Campeggio that her marriage to Prince Arthur had never been consummated and she gave him leave to tell this to the Pope. She also swore a public oath to that effect.

On 30 May 1529 the King licensed the two Legates to proceed according to their commission and on the next day the trial began in the priory of the Dominicans at Blackfriars. Both Henry and Catherine were then cited to appear before the Legatine court on 18 June. But during the second week of May Campeggio knew of a devastating fact which was bound to influence all the proceedings: the Emperor had decided to get the cause revoked to Rome.

II

Soon after Campeggio arrived in England in the autumn of 1528 Catherine told him that she was a foreigner without any friends, and when she made her last appearance before the court at Blackfriars she was to appeal against its jurisdiction in poignant terms, emphasizing that she was a stranger born out of the King's dominions. Catherine justly invites sympathy. She was now to be at bay in a country increasingly under the domination of a monarch of strong, determined personality. She needed friends and trusted counsellors more than at any period of her life, but there were to be a good many defections by people whose continued loyalty might have been expected. Most of her allotted counsellors at the trial were sooner or later to desert her cause, but that event she had foreseen, because, as she asserted, no reliance could be placed on them, since they were the King's subjects. We catch again and again in so much of her correspondence with the Emperor or in her dealings with Campeggio the note of anxiety about her fate. No marriages, she said, would be secure if hers were dissolved. Her case should not be determined in England where she feared the influence of the King's power. There was no security for her proper defence, and that was the

constant guiding principle of her attitude to the Legatine court—
that and the unhesitating allegiance to her conscience. Soon her
actions were to be watched, and if we can believe the Imperial
ambassador in England, it was put about, to serve, apparently,
as an additional weapon in the King's case, that Catherine had
attempted his life, a thing so inconsistent with her character
that we may dismiss it for the absurd invention it was. There
seems, however, to have been some such gossip, for Warham and
Tunstall, two of her counsellors, asked her, at an interview
apparently arranged to discuss other matters, whether it were true.
She told them she could not imagine a more abominable invention, for the King knew well that she prized his life more than her
own. There was no need, therefore, to discuss such a question
and the meeting proceeded to saner matters.

English political affairs were being increasingly influenced by
the King. He was now, by the measure of Tudor times, a man of
middle age—powerful, arrogant, intelligent, resourceful, possessing "one of the most purely egoistic temperaments known to
history". The Tudor kingship, ably strengthened by Henry VII,
was, under his son, a thing of king-worship. But Henry VIII
does not seem now to have been different in essential nature from
the days of his youth: in 1516 when he was no more than twenty-
five years of age his own opinion of his exalted kingly character
was that he had "no superior on earth". Perhaps Erasmus, visiting
the royal children at Eltham in 1499, had unconsciously found
a clue to the King's personality when he spoke of the boy Henry,
only some nine years old, as having even then "something of
royalty in his demeanour". Erasmus, as the later events of the
King's reign unfolded themselves, might have amplified his old
opinion in the light of those events. The lighter, gay days of the
Court in the first decade or two of the reign were dominated
by an *enfant terrible* of a King, considerably gifted, physically and
mentally, spending recklessly his father's fortune, a central figure
to whom everyone was attracted and to whom everyone gave
adulation. What we are soon to see is a deplorable development
of his character under the influence of absolute power.

Henry, surrounded by sycophantic and self-seeking courtiers and councillors, on whose lips the biblical dictum, "The wrath of a king is death", was often found, had manifold advantages, but Catherine, despite her pessimistic sentiments, was not without friends and supporters in her anxious situation. It would perhaps be inaccurate, and even anachronistic, to speak of a "Queen's Party", for the support which she received in this country was diffuse, and her band of real friends was small. But, unlike the King's supporters, they were strongly-principled and often very courageous. They manifestly needed courage, because Henry, in the years to come, never forgot or forgave a persistent support of the validity of his marriage to Catherine. As More was to declare after his conviction: "Yet I know full well what has been the chief cause of my condemnation: it is that I would never give my approval to this new marriage".

There were among Catherine's supporters great figures like John Fisher, one of her counsellors at the trial, and More, the old friend of the King and herself. There were her minor counsellors, who, unlike most of the greater ones, were consistently loyal, such as Thomas Abell, her chaplain, soon to render her incomparable service, and Richard Fetherston, Mary's schoolmaster, and Dr Edward Powell, the gifted Welsh scholar and preacher, and out-spoken little Dr Robert Ridley. There were the valiant Observant Franciscans, of her own religious order, many of whom were to give their strong adherence to her cause and some to preach in her favour, and, in particular, there was Dr John Forest, her confessor. There were the Spanish members of her suite, like Jorge de Atheca, Bishop of Llandaff, her physicians, Fernando Vitoria and De La Sá or Sé, her sewer, Francisco Phelippes (or Felipez), and her apothecary, Miguel de Soto, and there was her old favourite lady-in-waiting, Maria de Salinas, who had married Lord Willoughby d'Eresby, but was now a widow. Members of Catherine's suite were the object of particular sus-picion, for the King said there was nothing to fear from the Queen, but he was not so sure of her servants, both English and Spanish, especially the latter. Of Englishwomen, there were her old personal friends like Mary, the King's sister, who, for the most part far away in Suffolk, did not forget Catherine, and Margaret Pole, still Princess Mary's governess, and the resourceful Marchioness of Exeter, and the old Duchess of Norfolk.

Against all the assistance and consolation rendered by her special friends and adherents must be set the background of the Queen's popularity in the country at large. In London she was held in high esteem by the populace. When, it was said, she was once leaving her royal residence through a gallery for the priory of Blackfriars, she was so warmly greeted by immense crowds, who openly wished her victory over her enemies, that the King ordered nobody to be again admitted to the place. She never lost that affection of the common people which she had captured when she came to England nearly thirty years before. If, indeed, the opinion of the whole country could have been taken at the time of the trial, a vast majority would very probably have been found unfavourable to the dissolution of the Queen's marriage.

Carefully watched by the King's supporters and agents, Catherine in these difficult days relied, for any delicate negotiations, on those persons who were of proved trustworthiness. These were, in particular, the Spanish members of her staff, people who spoke her native tongue and had an intelligent appreciation of her problems. In March 1527 she sent her Spanish physician, Doctor Fernando Vitoria, to Spain in order to inform the Emperor of the rumours of the King's intentions about a divorce. Catherine valued Vitoria's qualities highly and he successfully accomplished his mission. In the summer she sent Francisco Phelippes, who had served her well for many years, to the Emperor with further news, especially news about the King's actual intention to procure a dissolution of his marriage, an intention which he had recently communicated to Catherine.

The Imperial ambassador in England had at first tried to dissuade the Queen from sending a messenger to Spain, considering that the better course would be to write to the Emperor. These English, he said, were so suspicious at this time that no courier of hers would be allowed to sail. In the event, he was right about the suspicions, but Catherine felt that in her distressful position no one but the Emperor could help her. A trusted Spanish servant would be able to tell him by word of mouth so much of recent developments, and she needed the Emperor's advice and consolation. She therefore gambled valiantly on Francisco's reaching Spain, despite her awareness of the enemies about her. Would she win?

Considerable dissimulation was practised in the business by both Henry and Catherine. We are told that Phelippes had applied to the King for a licence to go to Spain because his mother was "very sore sick". The Queen, so it was said, refused her assent and laboured with the King to prevent it. But Henry "knowing of the collusion between the two doth also dissymule, feigning that Phelippes' desire is made upon good ground and consideration, and easily hath persuaded the Queen to be content with his going". If the Spaniard were captured by the King's enemies in France or on the high seas the King would, he said, willingly pay his ransom. All this Henry did to gain the messenger's confidence. Wolsey, who was at Calais, was called in to play his part. He was told that the Queen's agent must be stopped in some part of France, but it must not get about that his detention was the result of any machinations by the King, Wolsey or any of the King's subjects. The matter was apparently too delicate for that. Henry was aware that the only cause of this man's going to Spain was that he is "and hath been always privy unto the Queen's affairs and secrets". Phelippes gave the King to understand that he intended to pass through France, but if this was merely further dissimulation and he meant to travel by sea, then the English ambassador in Spain was to be notified, and he was to find out in every possible way all that the Spaniard said and did. It was a matter which the King regarded as highly important.

Francisco came across none of Henry's or Wolsey's spies, and evaded, no doubt with the aid of Catherine's friends in this country, the web of plotting which had been spun for him, and successfully reached the Emperor. Clearly, he was a man of address. Charles V was told of the Queen's affairs, of which, however, he already knew from the Imperial ambassador, and some English merchants in Spain had also gossiped about the business. But the Queen's agent was able to supply much confidential information.

The Emperor promised Catherine help and said that his latest despatch to the ambassador might be shown to her, if it was thought desirable for the tranquillity of her mind.

Wolsey found it necessary to attempt to counteract what had been done. Any rumour that the question of a divorce was in the air was false, he wrote to the two English ambassadors in Spain. If the Emperor referred to the matter, in view of what either Vitoria or Phelippes had said, the ambassadors were to give him "a prudent reply". No dissolution of the King's marriage was intended, but only "confirmation" of it, in view of French qualms. It was pretty feeble lying.

The King's chief minister was now becoming inordinately suspicious of the Queen's friends, and a few months after his return from Spain, Phelippes was examined "in the gentlest manner possible", presumably, though we are not told, to obtain vital information. Vives, another Spaniard, it is to be noted, was also examined. They were both prevented from leaving London or visiting the Court.

In anticipation of the trial to be opened in England, counsellors were appointed for the Queen in October 1528. That she was right in thinking that most of them would prove no impartial counsellors, since they were the King's subjects, is seen from the outset, for, in order to compel Catherine to take certain action, they were given a tendentiously-worded document entitled, *Advice to be given to the Queen's Grace by her counsel*. There seems little doubt that this was drawn up by the express desire of the King. It said that after search had been made in the royal treasury no Brief could be found corresponding to the copy which Catherine had obtained from Spain. The counsellors of the King, therefore, think that the Brief is a forgery. When the trial begins the Queen's certified copy will not help her case, and the King, for his part, cannot be satisfied with it nor ought he to be. Catherine must write to the Emperor for the original, which should be sent to England by way of Bayonne. If this is not done,

G

it will mean the ruin of her affairs and endanger her child's inheritance. The Emperor could have a copy made, it was complacently suggested: that would serve his purpose very well. Catherine should further tell the Emperor that she has promised to obtain the Brief within three months, failing which sentence will probably be pronounced against her. She must make a notarial declaration that she fully intends to take this action. There must be no risk of frivolous delay.

Somewhat later in the year Francisco Phelippes went again to Spain, this time in the company of John Curson, a groom of the King's chamber. He carried with him "letters of great importance." The King had agreed that Catherine should send Phelippes, and the French ambassador provided a safe-conduct through France. The "letters of great importance" probably included a request for the Brief. But Francisco broke his arm at Abbeville and was obliged to return to England. Curson went on to Spain. It was a curious incident.

Catherine then wrote to her nephew for the original Brief. She told him it had been asserted that the copy which she had obtained would not suffice to be read before a judge. She begged the Emperor for the love of God to help her to obtain justice. Her letter was to be conveyed to Spain by her chaplain, Thomas Abell, but with him she sent an old faithful Spanish servant, Juan de Montoya. She did not trust her chaplain.

What do we know of Thomas Abell? He had been educated at Oxford and was a distinguished theologian. In later years he was described as "Doctor Abell". It is not known when he was appointed as the Queen's chaplain, but it must have been before the beginning of 1528, for in that year the King made him a New Year's gift in common with other members of Catherine's suite. The Queen's distrust is somewhat curious, for he was to prove one of the most steadfast of all her friends and to be a martyr for his religious faith. At her trial he was chosen as one of her theological counsellors. Perhaps Abell was a rather grave, taciturn man, about whom Catherine, with all her insight into men's characters, could not make up her mind, but it is also possible that in her state of acute anxiety she felt unable to have much faith in anyone whose absolute loyalty had not been tested in some vital matter. A little earlier she had expressed fear lest the original Brief should fall into the hands of her enemies, for the persons whom the King would send to Spain would spare no trouble to get hold of it, particularly as there was no record whatever of it in Rome. But there were informers all round the Queen. The Imperial ambassador considered that Catherine should send a power of attorney to Rome, declining any tribunal in England, but the power could not be sent because she was surrounded by spies in her chamber and was allowed little liberty.

Abell was told nothing about his mission to Spain, except that it was the King's desire to obtain the Brief. De Montoya, on the other hand, was well primed. He carried no letter from England, but was coached assiduously by the Imperial ambassador in everything that he had to say to the Emperor, committing it all to memory.

And so the two messengers travelled in that grim winter month of January across the turbulent Bay of Biscay to Spain. But it was the distrusted Thomas Abell who immediately on arrival took over the reins from de Montoya and acted astutely for the Queen. And since he knew nothing of any secret instructions, it must have been de Montoya who confided them to him on the journey south. For it was Abell who wrote to the Emperor, telling him that, in no circumstances, must he give up the Brief, notwithstanding the Queen's letter to him earnestly asking for it: she had been compelled under oath to write in such a way. Moreover, the Emperor should ask his ambassadors to do everything possible to prevent the examination of the Queen's suit at any other place than Rome. They should complain that the Pope had given many injunctions against the Queen, without hearing all the particulars of her case.

The result of Abell's action was an interview with the Emperor at Saragossa—the city before which, more than seven and a half centuries previously, Charlemagne had appeared in his attempt to win Spain for Christianity, only to find the city gates closed against him by the Arab governor. At the interview were the two English ambassadors, Edward Lee and Ghinucci, the Bishop of

Worcester. But it is significant that while they were at Valladolid Abell did not come to see them, because, he said, *the Emperor had sent for him*. He had thus been able to concert with the Emperor, before the ambassadors arrived, the plan of campaign to be followed at Saragossa. They did not know of Thomas Abell's adroit move in the Queen's interests.

The Brief was produced and read. A statement was desired by the English ambassadors of all that was said at the meeting, and this was arranged. They pointed out how necessary it was for the discharge of the King's conscience, and the security and quietness of the realm, that the Brief should come safely to England, and for those reasons the Emperor, in sending it, need not be apprehensive. Smilingly, the Emperor replied that if things "were in better point than they are" he would not fear sending it, but his mind was not tranquil until he knew whether the Brief had been found registered at Rome. "*Master Abell was present at this interview, but said nothing.*"

A transcript of the document was prepared under the authority of three bishops who were present, that is to say, it was a properly-authenticated copy, a legal instrument, which the Imperial ambassador had suggested should be made months ago. During the reading of the Brief, Lee noticed, so he said, some words to the effect that the Queen had been known in marriage by Prince Arthur, though he admitted to Wolsey: "I may, peradventure, mistake the words of the Brief, for I only heard it read". The other ambassador also alleged he had noticed the words. But Thomas Abell told Lee that Catherine had taken an oath that she had not consummated the marriage. Perhaps it was inevitable, knowing Wolsey's precarious position, the precise desires of the King and because of their own lack of success in obtaining the original, that the ambassadors should be full of suspicion about the way the document had come to light and also declare it to contain flaws.

III

If there were any doubt of Wolsey's almost morbid anxiety

in these months before the commencement of the trial at Black-friars, it would be dispelled by the many references that he and others make to the disastrous consequences of a result unfavourable to the King. Should assent not be given promptly to the royal desires, he said to the Pope, the King would be driven by divine and human law to seek his rights from the whole of Christendom, a possible by-passing of the Pope's jurisdiction which was perhaps already not absent from the King's mind. The authority of the Apostolic See in this kingdom, he said later, would be annihilated. In January 1529 the Imperial ambassador declared that the King was beginning to blame the cardinal because he did not fulfil his promises, a statement which indicates that Wolsey's stock was perhaps beginning to fail. Moreover, Anne Boleyn, a malicious enemy to have, suspected the cardinal of placing obstacles in her way, because, if she became Queen, his power would decline. This was rather unjust to him, as he was, in fact, taking every possible measure to promote the King's object.

Wolsey was never a friend of Catherine's and was not likely to approach her directly in matters which concerned her so intimately at this time, but in the late summer of 1528 he tried to influence her by sounding an able protégé of his, Robert Shorton, her almoner. His career before he became almoner illustrates the extent of the value of his services to the Queen.

Shorton, now a man in early middle age, had been a scholar of Jesus College, Cambridge, and had had a distinguished academic career. He seems at an early age to have come under the notice of Fisher and he did superlatively good work in the foundation of St John's College.

The foundation of St John's was the result of Margaret Beaufort's munificence and her great interest in learning. She had left a considerable legacy to establish a new college at Cambridge for a master and fifty scholars, besides servants, and also buildings and endowments. Under Fisher's *aegis* this college became St John's. Much of the necessary work devolved upon him, for he was one of the executors of Margaret Beaufort's will, and the other executors left to him the important task of drawing up the statutes of foundation. Shorton, most probably owing to

Fisher's influence, was appointed First Master of St John's. He was that rather rare combination, an able scholar and excellent man of business. He superintended the erection of the college buildings, supervised the expenditure, and guarded the revenues, which continued to flourish during the whole time of his Mastership. He resigned his post in 1526 to become Master of Pembroke Hall; and it was at this stage of his career that he attracted the patronage of Wolsey, who employed him, obviously on account of his invaluable work at St John's, "in stocking and cultivating" the cardinal's new foundation at Oxford. Wolsey thought highly of him, making him the Dean of his own chapel and employing him as an examiner of heretics, for Shorton was a religious conservative. A large number of ecclesiastical posts which he held was doubtless due to Wolsey's influence. In 1527 he became Dean of Windsor, an appointment which brought him into close association with the Court, and probably about this time he became Queen Catherine's almoner. The latter appointment is likely to have been due to Fisher's recommendation.

The post of almoner was of mediaeval conception and had for its basis the necessity of dispensing Christian charity. Such posts existed in monasteries and in great lay households. It was an important office in itself, but with Catherine, as a fervent lay Franciscan, it assumed added significance. She was noted for her works of mercy among the poor and even Wolsey was obliged to admit that she was very charitable. Her appointment of Robert Shorton seems to reveal a hitherto unnoticed aspect of his character: he was not only an administrator of proved ability, but he must also have possessed a sense of discerning sympathy for those to whom alms were dispensed out of the large sums which Queen Catherine had available for the purpose.

No necessitous person ever came to the gates of any of the royal palaces without obtaining relief from the Queen. She required her almoner to be diligent in the distribution of alms and to have a special care for the impotent and aged, for they moved her heart much. In whatever towns and villages she resided, she would steal forth in disguise to discover what particular kind of relief was needed—whether shirts or smocks or money—or she would visit women in child-bed, causing bread and ale and candles to be brought, or sheets or linen.

But when Wolsey saw the Queen's almoner in 1528 it was not about Catherine's Christian works that he wanted to talk: he wished to know from him what recent tidings the Queen had heard in the King's Matter. Shorton's answer was that there were none, except that Campeggio was coming to decide the matrimonial suit. The cardinal then spoke much of the benefits which the King had conferred on Shorton—no doubt through Wolsey's influence—and emphasized Shorton's obligation to be "true and faithful". He asked him to keep their conversation as secret as if under the seal of confession. What, asked Wolsey, were the Queen's "intentions" in the matter of the suit? Shorton had often heard the Queen mention, he said, that if she could enjoy "her natural defence and justice", she trusted it would take such effect as would be acceptable to God and man. She based the strength of her case on the fact that she had never been known by Prince Arthur. She asserted that neither of the two Legates was competent to judge her; that she had never been heard in her defence; and that the Brief from Spain, of which she had copies, removed all the impediments to her marriage.

Wolsey was obviously very annoyed and expressed himself forcefully to the almoner. He marvelled not a little at the Queen's "indiscreet and ungodly purposes and sayings": she was not of such virtue and perfection as he once thought her to be. He proceeded to rebut her opinions in detail, pointing out the dire consequence to her if she persisted in maintaining them.

But it all made little difference to Robert Shorton. He was a better man than the cardinal and from constant association with the Queen had acquired a true appreciation of her worth. He was to remain her friend and supporter.

CHAPTER 7

Queen's Counsellors

I

Soon after Campeggio arrived in England the King consulted Catherine about the appointment of her counsellors for the coming divorce trial. She much desired to have Spanish advocates and proctors, but Henry, whose watchword was now haste, would not agree to that course because, so he said, they would take such a long time to come. But he allowed her to ask for two good lawyers from Flanders and accordingly she wrote for them to the Archduchess Margaret, Regent of the Netherlands. They came. They were de la Blekerie and Van Scoere, who, though young, were excellent jurists. And it was agreed that Vives, Catherine's old friend, should also be appointed. But the two Flemish lawyers left soon after their arrival, apparently because the time was not yet ripe for action: no process was in being and there seems to have been nothing for them to do.

Catherine's English counsellors were a commendable and not unformidable array. They were in each case comparable in proved ability and distinguished attainments with any advocate on the King's side, and, in allowing them to act for Catherine, the King was not being unreasonable. Two were major theologians: one, John Fisher, Bishop of Rochester, the Queen's old friend, she herself had chosen with the King's approval; the other was Henry Standish, Bishop of St Asaph. There were four other theologians, sometimes regarded as lesser lights, but who were nevertheless conspicuously able; and in the case of one of them, Richard Fetherston, still Princess Mary's schoolmaster, we again see the direction of Catherine's wishes. Thomas Abell, her chap-

lain, another of the theologians, may have been added at a later
stage with her concurrence. The remaining theological advisers
were Dr Edward Powell, a Welshman of considerable academic
qualifications and a notable Court preacher, and Dr Robert
Ridley, to prove himself a dauntless advocate for the Queen. It
was almost inevitable that her Spanish confessor, Jorge de Atheca,
Bishop of Llandaff, an obscure but faithful figure, and for long a
member of her suite, should be added to the others. But he played
little active part in the proceedings. Of particular significance is
the fact that no less than four of the six theologians, Fisher, Abell,
Fetherston and Powell, were to be undeviatingly loyal to
Catherine's cause and to die one day for their religious convictions.

The civil and canon lawyers were not less men of pronounced
ability: Thomas Warham, Archbishop of Canterbury, Cuthbert
Tunstall, Bishop of London, Nicholas West, Bishop of Ely, and
John Clerk, Bishop of Bath and Wells. All were religious conservatives, but they were without the steel in their characters that
most of the theologians possessed, although Warham, towards
the end of his long life, was to show that he had the makings of a
martyr, whilst Tunstall gave more resistance to ecclesiastical
innovations than did many of his fellow members of the hierarchy.

Fisher had early made known the nature and extent of his
views on the divorce question, and had become increasingly
feared and disliked by both the King and Wolsey. To Catherine
he was a source of inspiration and fortitude. Invariably fearless in
expressing his views once he had made up his mind, he was uncompromising in his attitude, but scrupulous and scholarly in his
examination of any problem presented to him. He found, he said,
that the authorities he had consulted about the validity of the
dispensation for Henry's marriage greatly differed among themselves: some declared that the marriage was prohibited by divine
law, others that it was lawful. After mature consideration he
affirmed that he saw an easy answer to those who denied its
lawfulness, but not to those of the other side. He perceived, too,
what others did not, or were in course of time unwilling to see,
because they were the King's men, that the question of granting
a dispensation was inevitably linked with the unique authority

given to the Pope by Christ. Who can deny, he said, that the Pope may grant a dispensation, in virtue of that authority, for any serious cause? But even if it were admitted that the arguments were balanced on either side, Fisher would be decided by the fact that it belonged to the Pope to pronounce on ambiguous passages of Scripture, after hearing the views of the best divines; otherwise it was in vain that Christ had granted to His Church powers to loose and bind. Thus had the Pope more than once declared that it was lawful to dispense in such a case as the King's. That, Fisher thought, should determine the question.

Henry Standish was from the outset the most doubtful of Catherine's theological counsellors and, perhaps inevitably, from a conspectus of his earlier career, was to range himself subsequently on the King's side. He had studied at both Oxford and Cambridge, had joined the Conventual Franciscans (he was, it should be noted—in view of subsequent important events in which the Observant Franciscans were involved—never an Observant), had become Warden of the Grey Friars at Newgate in London and then Provincial of his order. He early came under Henry VIII's notice and was for years a Court preacher. It is not without significance that in the situation which arose from the *cause célèbre* of Hunne in 1515, he displeased Convocation by his opposition to clerical immunity, but obtained the King's protection and so received no punishment. Three years later he was made Bishop of St Asaph. Richard Pace, the King's Latin secretary, had expressed to Wolsey an unsympathetic view of Standish's probable episcopal appointment when he heard of the King's intentions: he would be "right sorry for the good service he [Standish] was like to do the Church", and he is mortified to think that the promotion will go to him. All this did not prevent the bishop from speaking somewhat in Catherine's favour, but she distrusted him and her distrust was not misplaced. He became later entirely the King's man and was one of the three bishops who consecrated Cranmer as Archbishop of Canterbury in 1533.

Of the lesser theologians, Dr Robert Ridley was the kind of man, learned, of firm character and an outspoken advocate, whom Catherine needed. He came of an old-established, gentle family, which for some three hundred years had had its seat on South Tyneside. The Ridleys were influential in Northumbrian affairs and the religious conservatism of the North was not without its effect on the formation of Robert Ridley's Catholicism. He studied at Cambridge and the Sorbonne, became an able scholar, and at Cambridge and in London emerged as a figure of importance. Pronouncedly on the conservative side in religion, as he was, he took an active part in the trials of heretics, but, paradoxically enough, he was the uncle of the eventual Protestant martyr, Nicholas Ridley, for whose education at Pembroke Hall, and also at the Sorbonne, Robert Ridley provided. Nicholas himself studied for the Church, and either Fisher or Bishop West of Ely, a canon lawyer and advocate for the Queen, ordained him. Another of Catherine's counsellors, Cuthbert Tunstall, was Robert's kinsman, and it may have been Tunstall's final acceptance of the Royal Supremacy, after some opposition and hesitation, which contributed to Robert Ridley's own act of conformity. But this was much in the future and does not minimize the value of the noteworthy support which he gave to Catherine's cause at the trial.

The influence of Robert Ridley on Thomas Cranmer is not well known. When Cranmer was in Germany in 1532 he told Cochlaeus, the distinguished German Catholic theologian and the associate of Campeggio some years before the divorce, that he held Ridley in high esteem, regarding him as his teacher and as a source of his inspiration in philosophy. Cranmer brought back from Cochlaeus a letter for Ridley. Perhaps Ridley's influence had been manifesting itself in a specific direction, for, when the divorce was the most vital concern of English political affairs, not only were some English ambassadors abroad not being particularly loyal to Henry, but also, indeed, Cranmer, who was actually betraying the King in his talks with foreign rulers. Was this another of the tergiversations of that famous scholarly, timid mind, of the man brought from the quietude of his Cambridge study to become, at a most crucial moment of English history, a man of affairs to promote the King's great object? In any case, Granvelle, the Emperor's chancellor, later wrote to Chapuys, the

Imperial ambassador in London, telling him how surprised he was at what Cranmer had done against Catherine and Princess Mary, because, when Cranmer was at Ratisbon—he was there in the first half of 1532—he blamed exceedingly what the King, his master, and his ministers were doing in the matter of the divorce and against the Queen and her daughter. This was only a year before Cranmer's consecration as Archbishop of Canterbury and, in England, he had already taken a prominent stand against the validity of Henry's marriage to Catherine.

Dr Edward Powell, the last of the assembly of the Queen's theologians, was the able Welshman who, at this time and in the years to come, was a valiant defender of her cause.

The most notable of Catherine's canon lawyers, Thomas Warham, Archbishop of Canterbury, was now a very old man. He was a Wykehamist who had been elected to a Fellowship of Winchester's sister foundation, New College, Oxford, more than fifty years previously. A grave, devout, learned man and one of the leading humanists of the day, his attitude to the divorce, which was on the whole in the King's favour, may, perhaps, partly be explained by some qualms about the validity of the dispensation for Henry's marriage which he felt at the time, and partly, perhaps, by his constitutional timidity and rather complacent nature.

In the summer of 1527, when Wolsey was on his way to France, he went to see Warham at Dartford before visiting Fisher at Rochester. Wolsey was now becoming deeply involved in the King's Matter. He spoke to Warham about it and of how the knowledge of Henry's attitude had come to the Queen's ears, of how "displeasantly" she had heard of it and what the King had done for the "pacification of her". Warham was naïve enough to believe that the King's grace intended nothing more than the "searching and trying out of the truth", because of the doubts supposed to have been expressed by the Bishop of Tarbes about Princess Mary's legitimacy. The Archbishop wondered how the Queen could have arrived at her particular knowledge, forgetting, or being unsuspicious of the fact, that she always had eager informants. He added that, however "displeasantly" she took the matter, truth must prevail and judgement according to "the law" take place. "I have sufficiently instructed him", finally Wolsey tells the King, "how he shall order himself in case the Queen demands his counsel." It did not seem likely that he would prove a strong advocate for Catherine.

But in the year of his death, 1532, by which time he had been able to observe the recent sinister drift of ecclesiastical affairs, it is clear that his attitude had undergone a significant change and it seems morally certain that he would have ended as a martyr for his religious views. In March of this same year, when Parliament met to discuss the business of the divorce, the Archbishop spoke against the King much to his indignation. The King used foul language to him, declaring that were it not for Warham's age, he would make him repent of what he had said. And an unknown correspondent of Cromwell's, after Warham's death, testified to the Archbishop's change of attitude. This correspondent had spoken to Cromwell about Catherine's cause and had declared his opinion against her purpose, adding "that he never did speak *for* her, but when he was enforced by the late Archbishop of Canterbury".

More important than this evidence was the draft speech which he prepared shortly before his death, in answer to a charge of praemunire: it shows him in a strong light of defiance. He had been threatened with praemunire because, as long ago as 1518, he had, it was asserted, consecrated Henry Standish as Bishop of St Asaph without waiting for royal confirmation of the temporalities of the See. The reply he intended to make emphasizes in clear, incisive terms the importance with which he viewed the spiritual power as compared with the temporal power. "I intend", he says, "to do only that I am bound to do by the laws of God and Holy Church". The spiritual power of the Archbishops should not depend on the temporal power of the prince and thus be of little or no effect. Warham was mindful of the struggle of Thomas à Becket against Henry II for the freedom of the Church. Becket, he said, "was rewarded by God with the great honour of martyrdom, which is the best death that can be . . . which thing is the example and comfort of others to speak and do for the liberties of God's Church. . . . I think it is better for me to suffer the same than in my conscience to confess this article to be a praemunire for which St Thomas died".

Erasmus had long ago lauded Warham's qualities of mind and character, even speaking of him in terms similar to those he used of Fisher. He was of great piety and charity, and he died, said Thomas More, incredibly poor, possessing not much more money than would pay his debts, a sufficient commentary on his benevolence.

Cuthbert Tunstall, Bishop of London, the kinsman of Robert Ridley, was another of Catherine's legal counsellors. Educated at both Oxford and Cambridge, but chiefly at Cambridge, he later went to Padua where he became a doctor of laws. He enjoyed the friendship of Warham, More and other humanists, and his exceptional learning received the praise of Erasmus. He was Warham's chancellor and in 1522 became Bishop of London. His religious conservatism, great erudition and piety gave promise of valuable defence of the Queen's cause, and during the early years of the divorce he supported Catherine and later offered some opposition to the royal supreme claims, but he became the King's man in the end.

A brilliant diplomatist in both Henry VII's and Henry VIII's reigns, Nicholas West, who had been at Eton and was a scholar of King's College, Cambridge, was rewarded with the bishopric of Ely for his diplomatic work. It is of interest that, like another of the Queen's counsellors, Edward Powell, Bishop West early came under the notice of old Bishop Smith of Lincoln, a man of orthodox religious views and of much perspicacity, who was responsible for West's early ecclesiastical progress and who may have brought him to the notice of Henry VII, for he became a royal chaplain. The business of the divorce has left few records of his work on behalf of Catherine, but we know that with Warham, Fisher and others he witnessed the Queen's written appeal to the Pope which was drawn up on 16 June 1529. He died at an advanced age in 1533, before the King's supreme claims had hardened into relentless fact.

We have more information about the activities of John Clerk, Bishop of Bath and Wells. Clerk had been at Cambridge and had afterwards studied at Bologna, receiving a doctor's degree in law there. His attitude towards Catherine's cause was vacillating. There seems at first to have been some hope of a forthrightness similar to Fisher's, for the day after the last appearance of Catherine at the Legatine court—an event which will be recounted—he came before it with Fisher, asserting, according to the Venetian ambassador, that, to prevent the King from falling into mortal sin, both he and Fisher would defend the rights of the Queen and would prove that she was his legitimate wife. (It was precisely on the ground that Catherine was held not to be his legitimate wife that the King said he had been living in grave sin all the time of his married life.) Fisher and Clerk presented a writ of appeal against the tribunal and rejected the two judges as suspect. But a few weeks after the revocation of the marriage suit to Rome, Clerk altered his tune. He thought that in consequence of the revocation, and of the fact that the judges' hands in England were now tied, Catherine ought not to attempt to advance her suit at Rome, but she trusted more, said Wolsey, to the counsel of strangers and the Imperialists than to her own English counsellors. Both Clerk and Tunstall, Wolsey went on to say, would, however, try to dissuade her from taking further action in that direction. He had told Clerk of the danger to the Queen if the King were cited to appear before the papal court or if any process were made against him in Rome. All this Clerk knew well and he protested that, if Catherine were wilful, he would not continue to act as her counsellor. He was not prepared to die in her cause.

Most of the Queen's advocates prepared treatises for her defence and these were used in the course of the trial. They were compositions in manuscript and termed "books" in the parlance of the time. Fisher wrote a good number and some were printed. Clerk wrote one book and Thomas More, some years after the revocation of the divorce suit, told how once he had borrowed it. But More would not meddle with the King's Matter and had therefore cast it aside. When he happened to come across it one day, he offered to return it, but Clerk said he had long previously "discharged his mind of that matter". He had, indeed, forgotten that he had given More a copy. And because "he no more minded to meddle anything in the matter", he had burnt his own copy. He desired More to do likewise. And so, said More, "upon my faith did I".

II

The most bitter disappointment to Catherine at this time arose in the person of Luis Vives, her protégé. She had every right to expect his active support. She had long ago befriended him in his need, ensuring that he was paid a pension, had welcomed him to the English court and made much of him. Both there and on those long summer days when visiting the Bridgettines at Syon, she delighted to talk with him in her native tongue on religion, philosophy and letters. Here, she must have felt, was a spirit of like nature to her own, who reminded her of far-off Spanish days and who was attracted to those things of the intellect and spirit which held her most. She appreciated the sound orthodoxy of his Catholicism and the warmth of his discerning humanism. He had helped her in the past in many ways, not least in the task of providing for the education of Mary. He would surely be a great source of strength in the crisis which now faced her. Either in England or at his home in the Netherlands he was near at hand.

It was, indeed, counsellors or advocates from the dominions of her nephew, the Emperor Charles V, whom Catherine wanted, because of her distrust of most of her English counsellors. Advocates from Spain had, however, been denied her, but she pressed strongly for canon lawyers from Flanders. Only four days before the opening of the court at Blackfriars wise Archduchess Margaret informed the Emperor of an urgent message received from Catherine, who wanted Flemish lawyers to help her to marshal all the arguments and allegations involved in her case, and to draw up appeals. But the Emperor's view seems to have been that, since Catherine's suit was not to be decided in England —he had, of course, already resolved that the proper place for it to be heard was Rome—no lawyers need be sent. The Queen, said Archduchess Margaret, was very perplexed.

Catherine was still more unfortunately placed when Mendoza, the Imperial ambassador, left England, for his successor, Chapuys, did not come till late August 1529, some weeks after the revocation of the cause to Rome. Mendoza, like the Archduchess, pleaded with the Emperor, and wrote to him from Brussels only the day before that on which Catherine was to appear before the Legatine court (18 June). He said that Catherine wanted the assistance of the two Flemish lawyers who had left England months ago. Could they return? He mentioned, as the Archduchess had done, the work they would be required to perform. If advocates were not sent, the people in England who favoured the Queen's cause would think she had been abandoned. They do not seem to have been sent.

The Queen had consulted Luis Vives in the earlier days of her matrimonial trouble and he gave her the counsel and consolation she needed. She was anxious at that time lest she should be condemned unheard. Then in the autumn of 1528 she chose Vives as one of her counsellors, and soon afterwards there took place Vives' short detention in London in company with Francisco Phelippes. This act was the work of Wolsey, full of suspicion about Spanish activities. Vives had been asked to disclose what he had lately spoken about with the Queen, a proceeding which he regarded as an intolerable intrusion on the liberty of a private person. What, indeed, he spoke about, he said, would injure no one, even if it were publicized on church doors. But the example was a bad one, for a great part of the intercourse in life must rest upon trust and confidence, which, if destroyed, would put everyone on guard as much against a friend as against an enemy.

When Catherine selected Vives as an advocate, he considered that it would be unwise to defend herself before the Legatine court at Blackfriars, and he refused to act. But she had already petitioned the Pope that her cause should be heard by him and, what was to be made clear, Catherine actually took the course which Vives had recommended. Nevertheless, the Queen was angry, because, Vives afterwards said, he did not obey her will

H

but rather his own reason, and she took away the pension she had been paying him.

It is difficult to be certain that the Queen's great Spanish friend was to blame. But Catherine seems to have felt that in her great need of support at this time, Vives was one of the few suitable people who could give it. She was not the kind of character to reject an old friend without sound reason and on this occasion she was angry indeed. Even if she appeared to reject Vives' advice, there was much work, short of active advocacy, for him to do, and her subsequent, late appeal for help from Flanders proves her need.

Did Vives lack the necessary moral courage in the new situation? Something more was now needed than smooth words of comfort to a distressed woman, and for this he must forget the absorbing delights of study and speculation in a congenial library. We know that Vives was a nervous man and that the work of editing, at the request of Erasmus, St Augustine's *The City of God* had caused a nervous breakdown in 1521. He retired to Bruges and his recovery was slow. But even nervous men frequently act with consummate courage in a crisis. Was his recollection of his recent examination in custody at Wolsey's direction too anxiously vivid, and was he fearful of another spell of imprisonment? Yet there remains the fact of the advice which he gave Catherine, whose subsequent action accorded with it. Certainty about the entire blameworthiness of Vives eludes us.

The two appeals which Catherine was to make in person against the competence of the Legatine court to judge her were extremely able. Who advised her in the details of their making? Vives was in Flanders, having washed his hands of active measures. Fisher, the one great friend among her counsellors, was much too closely watched by Wolsey and his agents. It is a matter of puzzling surmise. But one man who seems to have been capable of giving assistance of the kind required was close at hand: Thomas Abell, her astute chaplain and appointed counsellor, who had already proved his worth in a difficult mission. That he studied the whole problem of the marriage case assiduously and thoroughly his long, erudite, distinguished work, *Invicta Veritas*, to be printed in a year or two, was to prove. Although he was a theologian rather than a canon lawyer he knew enough of canon law to deal with legal aspects of the marriage and to assist Catherine in her precise object. And what exactly had he discussed with the Emperor in Spain, if not all the aspects of Catherine's problem, not excluding perhaps the terms in which she should lodge an appeal against the competence of the Legatine court? It was only some five weeks after the vital meeting at Saragossa that Campeggio was writing about the Emperor's decision to get the cause revoked to Rome, and it could not have been more than a comparatively short time before the opening of the court at Blackfriars when Thomas Abell returned to England. He appears, indeed, to have been the one knowledgeable, judicious counsellor whom Catherine was conveniently able to consult at short notice when the Flemish jurists for whom she was pressing did not arrive—the chaplain who had aroused no suspicion of any partiality towards Catherine's cause in England, or in the minds of the English ambassadors in Spain. And to throw any inquisitive spies off the scent he could always, if necessary, converse with the Queen in Spanish, a language which few about the royal court knew.

Two days before Catherine's appearance at the Legatine court on 18 June 1529 she went to see Campeggio on her way to Greenwich. She was very worried. The Flemish lawyers had not come and she was anxious to have various particulars about the state of her case, especially whether it had been revoked to Rome by the Pope. The Pope, Campeggio told her, could not take action of that kind without much consideration, since two Legates had been appointed for the trial in England.

Meanwhile, the King's party were doing their utmost to ensure that the cause should be tried and determined in England. What, said Campeggio, Catherine would do in those circumstances, was unknown. Some people thought she would object to the place, some to the judges. Some thought she would appear before the court, others that she would allege some impediment in its constitution. But Catherine knew well what she would do. She was hardly likely to tell Campeggio.

When the court at Blackfriars met for the first time on the last day of May, Henry and Catherine were cited to appear on 18 June. The court then adjourned. The Queen came on the day arranged. She refused to recognize the competence of the tribunal. How could its members be competent? she argued. Wolsey was an Englishman, the King's chief minister; Campeggio, the judge, held the bishopric of Salisbury; the other members were the king's men, who would obey his behests. The proper person to judge her was the Pope. The court said it would reply to her protestation on 21 June.

On that day the King and, unexpectedly, the Queen, appeared in person. The court was crowded. Besides the two judges the King's and Queen's counsellors and proctors, there were the remaining English bishops and the scribes and all the other officers of the court, and many privileged spectators. Two of the Queen's counsellors are specially singled out by Cavendish, Wolsey's gentleman-usher, who wrote the cardinal's life and was very probably an eye-witness of the scene. One of these two was Fisher, tall, frailly thin, of greatly dignified bearing, with the mark of scholarliness and sanctity in his pale face—"a very godly man", says Cavendish, "who after suffered death . . . which was greatly lamented through all the universities of Christendom"; the second was a very different man in appearance, one of the Queen's lesser theologians, "ancient Doctor Ridley, a very small man in stature, but surely a great and excellent clerk in divinity".

After the required preliminaries were completed, the court crier called the King: "King Henry of England, come into the court", and the King answered, "Here, my lords". Then the Queen was called. She did not answer, but rose from her chair, a short, stoutish figure, but immensely dignified, and cast herself at the King's feet in full sight of the court. There was tension in the silence which her action had evoked. In her broken English she spoke, we may infer, fluently, emphatically, feelingly, because of the things that must be said, and all in that place—the judges, her counsellors and old friends, even, perhaps the King himself, for he was an emotional man—must have been moved by her sheer sincerity and by the high drama of the moment.

Catherine begged the King, for all the love that they had had for each other and for the love of God, to grant her justice and to show compassion on her. She was, she said, a poor woman and a stranger from abroad. She had no sure friend, and no impartial counsel. (This was not altogether an accurate statement, but perhaps was an excusable, rhetorical flourish.) She came to the King as to the fount of justice in the kingdom. In what way had she offended him? God and all the world were her witnesses that she had been a true, obedient wife for twenty years. She delighted in all the things in which he delighted and loved all those whom he loved, whether they were her friends or enemies. She had borne him children, and although God had called them from this world, this was no fault of hers.

Then she made the point which was so vital in her cause. "When ye had me at the first", she asserted, "I take God to be my judge, I was a true maid . . . and whether it be true or no, I put it to your conscience". If she was in any way to blame she was ready to depart, to her "great shame and dishonour", but if she was not, then she pleaded to be allowed to remain as wife and Queen and to have justice at the King's hands.

She reminded the King that his father was of such good sense that he was called the second Solomon, and her own father, too, was one of the most intelligent of princes. They had prudent counsellors about them. There were, indeed, in those days as learned and wise men as there were now—men who had thought her marriage to be right and allowable. "Therefore, it is a wonder to hear what new inventions are invented against me that never intended but honesty. And cause me to stand to the order and judgement of this new court, wherein ye may do me much wrong". Her counsellors could not be impartial, since they were the King's subjects and chosen from among the members of his own council: they dare not oppose the King's wishes having been made aware of them. She begged the King to spare her "the extremity of this court, until she had had advice from her friends in Spain". If that were not granted, then to God she would commit her cause.

She then rose, and making a deep curtsy to the King, departed.

Many thought she would have returned to her former seat, but she went straight from the court, supported on the arm of her Receiver-General, Master Griffith. The King, learning of her departure, ordered the crier to call her back. And he called her: "Catherine, Queen of England, come into the court". With that Master Griffith said to her: "Madam, ye be called again". "On, on", she said, "it maketh no matter, for it is no indifferent court to me, and therefore I will not tarry. Go on your way." And so she went, not making any further answer. Nor did she ever appear in that court again.

It was said that after the Queen's departure the King spoke to some bishops about his scruples concerning the marriage and of mentioning them at one time in confession to the Bishop of Lincoln. He had afterwards, he continued, asked Warham "to put this matter in question . . . and so I did of all [of] you, my lords, to the which ye have all granted under all your seals". But Fisher maintained at the court this day, in a sharp exchange with the Archbishop, that he was not to be aligned in this matter with the other prelates present. For him, it would seem, there was no question at all: his mind was quite clear that the marriage was a valid one, and so, it would seem, he had previously told Warham.

Either in the same session or a week or two later—the precise date is uncertain—there was a significant altercation between Wolsey and both Fisher and Dr Robert Ridley. The King's counsellors had declared that the marriage between Henry and Catherine was void from the beginning, because of the alleged consummation of Catherine's union with Prince Arthur. There seem to have been some forthright passages of denial and counter-denial, and then it was said that no man could know the truth about the matter. But Fisher, taking the discussion to a higher plane, affirmed that he knew the truth. "How know you the truth?" asked the cardinal. "Because", replied Fisher, "I am a professor of the truth. I know that God is truth itself, nor He never spake but truth. Who said: What God hath joined, let not man put asunder. And forasmuch as this marriage was made and joined by God to a good intent, I say I know the truth." The union could not, added Fisher, be broken or loosened by the power of man. "So much doth all faithful men know", said the cardinal, "as well as you. Yet this reason is not sufficient", and he pursued his line of argument.

The King's counsellors, said Wolsey, had brought forward "divers presumptions" to prove the marriage of Henry and Catherine not allowable at the beginning. Therefore, said the counsellors, with a semblance of syllogistic reasoning, it was not joined by God, and therefore the marriage was not lawful, for He ordains nothing without "just order". Hence, it was not to be doubted but that the "presumptions" in question were true. It all depended on "the presumptions", and Ridley challenged the reasoning and attacked the validity of the "presumptions". It was a shame, he said, and greatly to the dishonour of everyone assembled, that any such presumptions should be alleged in that open court: they were to all good and honest men "most detestable to be rehearsed".

Ridley, it seems almost certain, seems to be referring to depositions, some of them markedly repulsive in nature, which had been collected by the government about what was said to have taken place at the time of Catherine's marriage to Prince Arthur almost thirty years previously. Wolsey asked Ridley to treat the "presumptions" (or depositions) with greater respect. "No, no, my lord", said Ridley, "there belongeth no reverence to be given to these abominable presumptions, for an unreverent tale must be unreverently answered". And they proceeded no further, we are told, at that time.

As the Queen had already appealed to Rome against the jurisdiction of the Legatine court, she had been pronounced contumacious. The court sessions dragged on for week after week. At one session towards the end of June Fisher rose to say that on a former occasion he had heard the King discuss the marriage cause, asserting that his sole aim was to obtain justice and to relieve his conscience. Henry had invited all present to throw whatever light they could on the matter because his mind was perplexed and distressed. For this reason, Fisher now came forward to state what he had discovered after two years' most diligent study. He desired neither to be unfaithful to the King nor, on the other hand, to incur the damnation of his soul by failing in what he owed to the truth in a matter of such great importance. He then declared, giving the strongest reasons, that the marriage of the King and Queen could be dissolved by no power, human or divine. For this opinion he would even lay down his life, and his death would be not less meritorious than the death of St John the Baptist. He presented to the court a book that he had written on the subject.

Fisher's speech was quite unexpected and held everyone in wonderment. The King was furious, because of the implied comparison with Herod Antipas. He made a bitter reply.

The trial went on long into the July of that historic summer. After the withdrawal of Catherine, Campeggio had become unhappy about the management of the court proceedings. They conducted the trial, he said, in such a manner that, in many instances, it was impossible to act according to the evidence, except after their own fashion: they did whatever they liked and used all those arts which could make for a result in their favour. On 23 July the court re-assembled. Everyone expected that sentence—a sentence favourable to the King—would be pronounced. But Wolsey had the day before heard of the Pope's decision, which had been confirmed in Consistory, to revoke the cause to Rome. Campeggio must have been well aware of it, also. He produced his trump card: he adjourned the court for the vacation till 1 October, assuming for the purpose that it was part of the Roman Consistory. Then fury broke loose from the King's party. "It was never merry in England", said the Duke of Suffolk, "while cardinals were with us". The court never met again.

CHAPTER 8

Divorce and Revolution

I

THE revocation of the divorce suit to Rome was the real genesis of all the future anti-papal legislation of the reign: it was an indication to the King that, with the flight of time and the dilatoriness which had accompanied the divorce trial proceedings, he might not after all obtain his paramount desire from the Papacy. When he was cited with Catherine to appear, either personally or by proxy, before the papal court his wrath was boundless and his self-righteousness considerable. Was he, the King of England, to acknowledge a jurisdiction outside his own country when a tribunal had been specifically established to pronounce on his cause, and to pronounce, so he always believed, judgement in his favour? The King's enormous pride was grievously assailed, and not for the first time in history did the frustrated will of a man of ability, strong personality and power provide the motive force for subsequent radical acts. We see this at work, consciously or unconsciously, in so many of his future dealings with the Papacy or the clergy. He soon began to make plans for attacking the Church, plans which would invite considerable support from the English laity, for, although the divorce lacked popularity almost everywhere in the country, the clergy were disliked for a variety of reasons. It was an adroit move, for attention would be diverted from an unpopular cause. All the people here, the Imperial ambassador was soon to say, hate the priests. And in his contest with Pope and clergy, Henry would invoke the aid of Parliament, whose proceedings he would manage with deftness. He lost little time, and within a few weeks of Campeggio's adjournment of the Legatine court, a writ was issued for summoning a Parliament to meet in November.

One important consequence of the revocation was the fall of Catherine's old enemy, Wolsey, who had himself always predicted his disgrace if the King's wishes were not met. "There was never a fall so complete, so simple in its method, and yet so devastating in its effect". But it was not precipitous, and the full extent of the fall was not seen till 1530. In 1529 he was found guilty of praemunire and there was not a word of protest from the Pope. Next year he was charged with high treason, but his death saved him from execution.

During the autumn of 1529 future revolutionary events were already casting their shadows before. After Wolsey was ruined or dead, the French ambassador was writing in October, "the Lords intend to impeach the state of the Church and take their goods. . . . They proclaim it openly. I expect they will do fine miracles." Nevertheless, Henry had as yet no intention of a definite break with Rome, for the Pope might be intimidated into meeting his wishes; but the King would show himself to be both powerful and in earnest, and he began an assault on the outer defences of ecclesiastical strongholds by inducing Parliament to pass three important statutes: the Act by which mortuary dues were regulated, the Act imposing fixed payments for probates of wills, and an Act against the non-residence of clergy. These matters were old evils and there was nothing unorthodox in providing remedies for them. The attack on the Church had indeed begun, but whether it was to continue would depend on the Pope.

There was an important development in 1529 and 1530 of the affair of the divorce. Thomas Cranmer, the Cambridge divine recently brought into prominence by an introduction to the King, made in 1529 the ingenious suggestion of an appeal to the English universities and some foreign universities on the question of the validity of Henry's marriage. The result of this course which began in the autumn of 1529 and extended well into 1530 was, first, a majority at Cambridge in the King's favour and then a narrow majority at Oxford. In attempting to secure favourable results abroad, money flowed like water from the King's coffers, and in Italy, where Dr Stokesley, soon to be rewarded with the see of London, was very active on Henry's behalf, there were both bribery and some bullying. The universities of France, England's political ally, favoured Henry, but the university of Paris by only a narrow majority. Needless to say, the Spanish universities were wholly on the side of Catherine. In the end neither Henry's nor Catherine's cause could point to anything conclusive, but the results favouring the King furnished him with some useful, flexible material for propaganda.

In July of this same year (1530) the nobles, spiritual and temporal, sent a petition to the Pope asking for an early pronouncement in the King's favour. It was prompted by a number of the results from the plebiscites in the universities. At least some of the signatories to the petition were obtained by royal pressure and the rest probably through the intimidating effect of what had already taken place. The document reflected the King's confidence in the justice of his cause and it threatened the seeking of redress elsewhere if his wishes were not met. The Pope's reply some weeks later was friendly, but uncompromising on matters of principle. Six months afterwards the Pontiff issued a brief which forbade the King to marry until his cause had been decided in the Papal Curia.

Considerable advance was made in the winter of 1530-31 towards royal control of the Church in England, for the whole of the clergy were indicted for praemunire because they had exercised the Courts Christian. They pleaded guilty, and after some hard bargaining on the part of the King, it was proposed to them that, in making their submission, Henry should be described, in addition to his usual kingly title, as "Protector and Supreme Head of the English Church and Clergy", the significance of which was not lost upon a dismayed clergy. But Convocation of Canterbury, in debating the matter, displayed some courage after recovering from the first shock of the assault. The King prevaricated and explained: Convocation debated and bargained; and Henry at length won them over by saying that he intended no religious innovations by his proposal, though his purpose was clear enough. But Fisher commendably managed to get inserted into the formula of recognition of the King's position as Supreme

Head, the qualifying clause, "so far as the law of Christ allows", and so the ambiguous title was accepted.

Convocation of the northern province met a little later to consider the new title. This eventually received their assent, but not without protest from Tunstall, Bishop of Durham, who was careful to see that his protest was noted in the proceedings. "If", he said, "these words, 'So far as the law of Christ allows', are understood of spiritual matters, the King is not Supreme Head of the Church, since this is not lawful according to Christ's Law."

The considerable opposition shown at this time by some of the clergy to the royal encroachment on the freedom of the Church is not perhaps generally known. The Imperial ambassador in London informed the Emperor that ecclesiastics of the province of York and of the diocese of Durham had sent "a great protest" to the King against the unique sovereignty which he wished to claim, whilst clergy in the province of Canterbury had also published a protest. Some of Catherine's clerical friends were among those in opposition; and we find that the protest was signed, on behalf of the clergy of Canterbury, by, among others, Robert Shorton, the Queen's almoner, and Richard Fetherston, Princess Mary's schoolmaster, and, on behalf of the clergy of London, by Dr Robert Ridley. The clergy of four dioceses in the southern province were represented, and, apparently due to Fisher's influence, there were signatures by Nicholas Metcalf, Archdeacon of Rochester and Master of St John's, Cambridge, and also by two other clerics on behalf of the chapter of Rochester and clergy of that diocese. These protests highly displeased the King.

Parliament reassembled in January 1532 and it seems clear from two important measures soon to be considered that the King was vigorously recharging his guns for a further assault on the Pope and the clergy. The first measure, the Annates Act, directed a financial blow at the Papacy. A bishop on his appointment was always obliged to pay the Pope an amount equivalent to one-third of his see's annual revenue. It was now proposed to abolish this tax, but the Act was made conditional, for there was a provision that it should become law only at the royal discretion.

The measure was, in fact, an attempt to force Clement to grant the King's wishes for a divorce by threatening to withhold a substantial portion of the papal income from England. All the bishops and those abbots who were spiritual peers opposed the bill in the Lords.

The other important measure was the Submission of the Clergy and it meant the final collapse of the revivified opposition to Henry's attacks which Convocation had recently shown. The measure originated in the Commons' Supplication, which set forth, chiefly in general terms, what were conceived to be the laity's grievances about clerical abuses. The motif of the whole catalogue of complaints is the evil that the Commons, as the King's subjects, obey laws that were made not by him or Parliament, but by the body ecclesiastical.

The bishops replied to the Supplication in the Answer of the Ordinaries. The Answer was in strong terms. There was some bargaining with Henry, and then he appeared in Parliament announcing that he had discovered that the clergy were only half his subjects, for the prelates, he asserted, "swore an oath quite contrary to the oath they swore to the Crown: so that it seemed that they were the Pope's subjects rather than his". A fortnight later Convocation made a complete submission to the King. Fisher was absent from the sessions of this Convocation, whilst Clerk, Bishop of Bath and Wells, voted against the government in the final vote. Henry had obtained a resounding victory and was now on the way to a definitive statement of royal supremacy.

Significantly, on the day after the Submission reached Henry, Thomas More, the great friend of Catherine, and, with Fisher, the main support of the clergy, resigned the Chancellorship.

So far as the marriage question was concerned events began to move quickly in the autumn of 1532 and the succeeding year. There were some meaningful portents. Anne Boleyn was created Marchioness of Pembroke in September and, loaded with Catherine's jewels, went to Calais in ostentatious, semi-regal state. The Pope in November warned the King not to divorce Catherine or to marry Anne or any other woman, pending a

papal decision: the penalty if he did so was to be excommunica-
tion. But what did Henry, in his increasing self-sufficiency, now
care for any thunders of the Vatican? He married Anne secretly
in January 1533 and at least by the end of the month she was with
child. During the next few months secrecy continued to dominate
the King's activities, and the precise reason for concealment was
his determination to divorce Catherine and to legitimize his
marriage with Anne and the child to be born. To secure these
objects, Cranmer, who had been earmarked for the see of
Canterbury following the providential death of Thomas Warham
in 1532, was to be consecrated Archbishop. Bulls for the consecration were granted by the Pope with unaccustomed dispatch, a
dispatch apparently influenced by the omnipresent possibility of
enforcing the inimical Annates Act. On 30 March 1533 Cranmer
was consecrated. In order to permit of the issue of the necessary
papal Bulls, the Archbishop-elect had sworn an oath of allegiance
to the Pope, an oath he had previously declared with egregious
deceit that he had no intention of keeping.

The country was prepared for the ultimate, complete defiance
of papal authority by two events: first, the passing in March
1533 of the highly-important Statute of Appeals, which entirely
destroyed papal jurisdiction in England, so far as the laity were
concerned. Appeals about wills, marriages, tithes and the rest
were not to go to Rome, but were to be determined in this
country.

The other event concerned two votes in Convocation: the
first on the theological issue that a Pope could not validly dispense
for a marriage between a man and his brother's widow; and the
second on an issue of canon law that there was legal proof of the
consummation of Catherine's marriage with Prince Arthur by
the mere fact of marriage. A similar pattern of opposition was
created by the Queen's faithful theological friends on the first
issue, as in the case of the question of the Supremacy in 1531. They
were not concerned on the second issue, which was a matter for
the clerical lawyers, but it is perhaps worth noting that Clerk,
Bishop of Bath and Wells, voted against the motion. In each case
there was a great majority for the King.

Thus had recent events put Henry and Cranmer on firm ground. They had had considerable good fortune. Seldom has a revolution in its vital early stages proceeded with greater audacity, lack of scruple, comparative speed, and evoking such little effective opposition. So much had been accomplished that was orderly and legal, and with the support of a Parliament carefully managed. And now the new Archbishop proceeded to the great act of his archiepiscopal career.

In May 1533 Catherine was cited to appear before a court held in a house of the Austin Canons at Dunstable and presided over by Cranmer. The venue was only a few miles from Ampthill where the Queen had been sent to reside. It was said that Dunstable had been chosen because it was a solitary place and sufficiently far from London to preserve secrecy, for if the court had been held in the capital the affair would have been on too many people's lips and there might have been rioting. Persistently, Catherine refused to appear at Cranmer's court, was pronounced contumacious and in less than a fortnight sentence of divorce was given. Shortly afterwards Cranmer gave a second judgement, by affirming that the union between Henry and Anne Boleyn was a valid marriage. On Whit Sunday, 1 June 1533 Anne was crowned Queen.

At last, the Pope was stung into action. On 4 July he excommunicated Cranmer for giving judgement on the divorce suit. He also excommunicated the King, but the sentence was not to become effective until September, so that, it was said, he might have an opportunity of resuming his marriage with Catherine, a fatuous condition enough, if it were not apparently a formality born of despair. The King replied by breaking off diplomatic relations with the Vatican and later by appealing to a general council against the Pope. In September the child Anne had been bearing was born: it was a girl, the future Queen Elizabeth.

The spate of anti-papal legislation during the period, 1532-4, culminated in the Succession, Supremacy and Treason Acts of 1534. The Succession Act, the first of a series of such Acts, regulated the succession to the Crown. Henry's marriage with Anne Boleyn was declared valid and his marriage to Catherine contrary to the law of God. Anyone who, with malice, "disturbed" the King's title to the Crown or slandered his marriage to Anne was declared a traitor. A corporal oath had to be taken by everyone not only to acknowledge the royal succession, but also "the whole effects and contents" of the Act, including the rejection of the Pope's power to dispense. Queen Catherine was to be known as the Dowager to Prince Arthur.

The climax of all the anti-papal measures was the Supremacy Act, which received the royal assent in the winter of 1534. In brief form it set forth the King's Supremacy definitively: he had full power and authority in all matters over clergy and laity alike. He was "the only supreme head of the Church of England called Ecclesia Anglicana". Closely associated with this measure was the Treason Act of 1534 which accused of treason anyone who, after 1 February 1535, "maliciously" sought to deprive the King "of any title or style", by writing, speaking or by deed, or who called him a heretic, schismatic or tyrant. Refusal to acknowledge the Royal Supremacy was also made treason. The Act, which made an invidious encroachment on the fundamental liberty of the subject, did not pass through Parliament without much searching of political consciences and some demonstrations of dislike. The suggested word "maliciously" was accepted for insertion in the statute in an attempt to placate the Commons' qualms, but the effect was quite nugatory, as the course of trials for treason was subsequently to prove. It was under both the Supremacy and Treason Acts that a number of Catherine's friends, including Fisher and More, were brought to trial and condemned.

Before the work of this eventful parliamentary session ended sentence was at length given by the Papal consistory in favour of Catherine—on 23 March 1534. And a week later, 30 March, the day on which Parliament was prorogued, all the members took the oath under the Succession Act.

The divorce issue, it may be stated, did not of itself bring about the Reformation, for there was strong national feeling against the wealth and corruption of a Church in decline. The important factor in the whole crisis was the strong influence of the Crown. If the divorce question had not existed, however, there would perhaps have been no Reformation, at least, not the Reformation as we know it, because a religiously-conservative and powerful King would have been against it. As it was, Henry achieved all that he set out to do. Even before 1534, the year of statutory royal supremacy, he knew he had won over the nation to his designs. He had achieved it all without a standing army, without even an effective police force, and with local administration in the hands mainly of the gentry, all by his dominating, egocentric personality, assisted by a minister of genius, Thomas Cromwell, adroit and enormously efficient. And in 1534 there commences that period of pronounced despotism in which all the more deplorable aspects of the King's character were seen in a strong light and in which the monstrous logic of the position he had reached made him increasingly realize the supreme value of state trials for eradicating all opposition to his will.

II

Catherine's personal position deteriorated as the power of the King grew, as the bonds with Rome loosened, and as one event succeeded another to the definitive stage of divorce and the achievement of the Supremacy. But in the first year or so after the fatal day of July 1529, Henry's relations with Catherine, though now never or rarely cordial, were not strained to breaking point.

The Queen, whilst always anxious about the state of the marriage suit in Rome, never lost the clear-sighted conviction of the truth of her cause or her high courage. And she now had an able adviser and supporter in the new Imperial ambassador in London, Eustace Chapuys, a talented Savoyard lawyer, who had come to England soon after the collapse of the Legatine court. His despatches are lively and detailed, and though he listened to much gossip and regaled it for the Emperor's benefit, and though he is sometimes naïve and often necessarily biased, he told the truth. His correspondence is largely the story of Catherine at this time and is of supreme value.

Chapuys, said Catherine, was very wise, encouraged her continually and assuaged her sorrow. He was a learned and experienced lawyer and displayed tact. Some of her former councillors assured her that the Emperor could not have chosen a better representative. His approaches to the King and Cromwell were generally flexible and skilful, and he was able to do much for Catherine in a maze of unending difficulties. He was, in short, an admirable contrast to such former envoys and grandees as Fuensalida and Luis Caroz, stiff, arrogant survivals from a past age who would have been insufferable to Henry VIII and his council.

In these earlier days, when Catherine was still at Court, it was to be expected that, with the marriage suit uppermost in their minds, there should be fertile ground for dissension between her and the King. On St Andrew's Day (30 November), 1529, for instance, she dined with Henry and chided him on his neglect. He had been refusing to dine with her and she complained that he had not visited her in her apartments. He made excuses for his neglect and then, inevitably, entered on the subject of the marriage question. He repeated the old arguments, saying he was not her true husband, and especially mentioned the views of his almoner, Dr Lee, elect of York, who had, so he said, once known her in Spain. She countered them all vigorously. As for his almoner's opinions she did not care a straw for them. In the middle of the intense dispute the King left her suddenly. Chapuys was told by some of those present that Henry was very disconcerted and disconsolate. The Queen had been more than a match for him. Almost immediately he ran into Anne Boleyn, who noticed his downcast looks. When she learnt the cause she was furiously indignant. "Did I not tell you" she said to him "that whenever you disputed with the Queen she was sure to have the upper hand? I see that some fine morning you will succumb to her reasoning".

But the intervals between the King's visits to Catherine increased. For a month after the Feast of the Three Kings (6 January 1530) she had not seen him at all. She was subject to continual annoyance and Henry renewed his attempts to make her a nun. The King, she said pathetically and rather ingenuously, was not to blame for all that has happened to her, but "the inventors and

abettors of this cause". She trusted much in Henry's natural
goodness, and if only she could have him for two months with
her as he used to be, she alone would be strong enough to make
him forget the past; but as the "inventors and abettors" knew
that to be true, they would not let him live with her.

The only way to silence her enemies, she told the Pope, was a
sentence in her favour, a plea that was to be repeated with weari-
some regularity during the next few years. It was all fruitless,
for the Pope seemed as unresponsive to the pleadings of Catherine
as to the manoeuvrings of Charles V. The King's honour and
reputation were diminished and his conscience imperilled, said
the Queen, by the Pope's delay. She was amazed at his behaviour.
If he did not act soon, she would have to declare that he was without charity. She had suffered as much as she could bear. But the
time was not yet.

The King in his personal relations with Catherine was influenced
by English and international political events, but, naturally, also
by the activities of Anne Boleyn, advancing temerariously to an
uneasy achievement and creating enemies on the way. Absence
from Catherine was not making Henry's heart more tender.
Anne was sure, said Chapuys, that she would marry the King
and was braver than a lion. She told one of the Queen's ladies-in-
waiting that she wished all Spaniards at the bottom of the sea,
and when she was mildly reproved, Anne retorted that she did not
care anything for the Queen; she would be hanged rather than
acknowledge her as her mistress. Two ladies-in-waiting, in whom
Catherine had found great comfort, had already been dismissed at
Anne's request.

Events were, in fact, in 1531, moving to something of a climax.
One day in May when Henry's behaviour seemed to be un-
wontedly pleasant, the Queen took advantage of the occasion to
ask for leave to visit Princess Mary, who had been ill. She might
go, said Henry brutally, if she wished, and stop there. Catherine
replied graciously that she would never leave him for his daughter
or for anyone else in the world. And there the matter ended. But
Henry's remark was ominous, in the light of events later in the
year.

At this time the King wanted delay in the hearing of the marriage suit at Rome, as well as a change of place and of judges. He was obliged to think of many difficulties, not least of the possible cost of an open rupture with the Pope, a cost that might involve the creation of the Emperor as an embarrassing enemy. A great deputation of more than thirty temporal and spiritual lords, headed by the Dukes of Norfolk and Suffolk, therefore came to see the Queen on a day early in June to induce her to agree to the King's wishes. She was just retiring for the night, but had been secretly informed of the proposed meeting.

On this uniquely important occasion she was equal to the whole combination of these English lords. She knew them all, especially she knew Norfolk, of the House of Howard, old in the peerage, who was profligate, able, a strong supporter of the King and the uncle of Anne Boleyn. And how well she knew bluff Charlie Brandon, Duke of Suffolk, the complete extrovert, and the old tilting, convivial companion of the King, who was not more than of mediocre ability in political affairs or soldiering, and who had married Catherine's great friend, Mary, the King's sister. As we have seen, he had probably been in danger of losing his head after his secret marriage to Mary; and it was perhaps the consciousness of that mortifying episode that afterwards made him so careful of his ways and never an overt opponent of the King in all of the many vicissitudes of those revolutionary days.

Norfolk began by laboriously reciting the well-known facts and allegations in the marriage cause and referred particularly to the obstinacy of the Queen. Other lords supported him. She answered them all with her old accustomed spirit and adroitness. She was never so superb in courage as when, alone, she faced a crisis. And, in particular, her patience and singular courtesy allowed her opponents no chance of forcing a chink in the armour of her defences. She refused, of course, to meet the King's wishes.

When the long discussion was drawing to a close Catherine uttered one remark which has a sly touch of humour. She was greatly astonished, she said, "how and for what consideration" so many grand personages, "who could appal the world" had come in this manner to take her by surprise when she was alone and unfurnished of counsel. Norfolk and the Earl of Wiltshire were only able to make half-hearted replies and then left. Stokesley, now Bishop of London, the strong protagonist of the divorce, was urged to speak, but "when he had heard the Queen's reasons, he had not the courage". Others seemed vividly impressed by Catherine's answers and "secretly nudged one another when any point touched the quick".

The King was waiting anxiously for the outcome of the meeting. The lords told him of what had occurred. He was afraid it would be so, he said, considering the "courage and fantasy" of the Queen. But it would be necessary to take other remedies. And then he became very pensive.

At Whitsuntide Henry and Catherine were at Windsor. In the middle of July the King moved to Woodstock. He left the Queen at Windsor and did not say good-bye. She never saw him again.

Complete separation of the royal pair had begun. In August Catherine was ordered to retire to the More, a commodious, moated house belonging to the abbey of St Albans. Visits from people of the Court became rare and few consoled her. Princess Mary was sent to Richmond.

At her new residence Doctors Lee and Sampson, on behalf of the clergy, and the Earl of Sussex and Treasurer FitzWilliam, for the temporal lords, came to plead vehemently with the Queen, on orders from the King, to agree to a determination of the marriage suit in England. She assembled practically all the members of her suite, ostensibly that there might be many good witnesses of what was about to take place, and then she gave her answer. The King's men uttered in low tones the things they were commanded to say, but Catherine so spoke that all without difficulty might hear her replies. Complete refusal was only to be expected and in giving it she did not mince her words. The King's messengers did not know what to say.

Isolated from the Court and from many of her friends, Catherine was made to feel the full bitterness of her new position. She sent the King as a New Year's gift in 1532 a gold cup of great value and of exquisite workmanship. It was sent back. Henry was accustomed to send gifts at the New Year to all the members of the Queen's and the Princess's households, but this custom was now discontinued.

Yet Catherine's spirit did not decline. She was asked to give up her jewels to the King. She refused. It was against her conscience, she said, "to give her jewels to adorn a person who is the scandal of Christendom". But when the King expressly asked for them she sent all she had.

In the spring of 1533 she was ordered to go to Ampthill, the place in Bedfordshire which was close to the religious house at Dunstable where Cranmer was to give his sentence of divorce. She was escorted there with a large posse of horse and went in great haste, despite the impelling entreaties she made for delay, in order to provide her with necessities.

The invidious task of telling Catherine that she must no longer be known as Queen was allotted to Lord Mountjoy, her old chamberlain. This notification was, of course, a direct consequence of Henry's new marriage and was, so far, the greatest stab of all. Catherine was told that after Easter the King would no longer provide for her personal expenses or the wages of her servants. She replied as ever that she was the King's true wife and his anointed Queen. If the King thought her expenses too great he might, she said, take her personal property and put her wherever he liked, so long as she had a confessor and a few servants. If that were too much and there was nothing else for her to live upon, she would willingly go about the world, begging alms for the love of God.

All her servants were warned to perform their duties in the name of Princess Dowager. But they asked to see the authority for this change and Thomas Vaux wrote from Ampthill to Cromwell for a written declaration "touching the name and service of your mistress here", so that he and Mountjoy might be discharged from the suspicion imputed to them. Vaux was profoundly uncomfortable about the whole business. "I had rather die", he said, "in some other service of the King than continue here much longer."

The Queen's chamberlain and others tried again in July, but it was all futile. Catherine met their arguments clearly and forcibly

one by one. They threatened that if she continued to be so
recalcitrant the King might withdraw his fatherly love from her
daughter Mary. She replied that Mary was his truly-begotten
daughter, but not even for the threat which he now made—
and she certainly had great love for Mary—would she yield an
inch. As for her servants, she would never answer to any who called
her by another title than Queen. Cromwell could not help
saying that no one could have given wiser or more courageous
answers, and that God and nature had done the Queen great
injury in not making her a man, "for she might", so Cromwell
adds, according to Chapuys, "have surpassed in glory and fame
all the princes whose heroic deeds are recorded in history",
exaggerated language enough, but yet pointing to Cromwell's
spontaneously-expressed esteem.

A written report was made of this interview and Catherine
read it. She called for pen and ink, and vigorously struck out the
name of "Princess Dowager" whenever it occurred. She refused,
she said, to admit to having been the King's harlot for twenty-four
years.

Since the Queen was inflexible, her expenses were cut down
and towards the end of July she was moved farther away still,
to the manor of Buckden, a few miles from Huntingdon. There
was in those days a great park adjoining the manor. The situation
of the place was, however, unlikely to make for any comfort,
since Buckden is in the fenland near the Great Ouse, was then
subject to much flooding and was altogether unhealthy when
summer was past. But Catherine had no option. It was,
nevertheless, some pleasant compensation that when she departed
from Ampthill all the people in the neighbourhood assembled to
pay her honour and that all along the way to Buckden she was
greeted with affection. Though there was an order against it,
people called her "Queen", shouting it at the top of their voices,
and they wished her joy and prosperity, and to her enemies,
confusion.

With the approach of winter, however, Catherine could not
long continue to live at Buckden, for that would seem to court
illness and, possibly, death; and already in October it was being

said that the condition of the surrounding country would soon be so foul that it would be impossible for any provisions to reach her. Fotheringay, one day to be the prison of Mary, Queen of Scots, was mentioned as a new place of custody, but she was not sent there. In any case, life at Buckden was becoming burdensome and she was in great distress.

During the Christmas season of 1533, her household was reduced to a bare minimum. She was deprived of Mountjoy, her chamberlain, her chancellor, and other chief officers. She had now none of the appanages of royalty. All but a few of her remaining servants were cashiered and harshness was exercised in driving them away. Her own *femmes de chambre* were dismissed, but as the Queen said she would have no others, that she would even sleep in her ordinary clothes and herself lock the gates of the manor, two of them were returned. As for some new servants who came from the North, they were stated to have been more accustomed to war than to the ways of a court. She would look upon them as mere guards, since she was a prisoner.

The King's men tried at this time to remove her by force to Somersham, a far more marshy and pestilential place than even Buckden. She resolutely refused to go and they could do nothing. What a pity, they said, she could not be complacent, for the King would then treat her according to her merits and wishes. As it was, her wings must be clipped by taking away her state and servants. But she did not go to Somersham.

Catherine was still at Buckden when in May 1534 she was required to take the oath to the Succession. Two sets of commissioners came to proffer it. She, of course, refused. On the first occasion, instead of swearing, she read to the commissioners the papal sentence in her favour. The second band of commissioners was headed by Lee, Archbishop of York, and Cuthbert Tunstall, Bishop of Durham, who, though one of her counsellors at the trial, now gave the reasons for changing his views of the marriage and advised Catherine to change also. She was threatened with dire penalties, even with death, if she refused obedience. It was thus hoped to frighten her, but the effect was merely to strengthen her resolution. She would always regard herself as the King's lawful wife till her death. As for this divorce which they spoke of it was for her nothing at all and Cranmer who had pronounced it was a mere shadow. The Pope, who was Christ's Vicar, had given his sentence. That was the all-important matter for her. If, she said, she was to die, let her death take place in public and not in her chamber or in any other secret place. So, she must have reasoned, would the people, whose affection she always possessed, see execution done on an anointed Queen.

Her small staff of Spanish attendants, who included Jorge de Atheca, her physician, her apothecary, and her stalwart friend and now her *maître de salle*, Francisco Phelippes, also refused the Oath. For a time they were placed in custody, but were later released and this was a great consolation to Catherine. Shortly afterwards she was sent to Kimbolton Castle, which the King in 1522 had given to Sir Richard Wingfield. There she was to die.

CHAPTER 9

Five Great Ladies

A<small>LTHOUGH</small> the divorce was an unpopular cause in England, it was women, in particular, who manifested strong sympathy with the Queen. "Of the coming of this Legate Campeggio", says the chronicler Hall, "people, especially women and others that favoured the Queen, talked largely, and whoever spoke against the Queen's marriage was by the common people abhorred and reproved." The French ambassador, in the early days of the Legatine court, said: "If the matter were decided by women, the King would lose the battle". Affection for Catherine would, apart from other factors, have established for many a dislike of the divorce, but it was made more secure by the unpopularity of Anne Boleyn, whose increasingly arrogant ways at Court did not make her a more attractive figure. The possibility, too, that this ambitious, favoured lady-in-waiting, with her partiality for Lutheranism, might supersede Catherine as Queen was a galling thought to those people who held firmly to ancient religious ways. With Mary, the King's sister, however, it seems to have been grounds entirely personal which determined her continued attachment to Catherine. There appears to be no evidence that she was a pronounced adherent of the old Faith, nor, on the other hand, that she was attracted to any doctrine of the Reform. It would be hazardous even to conjecture that, had she lived to the time of undoubted Royal Supremacy, she would not have accepted her brother's high claims with few or no misgivings. In short, religious ideals did not apparently make any profound impression on her mind and her religious practice seems to have been of a formal nature. Nevertheless, she did not forget the friend who strongly influenced her early life and with whom she had lived at Court for so many congenial years. There was the added reason, perhaps, that she knew Anne Boleyn well.

Mary was interested in the King's Great Matter not merely because of the vital concern to Catherine, but because it aroused in her doubts of the validity of her own marriage. When, for instance, she married Suffolk, his previous marriage to Margaret Mortimer had been dissolved on the strength of a dispensation granted by the Archdeacon of London. Was that dispensation unimpugnable? To set the matter at rest Mary obtained a papal bull in May 1528, which ratified the dispensation and made good all defects of law and fact.

In the previous month of April the Duke of Suffolk had received an urgent summons to attend on the King. The commission to try the marriage suit had been issued to Wolsey and Campeggio, and Suffolk was apparently already aware of the fact. At the end of the month, Fox, one of the King's agents in Rome, arrived in London with the commission. The King commanded him to go at once with the news to Anne Boleyn, and by her he was "marvellously received". Both Henry and Anne were jubilant.

Suffolk arranged to go to Court with all possible speed and told Wolsey he would be with the King on St George's Day (23 April). He put his affairs in Suffolk in order and departed, but he left his wife distressed at the latest news. "The tidings", he said, "are somewhat heavy with the French Queen."

When Campeggio actually came to England in October for the divorce trial, he lodged, before reaching London itself, at Suffolk's mansion in Southwark, the "large and most sumptuous house" which Suffolk had built and which was situated almost directly against St George's Church. The duke had been summoned by the King to meet the Papal Legate. But when he had departed from his estates in Suffolk, Mary was "sorrowful and in tears" because of the purpose of Campeggio's coming.

The strength of the King's mounting determination to divorce Catherine and marry Anne did not alter the French Queen's sympathies, and some years later, in April 1532, there was a violent episode in Westminster which illustrates their unchanged nature. The Duke of Norfolk, Anne Boleyn's uncle, had recently come to Court by command of the King. At the time of his arrival twenty of his followers assaulted and killed in the sanctuary of Westminster the chief gentleman of the Duke of Suffolk. The whole Court was in an uproar about the affair and Suffolk set out to dislodge the assailants forcibly from the sanctuary, but was ordered by the King to return. Henry himself settled the business, though the incident displeased him. Its origin, so the Venetian ambassador was informed, was "the opprobrious language uttered against Madame Anne by his Majesty's sister, the Duchess of Suffolk". Mary followed this up by stoutly refusing to go with Anne Boleyn when she went magnificently with the King to France in the autumn.

The French Queen died in June 1533 and was buried with great ceremony at the abbey of St Edmundsbury (Bury St Edmunds) in July. She had lived long enough to know of the divorce of Catherine in May, but she was dead before the birth of Princess Elizabeth.

Of all Queen Catherine's friends and intelligencers in the earlier days of the divorce one who remained most loyal and valuable was Elizabeth, wife of Thomas Howard, third Duke of Norfolk. As the eldest daughter of Edward, Duke of Buckingham, that magnificent English lord whom Henry had executed, her provenance and family associations provided a close bond with that other great friend of Catherine, Margaret Pole, for the duchess's only brother, Henry Stafford, had married Margaret Pole's daughter, Ursula. The duchess was on excellent terms with her brother and showed much affection for Dorothy, his daughter, who used to stay with her. She once wrote to her brother that, should he die (there is no evidence that his death was, indeed, probable at this time), Dorothy "shall not lack as long as I live, and she would be hard by me". As the Countess of Surrey, Elizabeth Howard took a prominent part with Margaret Pole at the christening of Princess Mary, bearing the child to the font.

She was a woman of culture and for this reason would have appealed strongly to both Catherine and the Countess of Salisbury. Skelton, the poet-laureate, was her protégé, and at the castle of Sheriff Hutton, the Yorkist stronghold where Margaret

Pole probably stayed as a child, the poet wrote for Elizabeth Howard his long poem, "A Goodly Garlande or Chapelet of Laurell", a description of the making of the "chapelet" by Elizabeth and her ladies. It was doubtless from the duchess rather than from the politically-minded duke that their son, Surrey, the poet, inherited his particular gifts.

Her relations with her husband were almost invariably inharmonious. The third duke was not a pleasant character. Brutal, unscrupulous, self-seeking, his dissolute private life was the main cause of the disturbed relations with his wife. There was frequent, violent dissension between the two, and, despite attempts by both the King and Cromwell to repair the havoc, the final break came in 1534. But the duke's political position was significant: he was the most important of English nobles, and not only the Lord High Treasurer and one of the foremost of his councillors, but also the uncle of Anne Boleyn, who frequently displayed notable antipathy to the duchess. This antipathy was very marked when the proposal was made for the marriage of the duke's daughter, Mary, to Henry Fitzroy, Duke of Richmond, the King's natural son. Anne strongly opposed the match and used such vituperative language that only very narrowly did the duchess escape dismissal from Court.

As the wife of one of the King's chief councillors, Elizabeth Howard was in an exceptionally favourable position to pass on to Catherine any items of vital news which she learnt at Court, and her eagerness to do this was quickened not only by her friendship with the isolated Queen, but also by the feminine animosity she bore to the Queen's supplanter. We have in November 1530 an illustration of the kind of service at work, for the duchess sent Catherine a gift of poultry accompanied by an orange, and inside the orange was a letter from Gregory Casale, the English ambassador in Rome. Though the contents of the letter are not disclosed, they must have been extremely useful, for Chapuys sent a copy to the Emperor. The only disadvantage—and it was considerable—was that the duke was made aware of the business, and for this reason it would be necessary, said Chapuys, to dissemble more effectively in future.

The duchess remained strong in her allegiance and two months later she sent a message to Catherine to say that, if all the world were to attempt to advise her to abandon support of the Queen's cause, she would, nevertheless, remain perfectly loyal. Catherine's opponents had apparently been trying to enlist the duchess in their ranks. She bade Catherine be of good courage, for her enemies were faced with difficulties and were at their wits' end to know how to solve them.

In the spring of this same year, 1531, the year in the summer of which came the definite break in Catherine's relations with Henry and she was removed to the More, the duchess was her frequent informant from the Court. Anne Boleyn's dislike of Princess Mary was now as considerable as her dislike of the Queen, and her conduct became at times most irritating to the King. She used such ill words, Henry complained to Norfolk, as Catherine had never in her life used to him. The duchess reported it all to the Queen, telling her, moreover, that the duke was in great distress because of Anne's troublesome attitude. Anne Boleyn was having her brief time of deceptive domination, but she was evidently putting difficulties in the way of her adherents.

The Duchess of Norfolk some time later visited Catherine and gave her important news about the divorce which had been received at Court. What this was we do not know, but it deeply depressed the Queen. Chapuys was able, however, to give her an optimistic explanation and she was considerably relieved. Even the duke, seeing her emerge from her apartments at this juncture, noticed her changed demeanour. He asserted that she was confident of the justice of her cause and that her courage was "supernatural". It was "the Devil and nobody else", he affirmed, "who was the inventor of this accursed dispute". Yet in June he headed the deputation of the lords to Catherine to try to induce her to stay her hand in the prosecution of her suit at Rome. It was altogether improbable that he would desert the King's side, and he remained, in fact, very much the King's man. Elizabeth Howard did not waver.

Distress and misfortune were, however, in store for the duchess, whose forthright, antipathetic conduct was too much for Lady Anne. She was dismissed from Court in May 1531 because she spoke her mind too freely and declared herself for the Queen more than was liked. A year or two later the duke was completely wrecking his marriage because of his liaison with one of Anne Boleyn's ladies, Bess Holland.

The duchess lived on throughout the following two reigns and died shortly after the accession of Queen Elizabeth, four years later than the duke. She was buried in the Howard chapel. Her brother, Henry Stafford, proved his enduring attachment to his sister by the affectionate terms of the epitaph he wrote for her tomb.

The Duke of Suffolk did not long remain unmarried after the death of Mary, the French Queen. In September 1533, only six weeks after her death, he married Catherine, the daughter of the Queen's old Spanish friend, Maria de Salinas, Lady Willoughby d'Eresby, one of her ladies-in-waiting. Catherine d'Eresby, after the death of her father, had been made a ward of Suffolk's and seems to have been brought up with Mary's own children at Westhorpe in Suffolk. Maria, her mother, had long been in England, but when exactly she came from Spain is not known. She was not in Princess Catherine's entourage in the year of her arrival in this country, and, although she may have shared the Princess's drab existence in Durham House, there is no record that she lived there. The earliest clear evidence of her close association with Catherine emerged in 1514, when Luis Caroz, the Spanish ambassador, made some petulant observations on Catherine's conduct and the influences that were moulding it. The Queen of England, he considered, greatly required some discreet and intelligent person who would take care not only of her soul, but also would be able to manage her house and give advice about the attitude she should bear towards both the English and Spaniards. She had, of course, very good intentions, but there was really no one at hand to show her how she should properly serve her father. The chief culprit was her Spanish confessor, Fray Diego, who had told the Queen that she ought to forget Spain and everything Spanish, in order to gain the love of the King of England and of the English. This advice could scarcely have been better.

There were only a few Spaniards left in the Queen's household, the ambassador went on to say, but these preferred to be friends of the English and they neglected their duties as subjects of the King of Spain. The worst influence on the Queen—Caroz seemed momentarily to have forgotten Fray Diego—was exercised by Doña Maria de Salinas, whom she loved more than any other mortal. Because of her machinations, Caroz could never make use, in the negotiations which his office compelled him to conduct, of any power which Queen Catherine possessed in England, nor could he obtain through the Queen the smallest kind of advantage. He was like "a bull at which everyone throws darts". Even King Henry treated him most offensively, and if King Ferdinand did "not put a bridle on this colt", it would be found impossible to control him. The English handled Spanish sea-captains badly, the Spaniards complained bitterly of it, and they were forced to sail from England with empty ships. He begged to be relieved of his post, for he thought that any other ambassador would find more willing ears than he. And, perhaps, after this self-revelation of his ineptitude, he was right. So much for the influence of Maria de Salinas.

In June 1516, Maria married, as his second wife, Lord Willoughby d'Eresby, who had served Henry VII competently and in his son's reign had, among other activities, seen some soldiering in France under the Duke of Suffolk. The marriage seems to have been foreshadowed in the previous autumn for the Queen wrote to Ferdinand, her father, commending Maria for her faithful services, saying that she had always comforted her in her hours of trial. Shortly before her marriage she was naturalized as an Englishwoman.

Even after she married, Maria de Salinas spent much time at Court as a member of Catherine's suite, and when her husband died in 1526 she had greater freedom for her court duties, though a sequence of law suits with Sir Christopher Willoughby over her inheritance seems to have caused her much work and embarrassment.

The marriage of her daughter to Suffolk in 1533 was of considerable significance in increasing the assistance and support which Maria was able to give Catherine at a critical time. And when Suffolk and his assistants went to break up Catherine's household during the Christmas of that year, we seem to be cognisant of certain influences at work behind the scenes, for it was Maria de Salinas who told Chapuys of Suffolk's distress because of the work he had been commanded to do. He was to take Catherine by force to Somersham, that unhealthy and pestilential house in the Fens which was surrounded by deep water and many marshes. Catherine realized the great danger to her life, and it was indeed said that the King had agreed to place her there at the earnest solicitation of Anne Boleyn, in order, possibly, that she might die at an early date and by non-violent means, or at least in order to ensure that her captivity was effective, for the house was strong. But Catherine, although they loaded her baggage, and got the litters and horses ready for her to mount on, refused to move. She locked herself in her room, and when Suffolk's men came to take her away, she told them through a hole in the wall that they must break down the door if they wished to take her. This they dared not do through fear of the people assembled outside the house. But she never went to Somersham.

Time-serving Suffolk shows up better on this occasion. Maria de Salinas mentioned that he had "confessed on the Sacrament" that, fully aware as he was of the degrading nature of the task he had to do and the possibly disastrous consequences to Catherine if it were carried out, he wished that some mischief might befall him. Before Suffolk set out on his journey, Chapuys had some talk with him, apparently about the ill-treatment of Catherine and her daughter, and the conversation was reported to the King. Henry had not replied to the ambassador because that would not have pleased Anne Boleyn.

In these anxious days one of the most constant friends of both Queen Catherine and Princess Mary was Gertrude, Marchioness of Exeter, the daughter of Lord William Mountjoy, Catherine's

K

chamberlain of many years' standing. Gertrude had married in
1519, as his second wife, Henry Courtenay, Marquis of Exeter,
the son of Sir William Courtenay, by Princess Catherine, the
youngest daughter of Edward IV. Exeter was thus not only a
close kinsman of Margaret Pole and her family, but also of the
King himself: he had been "brought up as a child with his Grace
in his chamber". As the wife of a leading courtier and councillor,
who was so nearly related to the King, the marchioness had long
been the close companion of the Queen and Princess Mary, and
when great troubles arose her impeccable loyalty and undoubted
courage were to be of inestimable value to both Catherine and the
Spanish ambassador.

Anne Boleyn early became suspicious of any messengers to the
Queen, and in September 1530 she forbade those courtiers who
were in the habit of visiting Catherine, and from whom she might
learn about any matters of importance, to go to see her. Some
women were placed about Catherine to spy on her activities
and to report anything untoward or of interest that she might
say or do. And because the King had recently discovered that
there had been a leakage of some of the proceedings of his Privy
Council he had taken such measures as would prevent any news
from reaching the ears of the Queen. Perhaps the Duchess of
Norfolk or the marchioness had been busy. Lady Exeter was undoubtedly a useful, imperturbable go-between. She warned
Chapuys of the meetings which the King's council were holding
day and night for the sole purpose of reforming the Queen's and
the Princess's households, though, she said, they had not yet
formulated a solution. And Henry seemed to know of at least
this one important source from which Princess Mary was receiving
useful information. The Princess's movements had been closely
watched during the summer of 1532 and the Exeters were forbidden to visit her. About Christmas 1533 the King used very
threatening language to the marquis. Henry was of opinion
that Mary's wilfulness and obstinacy were due to the confidence
which she reposed in the Emperor, but she would soon be compelled to submit to the King's will and any persons who were
disloyal to the Crown would lose their heads. He would, also,

keep such good watch that no one would be able to send letters to the Continent or receive them without his knowledge. All this did not daunt the Exeters, and as late as November 1535 the marchioness, using a disguise for her visit, was still conveying useful information to the Imperial ambassador about the King's intentions regarding Catherine and her daughter, information which he, of course, at once passed to the Emperor.

Then, in January 1535, we are aware, through the Exeters, of perhaps the most definite sign, so far, of the King's disillusionment about Anne Boleyn. He had long possessed more strings to his amorous bow than the woman whom he had married three years previously, but there was nothing unusual in him about that. At the beginning of January 1536 Henry informed one of his confidants, so the Exeters told Chapuys, that it was by sorcery he had been driven to marry Anne and that God had undoubtedly shown the marriage to be invalid because no surviving male issue had been granted to him. The doom of the unfortunate new Queen seems heralded. It was made secure by the premature birth and early death of a male child a little later.

The actual execution of Anne Boleyn in May made a difference; and when Princess Mary, her mother dead and the King married to Jane Seymour, made her complete submission to the King in 1536, swore the oath of succession and renounced the papal supremacy, she took her place at Court again with people like the Exeters and Margaret Pole and her son Henry, Lord Montague. And when Jane Seymour's son, the future Edward VI, was christened, it was the Earl of Sussex and Lord Montague who carried the two covered basins for the ceremony, and the Marchioness of Exeter, assisted by her husband and the Duke of Suffolk, who bore the royal infant to the font. Then followed the Lady Mary, the King's daughter, who was to be the child's godmother, her train being borne by Lady Kingston. The King had had his way.

Margaret Pole remained as Mary's governess till the Princess's household was dissolved at the same time as most of Catherine's household officers were discharged in December 1533. Lady

Salisbury had had some bitter, perplexing moments earlier that year, the year which saw the consummation of all Anne Boleyn's hopes and aims. Her dislike of Anne was as real as that felt by any other of Catherine's friends, and we see it at work in July, only six weeks after Anne's coronation. The King demanded Princess Mary's jewels, but the answer of poor, harassed Lord Hussey, her chamberlain, was that he had never seen any jewels, except those which the Princess chose on occasions to wear. But Margaret Pole knew more than this.

Then, a little later, Anne Boleyn, not satisfied with all the precious things which Catherine had already given up to the King, audaciously asked for, in anticipation of the christening of the child shortly to be born, "a triumphal cloth" which Catherine had brought from Spain and with which she had wrapped her own children at baptism. It had doubtless been used at Mary's own christening, when Margaret Pole had carried the infant Princess for the bishopping in the Franciscan Observants' church at Greenwich. Catherine considered the request an outrage. "It has not pleased God", she replied, "that she should be so ill-advised as to grant any favour in a case so horrible and abominable."

But the demand for the jewels was urgently repeated, and Lord Hussey spoke to Lady Salisbury, who was showing herself to be tough. He asked for an inventory of them, but "the most that I can get my said Lady to do as yet is that she hath brought forth the jewels and made an inventory": she will not deliver them to the royal messenger for anything that he could say or do, unless Cromwell, to whom Hussey was writing, obtained a letter from the King addressed to her. He besought the King's minister to obtain it, "because of my poor honesty". Would to God, he added, that the King and Cromwell knew and saw what he had to do there of late. The jewels seem subsequently to have been sent, but a request shortly afterwards for Mary's plate was met with the brusque reply from Margaret Pole that it was in use at all seasons because the Princess was ill: it could not be given up unless new plate were bought. Nevertheless, the lady governess would send it if it were the King's pleasure.

For a short time after the birth of Princess Elizabeth, Mary's household continued on the same large scale as before. Lord Hussey remained as her chamberlain and there were her esteemed ladies-in-waiting, who included Lady Margaret Douglas, her schoolmaster, Richard Fetherston, and her two chaplains. Above all there remained her old friend and governess, Lady Salisbury. But soon radical changes were foreshadowed.

At the beginning of October 1533 Mary's chamberlain received a letter from Sir William Paulet, Controller of the King's Household. It bade her remove from her pleasant manor of Beaulieu in Essex. Paulet had, according to instructions, described her as "the Lady Mary, the King's daughter". She was astounded and distressed because of this mode of address. Was she, then, no more than a bastard? She wrote immediately to the King. She wondered much at the new title, thinking that His Grace was not privy to it. She did not doubt that he took her to be his lawful daughter, born in true matrimony. If she thought she was not, she would offend God. But in everything else she was the King's obedient daughter.

It was unlikely that Henry would be satisfied with those sentiments. He sent a commission consisting of the Earls of Oxford, Essex and Sussex, and Dr Sampson, Dean of the King's Chapel, to induce her to comply with the royal wishes. The commissioners used pleadings and menaces innumerable in an attempt to make her abandon the title of Princess. She met them all, as did her mother in similar circumstances in the summer of this eventful year, in the presence of all her staff, lest, Mary said, without many witnesses something might be reported that would not be to her advantage. She never lacked courage. She refused compliance. The spirit of her mother, even of her grandmother, Isabella, breathed in her. Margaret Pole must have looked on approvingly.

It was about this time that Catherine wrote Mary a memorable, undated letter, full of admirable advice and reflecting the Queen's high courage and the spiritual wisdom which guided her own life. She told Mary that the time had come when God would "prove" her. She was glad of it and besought her daughter to respond to His pleasure with "a merry heart", for He would not then allow her to perish. When the expected messenger from the King came, she must answer with few words and "meddle nothing", obeying her father in everything, except that she must not offend God and so lose her soul. In whatever company she kept and wheresoever she was, she must obey God's commandments. And then Catherine indicated how well she had taken to heart Vives' old advice for her daughter's instruction, for she told Mary that she was sending her two books in Latin: one, *De Vita Christi*, with the "declaration of the Gospels", and the other a book of some epistles of St Jerome. She trusted that in them she would see good things. Mary should have relaxation, too, and so she told her to play on her virginals sometimes, or on her lute. Above all, she should keep her mind chaste and her body free from all "ill and wanton company".

Catherine added that she never wrote a letter with a better heart, for she well perceived that God loved her daughter. "And now you shall begin and by likelihood I shall follow." She begged Mary to recommend her "to my good Lady Salisbury, and pray her to have a good heart, for we never come to the kingdom of Heaven but by troubles". Perhaps, one day, Margaret Pole would remember those words. And it was another great friend of Catherine's, Thomas More, who was wont to utter similar thoughts, for if his wife or any of his children had been ill or troubled, he would say to them: "We may not look at our pleasure to go to Heaven in feather beds: it is not the way, for Our Lord Himself went thither with great pain and by many tribulations".

Chapuys was deeply agitated at the treatment proposed for Mary. He sent her his advice and remonstrated with Cromwell. The King said he would deprive her of the people about her, because they put notions into her head and prevented her submission to him. Beyond any reasonable doubt, persons like Margaret Pole, and possibly Master Fetherston, were some of those whom Henry had in mind. The Imperial ambassador gave Mary excellent counsel on how to meet the King's aggressiveness, sending her a form of protest which made no admission of expressly or tacitly doing anything which would be prejudicial to her and mentioning many "fair and gracious remonstrances" she might use. This was to be a written protestation to the King which she should sign. She was to repeat before "her confidant"— who could surely have been none other than Margaret Pole?— some words of protest which the ambassador had suggested and which she should employ when the messenger came from the King.

But it was all futile: Mary was to go and attend on Anne Boleyn's child, who was taken early in December with great pomp and ceremony by a roundabout route to Hatfield, so that the populace could admire, so it was said, the true royal heir. The Duke of Norfolk then came to take Mary to "the Princess". Such a title, Mary told him, belonged to her alone, adding that what was proposed for her was strange and dishonourable. Norfolk said he came not to dispute with her, but to perform the King's will. Mary was allowed to go to her chamber for a half an hour and on her return asked the duke what company she should take with her on her journey. It need not be much, he said brusquely, for she would find plenty where she was going. She left with a very small suite.

Margaret Pole offered to follow Mary and serve her with an honourable train at her own expense; but that was out of the question, it was said, for then the King and those about him would have no power over her. And this circumstance, again, shows the measure of Lady Salisbury's influence. It was feared, so Chapuys alleged, that it was the intention that Mary should die, either with grief or otherwise, or to compel her to renounce her right, or to marry her basely, or in some way to stain her honour, so that there would be grounds for disinheriting her. Even if the ambassador was exaggerating, he seems to have been pointing with truth to Anne Boleyn's malevolence.

The Countess of Salisbury was one day to be reunited to her royal charge, but Mary was called upon to endure many tribulations and there was to be much national upheaval before that took place. Margaret Pole was to be greatly distressed to learn during the next few years of the persistent ill-treatment accorded to Mary, a solitary and forlorn figure in the hands of her enemies at those successive royal residences where Princess Elizabeth was lodged. After 1531 she never saw her mother again. She was made to feel the bitter dislike of Anne Boleyn and obliged to endure the humiliating treatment of her two governesses, the new Queen's aunts. She must have longed constantly for the company of sympathetic and strong-minded Margaret Pole. There was once even some violence when she was moved from Hatfield to another residence in the entourage of the infant Princess. There were problems of precedence whenever she was in the Princess's company. Her health suffered grievously. Chapuys could obtain from the King no alleviation of her treatment, but Cromwell, to his credit, at length wrung from Henry a half-hearted concession for Mary to go to a house near her mother's. The mainspring of all the trouble was Mary's undeviating adherence to Catherine's cause and her refusal to take the oath of succession.

The dissolution of Princess Mary's household radically changed Margaret Pole's mode of living and that change, with what she was hearing of the Princess's ill-treatment, may have affected her own health. She was no longer young; her old, traditional world seemed to be crumbling beneath her, and new adjustments to life were possibly becoming difficult to make. Her son, Henry, Lord Montague, wrote to Lady Lisle not long after Mary's departure—it was actually in February 1534—that his mother was at his manor of Bisham and was very weak.

CHAPTER 10

The Franciscan Observants

I

THREE religious orders were distinguished beyond all the rest for the vigorous opposition which they put up to the divorce and the Royal Supremacy: the Carthusians, the Bridgettines of Syon and the Franciscan Observants. The last-named were at once more numerous, more clamant in their protestations and, on the whole, perhaps less noted for a display of any considerable learning. They exercised their priestly functions in a more popular way and, in particular, they were almost universally acceptable preachers. Because of their devotion to the Queen and because of their plain speaking, they were feared by a government intent on the success of an unpopular cause. They were the English representatives of that movement in the Franciscan Order which, by the early part of the fourteenth century, had acquired such strength that it prepared the path for a resuscitation of the whole Order. The Observants, as their name implied, stood for a strict maintenance of the Franciscan Rule. They were to hold no property in common and were to renounce vested incomes and accumulated goods, in contrast to the Conventual Franciscans, who, like most other religious orders, held, in common, goods, income and property. The Observant Friars developed as a protest against a loose interpretation of the Rule, and in 1517 a papal decree established them as an independent Order of St Francis, that is to say, an Order entirely separate from the Conventuals.

The English Observants maintained their allegiance to the Rule till the end and were noted with the Carthusians and the Bridgettines for their adherence to a strict spiritual discipline. Only three years after their establishment as a separate order, for example, Wolsey, as Papal Legate, tried to impose on the English Benedictines, who were numerous and in many cases wealthy, a set of reforming injunctions. We do not know their nature, but whatever they were, they were accepted. The monks, nevertheless, felt bound to point out the problems that would arise. There should not be too much austerity and rigour, they said, for then there would not be enough recruits for the many, very great Benedictine abbeys. If there were in England as many houses of Carthusians, Bridgettines or Franciscan Observants, as there were of Benedictine monks, the multitide of religious necessary to maintain those houses would not be forthcoming. "For in these stormy times (as the world now decays towards its end) those who desire a life of austerity and of regular observance are few, and, indeed, most rare." Many years later Reginald Pole blamed Henry VIII for dissolving the three orders in question, for they were the only ones, he said, not to depart from their Rules. It was because of their unswerving fidelity to the Franciscan Rule that so many of the Observant friars refused to accept the Royal Supremacy. The reply of the Observants of Greenwich, for instance, to all the pressure of the Commissioners for the Oath was the devastatingly simple one "that they had professed St Francis' religion and in the observance thereof they would live and die".

The Observants had become associated with the English royal house in the last quarter of the fifteenth century and it was Edward IV who formed an establishment for them at Greenwich in the year before he died. The foundation of the first friary was laid in 1482 and the King bore at his own charge the cost of a site for both the friary and church. Henry VII confirmed his predecessor's gift and enabled the buildings to be completed. The charter which he granted mentioned King Edward's "pious intention and the good dispositions, devotions, expenses and labours of the said brethren day and night in orisons, prayers and fastings". There were to be at least twelve members of the community under the charge of a guardian. In course of time five other Observant houses were established in England, more than one being of royal foundation and all were assisted by royal grants.

The Greenwich friary adjoined the royal palace and its situation was significant in the light of the close attention which the community received from members of the royal family. The church fronted the Thames, but the longer part of the friary buildings ran to the south at right angles to the river. Near the western part of the church was the friars' garden and a path from it led to their wharf. Apparently in the west wing of the palace the community had another chapel and there Queen Catherine with possibly devout members of her own suite or of the Court took part in the religious offices. The brethren do not appear to have had a library in their own buildings, but they had complete use of the palace library, which they called "our library".

Throughout his life Henry VII maintained close and amicable relations with the Observants, especially with the foundations of Greenwich and Richmond, both of which were easy of access to the royal palaces. His own confessor was an Observant friar and the King's wife, Elizabeth, daughter of the royal founder, Edward IV, made the Greenwich friary an annual grant. It was probably at the friary church of either Greenwich or Richmond that all their children were baptized.

His favourite religious order was not forgotten in the first Tudor's will, and his legacies, while considerable to all six of the Observant houses, were specially munificent to the royal foundations of Greenwich and Richmond. He spoke of the Observants' necessities and said that he knew by experience, because of private conversation he had had with the friars, how urgent sometimes those necessities had been: if, indeed, "privy succours" had not been made to the brethren in their needs, they would often have been "in manifest peril of ruin" for lack of food. And so the King made his legacies because of his long-continued devotion to St Francis and out of charity to the friars, and in order that remedies might be provided in due time.

Nor was the young Henry VIII lacking in affection for the Observants, and he continued the royal practice of making gifts to them. He told Pope Leo X that he could not sufficiently express his admiration for the friars because they kept their vow of poverty strictly and because of their sincerity, charity and devotion. No religious order, he says, battles against vice with more perseverance and none were more attentive in their endeavour to keep Christ's fold intact.

The Observants were sometimes employed on royal diplomatic missions, and it was one of their Ministers whom the King sent to his sister, Queen Margaret of Scotland, to remonstrate with her for having separated from Archibald Douglas, Earl of Angus, the man she had married after her husband, James IV, had been killed at Flodden. The Minister arranged a reconciliation, but Margaret failed to keep the agreement he had made. James IV himself had great predilection for Observant friars, from among whom he chose his confessors. And it was after the great disaster of Flodden Field that Queen Catherine had employed the Provincial of the Observant Order on a mission of advice and consolation to Queen Margaret, so that she might be able to meet all the distressing problems that had arisen.

Brought up by his father in close association with the Franciscan Observants from his earliest years, Henry VIII scarcely needed the devotion of Queen Catherine to the Order for reinforcing his own, but Catherine's early acquaintance with the Observants in Spain was, in fact, a notable counterpart to his own experience. The celebrated Ximenez was confessor to her mother, Queen Isabella. Ximenez, a canon and civil lawyer, became, after a varied career as a secular priest, a Franciscan Observant in the royal city of Toledo and in 1492 was appointed confessor to Isabella. But he would accept the post only on condition of being allowed to continue his religious life in his monastery and of appearing at Court merely when he was wanted. At about this time he was made Provincial of his Order in Castile. Three years later he was chosen to be Archbishop of Toledo, but he refused the appointment, persisting in his refusal for months and accepting in the end only at the clear injunction of the Pope. The simplicity of his life continued, and he gave a great part of the very considerable revenues of his See for the relief of the poor and the ransoming of captives.

Catherine of Aragon in those years must have been profoundly impressed by the kind of religious life which he led—this man of great ability and distinguished culture who was an important prelate and yet remained the simple son of Francis. Long afterwards, when the daughter of Isabella was herself a queen, she may have remembered the simplicity of Ximenez the Archbishop, who agreed to wear prelatical dress only in such a way that his friar's habit was clearly discernible beneath, and who compelled his own brethren to observe so strictly the rule against holding property that many of them left Spain. He was, like Catherine, a great patron of learning, and about the year 1504, three years after she came to England, he founded the University of Alcalá.

The Queen's affection for these followers of St Francis never wavered and they repaid it with almost unexampled loyalty to her cause. As her affection began, so it ended. It was more in evidence after she became Queen. Before the birth of her first child, she vowed, when in labour, to present "to St Peter the Martyr" one of her richest headdresses and she despatched it to Spain by one of her maids. This particular Franciscan was apparently Peter of Sassoferrato, who had been sent to Spain by Francis of Assisi to preach the Gospel to the Moors and had been martyred by them at Valencia. His *cultus* seems to have had a considerable vogue in Spain. Catherine, in her poverty at her life's end, had little to leave and few requests to make, but one request she made in her will was for burial in a church of the Observants, forgetting, or not apparently aware, that the whole of the Order had been suppressed.

The Observants came into a certain amount of prominence a few years before the commencement of the King's Great Matter because of a visitation of them which Wolsey, as Papal Legate, was intending to make; and it is at this time that we begin to learn of the activities of John Forest, the Queen's Observant confessor and spiritual director, round whom were centred some crucial events in which the friars were involved at the time of the Divorce.

John Forest entered the friary at Greenwich when he was twenty years of age and afterwards studied with the Franciscans at Oxford. We do not know what, if any, degree he took, though he is referred to later in life as "Doctor Forest". Events were to show that he was a capable administrator and to Hugh Latimer he was one of the most learned men in the kingdom. When Wolsey's visitation was made he proved himself to be an earnest supporter of the cardinal's authority against his own recalcitrant brethren.

The question of a visitation of the English Observants had arisen a year before the affair actually took place (in 1525), for the Pope had written to Wolsey saying, what subsequent events were to disprove, that the friars were very ready to submit to his visitation. They were, however, jealous of their privileges and apparently deeply suspicious of any reforms which might be imposed on an ordinarily exempt Order by anyone who was outside the Order. The Pope warned the Cardinal Legate to proceed with caution and not to attempt anything which had not secured the Observants' good will. They had not, he said, obtained without grace and good will the esteem in which they were universally held. Would Wolsey therefore think of the good of Christendom and not that of England only, and use gentleness and tact rather than severity in admonishing the friars? The cardinal promised to use such moderation that no cause for complaint would arise.

We know little more about the business. The man whom Wolsey proposed to make the visitation was Standish, Bishop of St Asaph, an ex-Conventual Franciscan, who, as already mentioned, had incurred the animus of Convocation for his anti-clerical views in 1515, but had been protected by the King, and who eventually became the King's man at the time of the divorce. Some nineteen of the Greenwich community were displeased at the visitation and left their friary for other places. Perhaps they really objected to the person deputed by Wolsey to visit them and would have preferred a superior of their own Order, which had been made a separate Order so recently. In any case, Friar Forest, preaching at Paul's Cross, "accursed them that went out of the place", and though this can scarcely mean that he excommunicated them, for he had no power to impose such a ban, he was justified in his reproof. Wolsey had legality on his side and the Pope had explicitly supported him. The friars had apparently broken their vow of obedience and Forest had supported constituted authority.

This episode took place some three or four years before the marriage question began to agitate everyone's mind. When that question actually arose, it was the Greenwich community, in close contact with the Queen and with the Court, who knew much of what was politically taking place. But the King, on the other hand, was made aware of many happenings among the friars, for two of the brethren, one, John Lawrence, a priest, and Richard Lyst, a lay-brother, were spies for Cromwell and corresponded with him frequently. It is unfortunate that much of the information about the relations between the Court and the friars is contained in the communications which these two brethren made to the King's chief minister; but, allowing for the fact that they were both clearly out of place as members of so strict a religious order and were therefore discontented—"my head", Lawrence was to say, "has ever been tied under another man's girdle"—that they were sycophantic and looked for materialistic benefits as a result of their fawning correspondence, and betrayed inevitable bias in favour of the King, their communications are valuable. From the King's point of view it was necessary at this time to keep as close a watch as possible on the Observants' activities, since, as popular preachers and confessors, and as favourites with the Queen, they wielded considerable influence. Cromwell did not, however, invariably accept without critical assessment the information he received from the refractory brethren.

The first evidence of considerable overt opposition to the King did not emanate from Cromwell's informers, but was a sermon preached by the Observant Minister, William Peto, who had once been Princess Mary's confessor when she was very young and had also been at times confessor to the Queen. Years later he became a cardinal and returned to his Greenwich friary after it had been repaired and refounded by Queen Mary.

On Easter Day, 1532, the Minister preached a notable sermon which displeased the King. "The unbounded affection of princes

and their false councillors", he said, "deprived them of the knowledge of the truth." Henry spoke to Peto after the sermon, and
heard from him words which displeased him more, for the candid
Minister told him firmly that he was putting his crown at hazard
and that both the great and the common people were murmuring
at his designs for a new marriage. The King dissembled his displeasure and allowed the Minister to go to Toulouse, ostensibly
that he might take part in a general chapter, but in reality he went
to Antwerp to arrange for the publication of a book in the
Queen's favour, which, it was afterwards given out, had been
written by Fisher, Bishop of Rochester.

On the following Sunday, in Peto's absence, the King caused a
counterblast sermon to be preached by his chaplain, Dr Richard
Curwen, who wished, he said, Peto had been present to hear all
that he was setting forth. At this point the Warden, Friar Elstow
(or Elston), rose from the roof-loft to say that he would reply
on the Minister's behalf. He used, in truth, such forceful arguments that the whole congregation were astounded. There was
also much dissension between the two clerics, and the King became
very angry. This anger had not abated by the time of Peto's
early return from abroad. The Warden, Henry told Peto, ought
to be deprived of his wardenship and his errors amended, but
when the Minister refused to do anything of the sort, they were
both arrested. They informed the Imperial ambassador they would
rather die than change their opinions. Elstow, in particular,
incurred the severe wrath of the King, who told him in the course
of a stormy interview that he would throw him into the bottom
of the sea if he did not hold his tongue. "I never had any mis-
giving", Elstow is said to have replied, "about going to God as
quickly by water as by land."

Both Peto and Elstow were still under arrest at the beginning
of May 1532, when the Observants were told that the King, con-
tinuing to act on his angry impulses, had sent to Rome for a
commission from another religious order to try the recalcitrant
friars. The Queen and the Greenwich brethren wanted Chapuys
to write to the Emperor to stop the commission.

Shortly afterwards Peto and Elstow were allowed to retire to

7. JUAN LUIS VIVES
From the portrait at Valencia attributed to Ribalta.

ANNO DNI   1 5 + 4

LADI MARI   DOVGHTER TO

THE MOST   VERTVOVS PRINC

KINGE HENRI   THE EIGHT

THE AGE OF   XXVIII YERES

8. MARY TUDOR
Artist unknown.

the Low Countries, where they continued their vigorous activities in the Queen's favour. Peto published an answer to *A Glass of the Truth*, a work which had been circulated in England as propaganda against the King's marriage with Catherine and as preparatory ground for the proclamation of the royal supremacy. They had frequent communication with their English brethren and were helped in all that they did with money from this country. Much of what was taking place was made known to the Government by its alert spies at Antwerp.

It was apparently in the early summer, soon after Peto's departure abroad, that Father Lawrence commenced his pertinacious informing. He was always willing, he told Cromwell, to do the King a service. He had already preached in the King's favour and, in consequence, had to bear the considerable ill-will of his brethren, who had reported him to the Queen. Could he be allowed to see the King? He was in "great heaviness until he knows His Grace's pleasure". Father Curson was, according to Lawrence, a very troublesome Greenwich friar and should not be allowed to be at either Greenwich or Richmond, for, if so, he would do the King and Cromwell great dishonour. Both friaries were, of course, near the royal palaces. In the autumn Lawrence seems to have received a "kind offer" when he visited Cromwell. Was it a chaplaincy? If ever he were at liberty from his friary, he said, he would be a "profitable chaplain". But later he thought he had displeased the King's minister, who had probably been critical of him. Nevertheless, Cromwell would find him at all times "pliant and obedient".

Friar Forest appears to have been made Warden after Elstow left for the Low Countries and became increasingly prominent in the affairs of the Greenwich community. He was the subject of many of Lawrence's and Lyst's ill-natured machinations. A general chapter of the Order in England was held in August and it is clear that Forest, who had been known at Court for years, told the chapter he had "put the King beside his purpose to suppress the whole order". This achievement is a measure both of the King's intense irritation and of Forest's diplomatic skill.

L

There had, indeed, if we can believe Richard Lyst, been a rumour earlier in the year of an intention on the part of the King to dissolve the convent at Greenwich and remove the friars to the house of the Grey Friars in London. In this way, it was said, the Greenwich friary could be converted into a college. But Friar Forest seems to have suggested some conciliatory measures at his interview with the King. At first it was proposed to re-appoint de la Haye, a friend of Charles V, as Commissary of the English Observants, but a Frenchman was eventually appointed by the General of the Order. A French commissary, it was perhaps felt, would be more acceptable to the King. Lyst thought it would be well if Cromwell spoke to him as soon as he came, so that he might know how to proceed "concerning the King's honour". He came during the Lent of 1533, and was fully armed as visitor of the English province. But it was unlikely that he would for long still the troubled waters.

Father Lawrence maintained that there were others among the Observants who were prominently vocal in their opposition to the King's cause. He was particularly set against Father Robinson and told the King that this friar had been chosen as the "Discreet" for the convent at Richmond, though his election had not had Lawrence's vote. Friar Curson was another of the brethren now opposed to the King. He had been elected as "Discreet" for the Southampton friary and so the King's pleasure was "not justly pondered". Henry was annoyed at their election and wanted them removed, but this, according to the statutes of the Order, was not possible.

II

It was the lay-brother, Lyst, who, from February 1533, manifested the strongest feeling against the Warden, John Forest. He wrote to both Cromwell and Anne Boleyn about him, giving them details of his alleged derelictions. A recent interview which Forest had had with the King seemed to have gone well, but, said Lyst, the Warden was actually full of "unkindness and duplicity". The former Commissary, de la Haye, was ruled by

Forest and took the Queen's part. One Brother Raynscroft had died in the convent through neglect and Lyst implied that the Warden was responsible. Moreover, Forest was determined to make Father Lawrence contemptible in the eyes of the brethren and would like him expelled from Greenwich, because it was known that he would preach in favour of the King. On the other hand, the Warden had often said he himself would never favour the King's designs and had preached imprudent sermons at Paul's Cross, "speaking and railing about the decay of the realm". The Chancellor should not allow him to preach there again: it would be more appropriate for him to sit at home with his beads.

Brother Lyst told Anne Boleyn of all the rebukes and the troubles he had suffered. He had often, he told her, been derisively called "your chaplain", though he was not yet in priest's orders. He intended, however, to be a priest within two years or less and he would then say a hundred Masses for her. He was forty shillings in debt and there were things necessary for his mother, but he was ashamed to beg any more because Anne Boleyn had been so good to her.

When the King saw Forest a little later His Grace was thus well primed. It is not clear whether the accusing lay-brother visited the Court, as he wished, but his denunciations to Cromwell and Anne Boleyn were doubtless quite enough for their purpose. Forest's reception was hostile; and when he returned to his friary he turned whatever unfavourable charges the King had made against him "to the whole religion". In other words, it would seem that the Warden told the community of the King's attitude towards him and gave them a warning about future dangers.

It was obvious that Friar Forest could not much longer remain at Greenwich, and Lyst two months later is found petitioning the King's chief minister for his removal to Newark or Newcastle, where there were Observant houses. And so he went in April 1533, apparently through the action of the new Commissary, to "another convent of ours in the north parts". From the King's point of view it was indeed vital that Forest should go. The business of the divorce was reaching a critical stage and nothing could be allowed which might seem even remotely to disturb the King's plans. An able, popular, fearless preacher in a place which adjoined the royal palace could not be tolerated, and so Friar Forest went to a distant friary where, at any rate, his sermons could do less harm. "Your little friend and less lover and mine", said Richard Lyst to Cromwell, "for all his great cracks was now far away."

The two discontented friars both fade from the story. Lawrence seems to have departed from the Observants, whilst Lyst, who had once been an apothecary to Wolsey and had "made many waters for my Lord Cardinal", studied for the priesthood at Cambridge and finally became a secular priest. He was able, he said, to "serve God with more quietness than I could among the friars". While at Cambridge he kept in touch with both Cromwell and Anne Boleyn.

It did not need John Forest's attractive presence in the south of England to maintain the Observants' intransigence, and some of the friars continued to be most energetic in the Queen's interest. Two Observants visited Catherine in the summer of 1533 and were then discovered at Ware by Cromwell's spies. They were tracked to London and caught there. Cromwell interrogated them, but could find out nothing of importance. If they were examined under torture, he told the King, they might confess vital things. The new Warden of Greenwich asked for the punishment of them, ostensibly to save them from something worse.

There was also a traffic in friars from Father Peto in the Low Countries to this country, and later that year two Observant friars came to England for books relating to the marriage question and in connection with other "privy practices". Cromwell's agents had spotted them, but he considered it would be best to let them first speak to Catherine in order that their "further practices might be perceived and so their cankered intents be discovered".

Up and down the country the Observants were insistent and outspoken against the King. At Newark there were sermons of a "seditious and slanderous" nature and the precise nature of them was not denied by the preacher. What would happen, Cromwell was asked, if this sort of thing were allowed, considering the "credit among the people" which the sermons obtained? Friar Pecock, the Warden of Southampton, preached in the priory church of St Swithun at Winchester in favour of the papal supremacy and was, in consequence, taken into custody, but later seems to have satisfied the authorities. And in July 1534, John Hilsey, Prior Provincial of the Dominicans and Cromwell's agent, was found chasing two Observant friars all over the west country and then back to South Wales. They gave him a good run for his pains and were only at last seized at Cardiff, after having adopted secular disguise. They had everywhere been preaching in favour of papal supremacy and asserted their determination to die for it. They railed at the books issued as propaganda by the government, calling the people heretics who were distributing them. If the King's new marriage or Anne Boleyn or the infant Princess were discussed "they reported the worst they can and dare". And when they, as helpers at the christening of Princess Elizabeth, were asked whether she was christened in cold or hot water, they replied that it was in hot water, but that it was not hot enough. Their perseverance, however, did not outlive their outspokenness, and after a spell of ill-treatment in prison they submitted to the King and pleaded for deliverance.

It was perhaps inevitable that, after a wholesale refusal to accept the Supremacy, the Observants should be suppressed, and so it happened. Henry could not allow such favourites and supporters of Catherine to be at large to continue their subversive work. The Imperial ambassador told the Emperor that all the Observants had been driven from their friaries for refusing the Supremacy and had been sent to other religious houses where they were put in chains and worse treated than if they had been in prison. Two carts loaded with friars passed through the London streets to the Tower.

Not all the friars, however, were imprisoned. The total number of Observants in England was about two hundred and there are no details of the fate of all of them, but an apparently authoritative, informative list of a hundred and forty survives. Of these, some forty-odd are stated to be confined in other monasteries or with ecclesiastical or lay magnates; thirty fled to Scotland or abroad; thirty-six were exempt and thirty-one died. The deaths were most probably the result of ill-treatment. Of the death of one we have details. Anthony Brockby (or Browne), a noted scholar, who had been at Magdalen College, Oxford, was imprisoned and then tortured so mercilessly that "for twenty-five days he could not turn in bed or lift his hands to his mouth, and was strangled with his own cord". Two friars, Rich and Risby, were, as will be told later, involved in the business of the Nun of Kent. John Forest, the Queen's confessor, was to be relentlessly watched by the Government and was in due course to suffer death at its hands.

The brother of the Duke of Norfolk went to Scotland next year (1534) to request the extradition of those English Observants who had fled there and who were going about preaching that Henry was in schism or heresy. The pattern of opposition was the same in outlying parts of the realm. All the Observants in Guernsey refused the Supremacy and asked leave to return to Normandy. They had taken an oath, they said, to the Pope which they could not change. They were all bundled off to France. Even in Ireland, four years after the dissolution of the English friaries, the Observants there were held up to execration. "The blood of Christ", writes one of his agents in Dublin to Cromwell, "is clean blotted out of men's hearts by that monster, the Bishop of Rome and [by] his adherents, especially the false and crafty bloodsuckers, the Observants."

The members of no other religious order gave so many friends and supporters to Catherine of Aragon and few people there were who suffered so much in her cause.

CHAPTER 11

The Constancy of Thomas Abell

THOMAS ABELL continued to be Queen Catherine's loyal and valued chaplain during the anxious years that preceded the declaration of the divorce and for some months afterwards, until, in fact, the dissolution of her royal state was accomplished. During all that time, from the moment when he returned to England from Spain shortly before the opening of the Legatine court, his strong sense of attachment to the Queen and her cause never weakened nor did he relax his activities in her favour. These activities included both writing and preaching. And he was always at hand to advise her, if necessary, in countering the designs of her persevering enemies. His counsel and his consistent forthrightness of conduct were of considerable worth. Catherine was grateful for all he had done and was doing, and as early as June 1530 had presented him to the living of Bradwell-on-Sea in Essex.

It was the Queen's chaplain who, when the opinions of the European universities were being sought about the validity of the Queen's marriage, had the dubious honour of depressing the enthusiasm of the King. At first, when Henry learnt the news of the declaration of the University of Paris in his favour, he was exultant; but when he heard that the decision was far from the unanimity which the French ambassador had reported, and when he was told of what had actually happened, he was not jubilant at all, and the favour he usually showed to the ambassador was notably lessened.

Thomas Abell was the first to give the number of persons at the university declaring themselves in Catherine's favour, together with their names and the academic posts which they held. The occasion of his action was a summons to appear before the King's council to answer an accusation of having expressed the opinion in several places that all who advised the King concerning the proposed dissolution of his marriage were iniquitous people. He now boldly re-affirmed that opinion to the council, adding that, since the Church had approved the King's marriage and that it had endured for so many years, anyone who abetted Henry in an unrighteous act was a traitor to God and the King. The King did not forget the outspokenness of Abell, who had given by it so undoubted a hostage to fortune.

The corruption at Paris over the business of the plebiscite on the marriage was, as at other universities, such that no valid confidence could be placed in the decision which the university had reached. Thomas Abell produced before the King's council a list of forty-four doctors, "among the most learned and honoured in Christendom", who had voted for the Queen. This caused a minor sensation and it was said that when Norfolk saw the list, he turned to Robert Shorton and to the Queen's chancellor, both of whom seem to have been called to hear Abell's statement, and asserted: "Certainly, the man is right, and I must say it is a most wicked and treacherous act on the part of the French to have stated that the consent of the university had been unanimous". In fact, the total vote in favour of the King was only seven (or eight) more than that for the Queen. So much for the action of the great and ancient university of that kingdom which was Henry's ally and from whose monarch he expected to receive substantial support in his designs for a divorce.

The outspokenness of Abell displeased Henry extremely. He was banished from Court by order of the King, who afterwards sent Norfolk to Catherine requesting her to punish the chaplain for his insolence. The Queen replied that justice was a matter entirely for the King, but that it was not justice "to make anyone suffer for having rightly acted".

Shorton, the Queen's almoner, also acted fearlessly. Norfolk told him that since the University of Paris had decided against the Queen, there was nothing more to be said about the matter and that he should tell her it would be much better for her to agree with a good grace to the divorce than to go on opposing it. But he refused to do as Norfolk bade him: his duty, he said, his honour and conscience forbade it. Robert Shorton was still clearly the Queen's firm supporter, as in the days of Wolsey.

The narrow majority at Paris, of all places, seems to have galvanized Catherine's courage, for she was now said never to have been firmer in her intentions. She did not, it was said, care a straw for what had been done in the King's favour. One of the persons who had gone to Paris in order to agitate in Henry's cause told the Imperial ambassador that he had been surprised to find so many distinguished men in England now speaking boldly for the Queen.

But the King employed every weapon in his power to promote his purpose and it was perhaps inevitable that, just as he had sought at an early stage the aid of Parliament in his contest with the Papacy, the government should institute much propaganda to supplement parliamentary activity. Cranmer was first in the field; and when, during the winter of 1529-30, he was commanded to go to the house of the Earl of Wiltshire, Anne Boleyn's father, and there "pen his mind and opinion concerning the said Cause", the almost natural consequence was that the book he completed should be placed in the hands of leading Cambridge dons. Cranmer himself went to Cambridge to try, patiently in smooth speech, to convince them with the arguments he had recently clarified by his writing. He seems to have succeeded.

Then, later, appeared the *Determination of the Most Famous Universities*, concerning the marriage issue. According to the chronicler Hall the King had commanded "a determination of the universities and all the judgement of great clerks to be compiled into a book". It satisfied, he says, the "minds of all indifferent [impartial] and discreet persons, but some men were [so] partial that neither learning nor reason could satisfy their wilful minds".

The need for a reply to all this propaganda was urgent, and Thomas Abell supplied it by his *Invicta Veritas*, which met his opponents with potent, thorough, logical reasoning. Abell explains that his work is an answer to the *Determination*, which affirmed that for a man to marry his brother's wife, a widow, left without issue, is against the law of God and Nature, and that in such a case the Pope had no power to dispense for the marriage. Abell was compelled, he says, by his profession and by a promise "made unto our Saviour", to answer "this untrue saying". He dealt in much detail and with distinguished learning, with all the acute theological issues that arose, and supplied a wealth of supporting evidence from the Old and New Testaments. He quoted, in particular, from St Paul's Epistles, from the Early Fathers like St Jerome, much from Tertullian, and evidence from Origen, Basil the Great and Albert the Great. He answered opposing arguments one by one in a forthright fashion, and asked the reader "to weigh carefully" everything he had written, and, with great fairness, requested him to compare it with the book written on the other side. "Set aside, Christian reader", he wrote, "all blind affection and read this book with judgement, conferring it with the other book against which this is written; and I doubt not but thou shalt stand on the Queen's part as a favourer of the firm and invincible Verity."

Abell's book seems to have created much stir in restricted circles, for it was of marked merit, but its circulation, for obvious reasons, could not be widespread. It found its way with Fisher's own work on the marriage to that place of distinguished learning, the convent of Syon, and no doubt it went to other religious houses where there was a strong, religiously-conservative element favouring the Queen. There were inevitable replies by the King's partisans and one was "a confutation of Abell's babbling in his enterprise to defend the Marriage". But his book, nevertheless, may have had much influence at this time in Catherine's favour, for one Temses in the Commons motioned the House to make suit to the King to receive the Queen again into his company and also to avoid the bastardizing of Mary and other great mischiefs. The King was annoyed. He sent for Audley, the Speaker, and bade him tell the Commons "of the King's marvelling that the House intermeddled in a cause not determinable there". At this juncture Henry was trying to obtain all copies of Abell's book which had been sold. He caused the work to be examined at Oxford, but the authorities there seemed to find nothing to criticize. Again we learn of the unpopularity of the divorce, for the Imperial ambassador said that if the book had not been banned there would have been danger of disturbances in the country. The work touched the King to the quick.

The champion of the Queen was now living dangerously, but in great allegiance to his conscience. In August 1532 we hear of his imprisonment in the Tower because of the book which he had written and because of his preaching vigorously in Catherine's cause and the cause of the papal authority. He wrote to Dr Pedro Ortiz, the Emperor's proctor at Rome, informing him of recent happenings, and Abell's letter was shown to the Pope. Ortiz asked for a papal Brief to forbid anyone, pending the determination of the suit at Rome, to preach against the marriage, and also to grant the Queen's chaplain the title of Apostolic Preacher. The Brief was made out, but later the Pope had revised thoughts and would not send it. Ortiz was almost in despair. He was at this time pressing His Holiness to excommunicate Henry, but Clement, not unexpectedly, put the matter off. The Pope, indeed, judged the King to be in mortal sin, but other people might assert, he said, that it was the custom in England to converse with ladies! He could not prove that there was anything worse than that in this case. The King, too, might allege that his conscience forbade him to treat Catherine as a husband should treat her. Truly, the Queen had reason to complain of the Pope's procrastination.

Thomas Abell remained in prison for some months. He had been allowed by the Lieutenant of the Tower to say Mass during his imprisonment, an event which was duly reported to Cromwell by one of his minions. But Abell was liberated early in 1533 on condition that until after Easter he would neither write nor preach on the marriage. The condition is significant. Are coming decisive events casting forth their shadows? At some unknown date in January Anne Boleyn had married Henry secretly and the matter was kept so close a secret that even Cranmer, the favoured character of the coming drama, did not know of it till a fortnight after its occurrence. The world was not to know it till after Easter. We have seen the essential reason for the close secrecy, and a trusted chaplain of Catherine, who was a distinguished authority on the theology of the marriage question and a notable preacher as well, must be kept quiet until the divorce was proclaimed. There must be no risk of public disturbance.

Abell was henceforward closely watched. In the summer of this same year, Thomas Audley, the new Lord Chancellor, was looking for him everywhere in London, for it would seem that Abell had been responsible for issuing two warrants in the title of "Queen Catherine" rather than in the newly-prescribed name of "Princess Dowager". Audley could only assume that he was in Catherine's household and he was indeed probably being effectually hidden there. The Lord Chancellor was full of suspicion. "I perceive", he said, "that there is secret confederacies." But there seem to have been no untoward results. Abell in October was found in Catherine's household at Buckden.

The requirement of all Catherine's servants to acknowledge her as Princess Dowager instead of Queen, which business had begun earlier in the year, was pursued relentlessly in the autumn. Thomas Bedyll was the first to go on an errand from the King. He found on arrival at Buckden that all the Queen's ladies, Thomas Abell and her other two chaplains, her servers, ushers and the rest did everything for her in the name of Queen. They persisted in doing that because her proctor at Rome, so it was asserted (but it was greatly premature intelligence) had written to say that sentence had been given in Catherine's favour. Bedyll had been unable to catch even a glance at the proctor's letter, because, he said, he was "greatly misliked" among the household at Buckden. He spoke truly. As one of the more unpleasant of Cromwell's agents, he was employed a few years later in the visitation of the monasteries. "His coarse texture of mind and snuffling accents show to peculiar disadvantage against the foil of hard decisions and physical suffering accepted and endured by his victims; the most obsequious of men, he was quite untouched by finer issues." "His letters are almost universally repellent."

We can only guess at the extent of Bedyll's unpleasantness at Buckden, but, judging by what he himself said, it must have been real. At any rate, his mission was unsuccessful and a week later, poor Mountjoy tried his hand. He found it all a distasteful task and he recalled the mortifying experiences of the past. "What business", he says, "I have had in this matter [the King's Great Matter] since it began, as well in the cardinal's days as since, by the King's commandment, I have good cause to have it in remembrance, for [because of] the high displeasure which I have had for the same." Indeed, it seems to have been the irksomeness of accomplishing the King's will which had caused him to absent himself from Catherine's household. The members of her council and the officers of her household did not, in fact, address her as Queen, but her chaplains, on the other hand, told Mountjoy plainly that they could not perceive how the King could "discharge their consciences to call her Princess" since they had sworn an oath to serve her as Queen. Of that mind, too, were her own gentlewomen.

Tranquillity was evading William Blount, Lord Mountjoy, grown old in the service of Catherine. He had received sore words from her, he said, because of the messages he was obliged to bring and because of the King's commands. He wanted to be discharged from his office of chamberlain and was willing to serve the King in any other sphere. Would Cromwell be good enough to plead for him? But, so far as his service with Catherine was concerned, he had not long to wait.

Suffolk and his assistants came in December to disperse her household and induce her to go to Somersham. The duke's report to the King patently reflects the vigour of the proceedings. One more attempt was made to force her to agree to the title of Princess Dowager, but she persisted "in her great stomach and obstinacy", answering "with open voice" that she knew herself to be Henry's Queen and his true wife. Nor could her servants be sworn to take an oath acknowledging her as Princess. They stood stiffly to their opinions, and with much difficulty it was extracted from them that their attitude was the result of the counsel given by Thomas Abell and by another chaplain, Barker. The two were examined. They asserted that no one sworn to Catherine as Queen could change his or her oath without committing perjury. They persisted in that view because "their learning so informeth their conscience". They were committed first to the porter's ward at Buckden and later to the Tower.

New servants were installed in the household and oaths taken of them to serve Catherine as the "Princess Dowager". Jorge de Atheca, Catherine's Spanish chaplain and Bishop of Llandaff, was allowed to remain, because, if both he and Abell departed, there was no one left who could hear her confessions: she always made them, she said, in Spanish and could make them in no other tongue. Atheca, it was added, was a man of great simplicity of character "and shall do least harm to tarry and be her ghostly father". He refused, of course, like Abell and Barker, to take the oath.

CHAPTER 12

Dr Powell Preaches

THE PREACHING of John Fisher, of the Franciscan Observants, of Thomas Abell and of others on behalf of the Queen had its counterpart in the West Country where at Bristol in 1533 Dr Edward Powell, the Queen's counsellor, and William Hubberden, another secular priest, defended the marriage and religious orthodoxy. Their vigorous opponent was Hugh Latimer, the future Protestant martyr, whose activities in these years were bringing him particularly to the government's notice, though conservatives in religion were seeking to keep him in check.

Latimer had early become the friend of leading Protestant divines. The first stage of the troubles which his Reformist views obtained for him took place in 1525, when he incurred the hostility of Wolsey for his association with the celebrated heretic of those days, Dr Robert Barnes, a former Austin Friar. But it was Latimer's opposition on the question of the validity of Henry's marriage to Catherine which first made him prominent and set him on the road to substantial preferment. In 1530, as a Cambridge divine, he was employed by the King in endeavouring to obtain from the university a declaration that the marriage was contrary to Natural Law. He began to preach at Court and was soon rewarded by the Crown with the living of West Kington in Wiltshire, a place which was only some twelve miles from Bristol. In West Kington and the neighbourhood Latimer commenced to preach sermons attacking religious abuses, sermons which, with their homely imagery and forceful phrases, would make so great an appeal to the common man. In London and elsewhere, much later in his career, he would in the same style not only propagate Protestant ideas but also assail economic evils. Those sermons were to make him famous. But in his earlier days he proceeded with caution, and was credited with criticizing only the abuse of Catholic doctrines rather than the doctrines themselves.

For a whole year Hugh Latimer does not seem to have disturbed the calmer waters of orthodox religion. But early in 1532 he was in trouble. He received a summons to Convocation and was confronted with a set of sixteen articles of Catholic belief to which he was asked to subscribe. He made a complete submission after he had declared that such matters as the use of images, making pilgrimages, praying to the saints and the rest were of a voluntary character.

But in March of the next year he was again in trouble and the trouble arose out of an invitation by some of the Bristol clergy to preach in the city. He delivered two sermons and it was these sermons which began the religious rancour and turmoil that persisted till the middle of the summer of this year. Great troubles there were at this time all over England about preaching, says a local contemporary account, particularly in Bristol, where Master Latimer preached. Sermons against him were made by Master Hubberden and Doctor Powell, so that there were "great partakings on both sides". The mayor permitted even laymen to preach. Some priests were apprehended during the stirs and cast into prison. For a full understanding of these events it must be mentioned that the mayor was known as a man of heretical opinions and that Bristol itself had a tradition of substantial heresy, originating in the Lollardism of the fourteenth century. Wycliffe once preached there and towards the end of the next century many people were burnt for their unorthodox views, whilst other heretics submitted to authority. Then, about the year 1520, William Tyndale frequently made preaching tours in the city and in neighbouring Gloucestershire. His mind was at that time no doubt full of the tendentious ideas he would expand and incorporate in his translation of the New Testament four or five years later.

Latimer's preaching campaign of 1533 did not therefore commence on barren soil. But in other ways he had good fortune

9. THE PALACE OF GREENWICH

From a drawing by van den Wyngaerde. The Observant Friars' church is seen adjoining the Palace. The Friary buildings were further to the right.

10. SIR THOMAS MORE AND FAMILY

Painting by Rowland Locky, c. 1593.

my lord & beseke owyr sauyor iesu chryst to geue yor lordshyp aftr thys lyff, lyf
euerlastyng in heuy. amen. I humbly beseke yor lordshyp that ytt woll plesse y
to be so good lorde onto me, as to moue the kyngs grace to geue me lycens
to go to churche and say masse here wythin in the towyr and for to ly in so
howse vpon the grene. I haue ben now in close pryson thys iiij yers and a qr
co. ester, and yor lordshyp knowythe very well that ther was neuer man in thy
realme that euer was so oniustly condemnyd as I am. for I was neuer syns I con
hyther askyd nor examynyd of eny offense that shuld be layd onto my char
also master barker my felow was commyd hyther wyth me, and bothe of vs
for on thyng and dede, and he was examynyd and delyudyd. and I was
neuer spokyn to and yet condemnyd and ly here styll in close pryson. and all th
was put in my condemnacyo ys ontrew, as I haue wrytyn onto yor lordshyp
largely ons before thys tyme / and I iuge and suppose in yor lordshyp so mych
naturall pyte and so myche charytabull compassyon, that yor lordshyp wold of
yor owne mere gudnes haue mouyd and besowght the kyngs grace to hau
ben so gracyons lord onto me as to haue grauntyd me the lyberte wyche I
desyre, thowgh that I had ben culpabull, aftr so longe tyme of ponyshmet an
beyng in pryson as I haue ben. wherfore I do not dowt but rather trust th
yor lordshyp woll so do now for me. syng that yor lordshyp cleyrlye know that
I am innocent and haue so grett wronge. and therfore I do not reherse and
wryt of the dyuerse deseasys that I haue / nor of the grett myssy / nede, and por
that I am in, nor how that increasythe and waxythe more and more dayly
but all that, and thys lytyll petycyo of goyng to churche and lyeng owt of
close pryson I commytt holy onto yor lordshypys grett gudnes. the wyche I
humbly beseke yor lordshyp to moue the kyngs grace to grant me, and yu
so doyng yor lordshype shall bynd me to beseke almyghty god to geue yo
grace that yor lordshype may euermore here lyue, and lewd vand honor
hy acordyng to yor pynyst and profeffyo, that yo may haue aftr that the fy
and fruyssyon of hys most holy and gloryons godhed amen

by yor dayly bedman thoma
abell pryst   173

II. LETTER FROM THOMAS ABELL TO THOMAS CROMWELL
Probably written shortly before Easter, 1537.

in this year of grace, since the King's plans for divorce and rejection of the papal authority were becoming clear. The previous year had seen the Submission of the Clergy, the resignation of More, the death of Archbishop Warham, and there was increasing favour shown to Latimer's friend, Cranmer, soon to be promoted to Canterbury and to pronounce the divorce. Latimer was also on good terms with Ralph Morrice, Cranmer's secretary, and is found corresponding with him at the time of the preaching in Bristol. Probably the preacher was made aware of important news which had not yet passed from a very close circle in the Court.

We know of the ideas set forth in Latimer's first sermons only because of the complaints which some of the religiously conservative clergy made of them: the sermons themselves have not survived. Latimer seems to have attacked the prevalent abuse of Catholic doctrine, such as the superstitious honour paid to the saints, excesses attached to the cult of the Blessed Virgin, and the disproportionate attention given to the Ave Maria, as compared with the Pater Noster, whilst he had something to say about the perennial subject of indulgences. He disliked the idea of purgatory and told Ralph Morrice that "the provision" for Purgatory had brought thousands to Hell, because debts were not paid nor was due restitution made. On the other hand, a Bristol priest complained bitterly that Latimer had stated that Our Lady was a sinner and that good Catholics abhorred his preaching. He was to preach again in Bristol at Easter, unless he were prohibited.

There seems little doubt that, judging by the complaints which were made, Latimer had been provocative both in style and matter. Preachers, however, whatever their religious views, were nowhere in those days noted for their squeamishness of expression. It is very probable that Latimer said more annoying things than have come to light, and it seems almost certain that, as a leading protagonist of the divorce, he must have referred to some aspect of it.

The Protestant mayor invited him to preach again on the Wednesday of Easter week. But he did not, in the event, deliver another sermon till the middle of May. In the meantime, the

M

conservative element had been busy and had obtained, says Latimer, certain preachers to "blatter" against him. They were the two priests, William Hubberden and Dr Edward Powell. That they both agreed to preach against Latimer in these critical days and in a city which had a long tradition of Lollardry, and where the religious atmosphere had been greatly disturbed, says something for their courage. It was indeed their preaching which brought them to the notice of the King as outspoken critics of his religious policy and which seems, in the case of Hubberden, to have led to his imprisonment soon afterwards.

Of the two preachers, Hubberden was the smaller figure. He had been at Exeter College, Oxford, and less than two years previously had obtained a bachelor's degree there in both canon law and divinity. Much younger than Edward Powell, he was less experienced in preaching, and, by that measure, probably the more impetuous in the heat of controversy. He was, however, a popular preacher, though not of such erudition as his colleague. The general content of his religious conservatism may perhaps be gathered from remarks made by both Latimer and John Foxe, the martyrologist, even though these sources are palpably hostile. To the former Hubberden was "of no great learning, nor yet of stable wit", and he would preach whatever the bishop enjoined, though it is certain he would never have preached in an anti-papal sense, whatever else were a bishop's orders. To Foxe, Hubberden was "a right painted pharisee, and a great strayer abroad in all quarters of the realm to deface and impeach the springing of God's holy gospel".

Dr Edward Powell was a scholar of distinction and had long been known to Queen Catherine. It was no doubt his considerable reputation as a theological scholar and his incontestable religious orthodoxy which led her to choose him as one of her counsellors at the time of the divorce. He was a Welshman and was now some fifty-five years of age. He had studied at Oxford, had become a doctor of divinity in 1506 after studying at Paris, and about the same time was elected a Fellow of Oriel. Soon after taking his doctorate he gave a large sum for the roofing of the old Congregation House and for the decoration of its ceiling.

Powell early became the protégé of Bishop William Smith of Lincoln, that energetic prelate of traditional religious views and proved administrative ability who was the President of the Council of the Welsh Marches when Catherine of Aragon went there in 1501. But Smith's reputation is secure on other grounds. He was one of the founders of Brasenose College and was a valued counsellor of Margaret Beaufort, taking a share in the administration of her vast estates in the west of England.

It was Bishop Smith who collated Dr Powell to a prebend's stall in Lincoln, but from 1508 Powell was a prebendary of Salisbury, where he seems chiefly to have resided during at least the latter years of his active clerical career and whence he was called to preach in Bristol. Living in the quietude of the cathedral close with its exquisite view of the calm Avon and the river meadows, did he sometimes reflect on the activities of a great predecessor of his at Salisbury, Saint Edmund of Abingdon, scholar and Oxonian like himself, who, in 1222, became Treasurer of the cathedral, a post he retained till his election as Archbishop of Canterbury eleven years later?

Of Edward Powell's distinguished attainments there is no doubt and even Latimer himself was grudgingly obliged to acknowledge his "learning". His chief work, a defence of the Pope's authority and of the seven sacraments, which he had been preparing for a year, was published in 1523 and brought him immediately to the notice of the King. The treatise is in the form of a dialogue between Powell and Luther, and the King's interest would have been evoked in any case because of his own recent work against Luther. Powell's work is much longer than the royal dissertation, more comprehensive and more erudite. To it was appended a list of heresiarchs from whom Luther had borrowed his ideas and there was also a long list of errors which had been discovered in Luther's own works.

Those Englishmen of culture who had no tendencies to Reformist opinions were agreeably impressed by Powell's *Defence*. The University of Oxford gave it special praise: of all those who had attacked the Lutheran heresies, Edward Powell had done so with "extraordinary labours and most vigilant studies, and they expected no little honour from his work". Later, when the university wrote to the King in similar vein, they emphasized the frequent journeys he had undertaken in producing the work and the particular "vigilance" he had used. They are aware, they say, that the King already regards him with singular favour, but they hope that His Grace's esteem will be enhanced by their commendation, for Powell was a man of great learning and influence. And all this was doubtless noted and not forgotten by the Queen.

Edward Powell was, in particular, a preacher of ability and experience. He must have possessed all the vividness of a Celtic imagination, the quickness of the Celt's thought and his fluency of expression, the facility for making dramatic effects and for introducing apposite illustrations. He began preaching early in his clerical career, and there is praise for a Latin sermon, eloquent in style, which he preached in Lincoln Cathedral during a visitation by Bishop Smith. The text was appropriate: "Go and see whether it be well with thy brethren". And it was this acceptable, experienced Court preacher and theologian whom the conservative clergy of Bristol invited to preach, together with William Hubberden, during the Easter week of 1533. Their preaching, in the event, merely fed the flames of that conflagration which Latimer had weeks before enkindled. What they said can only be gathered from sources which are antipathetic, but the style of their sermons seems to have been as forceful as that of their opponent.

Dr Powell preached the more vehemently and the King, when he knew of it, was unlikely to forgive what he said. He spoke on St Augustine's Green "very seditiously, to the great inquieting and stirring of the people". He treated of the "Chair of Pestilence", on which which sat two kinds of people: the first kind corrupted and infected the people with open sinning and with evil examples, "as he that put away his first wife and taketh another without assent and dispensation of the Church". Especially was an act of that kind wrong in a head or a governor, such as a king, for it caused others to do likewise. King David in his adultery also sat in the Chair of Pestilence, an allusion which sounded to Powell's hearers "to the reproof of the King, their governor, and to their no little offence and grief". On the following Sunday Powell asserted that kings and princes were subject to priests and prelates, but he said nothing about the subjection of clerics to princes and governors, "which offended the people not a little".

William Hubberden, like Powell, was a vigorous supporter of the Pope's authority and, by implication, a defender of the Queen's cause. He declaimed against Latimer's sermons as being schismatic. Let all the kings in the world, he is alleged to have said, do the uttermost they can, they shall never destroy the Pope. Whoever opposed what the Sovereign Pontiff stated was a heretic. Bishops in England were formerly chosen in chapters under the influence of the Holy Spirit, but now they were chosen by the Crown.

Both preachers had been as outspoken as the Observants in London and Edward Powell, in particular, could not have been more condemnatory of the King than Fisher himself had been. The recent preaching, indeed, considerably aggravated the situation in Bristol, and Dr Nicholas Wilson, formerly the King's chaplain, who came down to the city and supported Powell and Hubberden, only increased the rancour. But the dice were heavily loaded against them; and when Latimer was allowed to preach in rogation week there was a more favourable background of national events. Nothing could more strongly have enhanced his self-confidence.

Two ecclesiastics made, in the midst of the hurly-burly, some significant changes of attitude. The first of these, John Hilsey, prior of the Dominicans, admitted that at the beginning of all the trouble the people of Bristol had been "not a little offended" at Latimer's preaching and that there were disturbing factions in the city. He thought it best to be silent about the matter at the time, but the sermons of Powell and Hubberden had caused still more trouble. He went over completely to Latimer's party. He had, he said, spoken to Latimer since his last preaching and found that his invectives were much more against the abuses of doctrines than against the doctrines themselves. He therefore recommended that Latimer, who had been banned from giving sermons in Bristol, should again be allowed to preach there. As we have seen, he actually preached during rogation-tide.

Hilsey had no wish to be on the losing side. A month after the coronation of Anne Boleyn his name was to head a certificate of various Bristol people in which the King's council would be informed of the "synystral" preaching of Dr Powell and Master Hubberden. He was duly rewarded. Cromwell appointed him in 1534 to be provincial of the Dominicans and in that year he was a commissioner with Dr George Browne, an Austin friar, for the visitation of all the friars in England. He was not a pleasant character, and both he and Browne were specially denounced by the Pilgrims of Grace for the way in which they conducted the visitation. After the death of Fisher the King gave him the bishopric of Rochester.

The second ecclesiastic who made a complete *volte-face* was Dr Baggard, the chancellor of Worcester, now acting as Ordinary of the diocese. He had forbidden Latimer to preach because of the disturbances his first sermons had caused. But Latimer had been allowed to preach again and he preached, says Baggard, "very well, with the approbation of his hearers". He gave Dr Nicholas Wilson licence to deliver sermons because, if he had refused it, "murmur" would have been created, "as people had such devotion and affection to his preaching". Hubberden, with his "indiscreet manner and lewd behaviour", he would not allow to come again, and as for Dr Powell he little esteems him, for "he is a man of small discretion, whatsoever his learning is".

Towards the end of June or the beginning of July a commission of enquiry was ordered into the whole affair and a report was sent to Cromwell. The report spoke of the commotion set going by Latimer and there was much complaint of Hubberden, who had remarked that "all Bristol was knaves and heretics" and who had used damaging words about the King. The business of setting down all the accusations was "overlong and tedious", and that we can well believe. Edward Powell was not mentioned. Largely, it would seem, as a result of what had been said, William Hubberden was imprisoned early in July in the Tower. He is not heard of after about 1535 and he probably died there.

Dr Powell's time was not yet. He returned to his cathedral close. Earlier in 1533 he had voted in Convocation in favour of Catherine's marriage to Henry and this with the things he had said in Bristol was sufficient to cause him to be carefully watched by the government. Hugh Latimer, though he had acknowledged his opponent's learning, spoke also of the "bitterness" he had shown. And the King himself would remember the part the former Court preacher and counsellor of the Queen had played in a considerable disturbance about the King's marriage and similar matters that had taken place in the greatest of the provincial cities.

CHAPTER 13

The Nun of Kent

THE COURSE of events in which Elizabeth Barton, the Nun or Maid of Kent, was the central figure is significant in the history of the divorce because it involved many people who were strong supporters of Catherine's cause. It concerned persons like Fisher and More, the Marchioness of Exeter, Catherine's old friend, and among others some conservative religious who were known to be opponents of the divorce, like the Carthusians of London and Sheen, the Bridgettines of Syon and the Franciscan Observants. More's own association with the Nun was patently non-political, as he was to show, and Fisher's association was hardly less innocent. The period 1533-4 saw the culmination of the whole episode. It was a period during which the government took determined measures to crush the marked antagonism to the King's new marriage which had developed. Yet it was inevitable that the government should take action in its own interests at this critical time, since the reputation of the Nun for sanctity of living was considerable and so was the opposition to recent national events which her mystical phenomena had aroused and stimulated. At the final stage a large number of people were included in the Act of Attainder of 1534 either for treason or misprision of treason, but only the Nun and four associates suffered the penalty for actual treason. More, after being in considerable danger, was eventually taken out of the Bill before it was passed, whilst Fisher, though his name remained, was allowed to escape from the penalties of misprision by paying a large fine. The executions constituted a warning—and were fully meant to do so—of the fate to be expected for maintaining explicit opposition to the King's marriage to Anne Boleyn. Those who suffered death have been called the proto-martyrs of the Catholic cause, and perhaps, in a sense, they were.

Elizabeth Barton was some twenty-seven years of age at the time of the divorce. We first meet her as a maidservant at the age of fifteen to one Thomas Cobbe in the parish of Aldington, Kent. In 1525 she became seriously ill and remained ill for some months. She began to have trances and to make prophecies. She had a vision of Our Lady who foretold her cure, and cured she was. Conviction that her visions and prophecies were not inconsistent with a divine origin seemed to be confirmed by her exemplary life: she was notably pious and all the spiritual counsel she gave harmonized with her virtuous living. The parish priest of Aldington, Richard Masters, dutifully reported the matter to Archbishop Warham, who entrusted an enquiry into the matter to the priest and to Dr Bocking, a competent theologian, at one time Warden of Canterbury College, Oxford, and afterwards cellarer in the Benedictine monastery of Christ Church at Canterbury. The next stage in Elizabeth Barton's religious career was her reception into the Benedictine convent of St Sepulchre's, Canterbury, and the appointment of Dr Bocking as her confessor and spiritual director. Her reputation for sanctity increased and the fame of her visions became widespread. She had become acquainted with the old Archbishop. She visited the Bridgettines and also the Carthusians at Sheen. She even, at one stage, went to see the King. The danger arose when her visions ceased to be edifyingly spiritual and assumed a political complexion.

Doctor Bocking was probably influenced in his spiritual direction of the Nun by his own opposition to the divorce and by the opposition to it that existed among her associates and followers. To that extent he can, perhaps, be held responsible for some of the untoward happenings that occurred, though it is unnecessary to accuse him of any conscious fraud or deceit: in the spiritual counsel which he gave to the Nun he doubtless proceeded in an orthodox, time-honoured manner. It was not, indeed, till years later, with the advent of Teresa of Avila, that anything at all scientific was formulated in regard to mystical phenomena. Finally, in attempting to assess the nature and value of the Nun's activities, it is perhaps worth noting that at least three of her closest associates who suffered death with her were not exactly nonentities in intellect: Dr Bocking was a competent theologian within limits, Henry Gold had been one of Archbishop Warham's chaplains, Dr Risby, the Franciscan Observant, was a Wykehamist and of New College, Oxford. Her spiritual qualities impressed Warham, Fisher and More. All this needs to be stated because most of the evidence about the Nun's later life comes from government sources and it is notably hostile: the government's intention was, of cour e, to prove that the Nun was a complete impostor from the beginning.

It is, nevertheless, intelligible that in the earlier years of the marriage question many people, strongly sympathizing with Catherine in her difficult position, should welcome what appeared to be authentic and prophetic information from an accepted visionary. The Nun spoke adversely of Wolsey and the King, and, if we can believe one deponent, she said that "an angel bade her to go to the King, that infidel prince, and command him to amend his life", adding that "if he married Anne the vengeance of God would plague him". The Imperial ambassador asserted that the Nun prophesied the King would lose his kingdom and that she had said she had actually seen the place in Hell prepared for him! Many had been arrested on suspicion of having encouraged her to make prophecies for the purpose of stirring up people to rebel. Her adherents were, indeed, accused by the government of sowing "a secret murmur and grudge" against the King and against "all his proceedings in the said divorce". The most celebrated of her political prophecies was the King's death after six or seven months (or one month, according to another assertion) if he married Anne Boleyn.

The government began to move in July 1533, only a matter of weeks after Anne Boleyn's coronation and some time before the birth of Princess Elizabeth. Able, merciless inquisitors conducted some gruelling examinations of the Nun and she seems to have made an admission of guilt at one of them. At a later stage the Nun and her associates were assembled on a scaffold at Paul's Cross to hear an abusive sermon by Dr John Salcot or Capon, abbot of the Benedictine monastery of Hyde, Winchester, who had rendered the King considerable service in the divorce and who later was to be rewarded with the bishopric of Bangor and then of Salisbury. At the end of this sermon the Nun appears to have signed some kind of confession, a proceeding which, together with her previous oral avowal, points to her lack of resolution at a crucial moment. There seems to have been no acknowledgement of wilful fraud. What all this had done, however, was to demolish her influence among her close followers and among people in the country.

The Nun was placed in the Tower, but the government did not intend to let the matter rest at denunciation, confession and imprisonment. Perhaps the occasion was too tempting for not inculpating some of the important people who had had dealings of some kind or another with the Nun. The net was spread wide and an unsuccessful attempt was even made to catch Catherine herself. To make sure of their intended victims the government rejected any notion of a trial and proceeded instead by the summary process of a Bill of Attainder, which was introduced into Parliament in the early part of 1534 and passed soon afterwards. The Maid and her associates, Dr Bocking, John Dering, who, like Bocking was a monk of Christ Church, Canterbury, two Franciscan Observants, Richard Risby and Hugh Rich, Richard Masters and Henry Gold were all attainted of treason. John Fisher, Thomas Abell and some other clerics with, at first, Thomas More, were accused of misprision of treason.

More had acted, as one might have expected, with the utmost caution and propriety. He told Cromwell that the Observants, Risby and Rich, came to him on brief visits. The former began to speak of the new marriage, but More refused firmly to hear of the Nun's revelations about it. Then Hugh Rich came. He commended the Nun's virtuous living, which was indeed beyond dispute, and asked More whether Father Risby had mentioned the prophecies concerning the King's Grace. "Nay, forsooth", said More, "nor if he would have done I would not have given him a hearing." Then the priest let her revelations alone and talked a little of the Nun's virtues.

Thomas More had actually once met the Nun when he made a visit to the Bridgettines at Syon. He learnt that she was in the convent and he spoke to her in a little chapel. His object in doing so did not arise from any curiosity about her: he wished to meet her because of the sanctity for which she was so well-known and which had endured for many years. He formed a good opinion of her piety. No word was spoken about the King.

After he left Syon More wrote to her wisely and warningly. He reminded her of the unfortunate Duke of Buckingham and his treason, which, since by that time More had entered the service of the King and was about the Court, he had reason to remember. He spoke of the duke's being "moved by the fame of one that was reported for an holy monk and had such talking with him, as far was a great part of his destruction and disinheriting of his blood, and the great slander and infamy of religion". The recollection of such a thing should prevent the Nun from talking to anyone, especially to "high persons", about princes' affairs or the state of the realm: only such things ought to be spoken of as were profit- able to the soul. Which was very sensible advice, indeed.

More was disillusioned after the Nun's confession at Paul's Cross: she was proved by that to be "a false, deceiving hypocrite". As for his own part in the whole affair, he said he had neither done evil nor said evil nor thought evil, but had rejoiced only at those things that were reported as good of the Nun.

By accusing him of misprision of treason, the government hoped to intimidate More into an acknowledgement of the King's new marriage. But Cranmer and his colleagues seem to have been certain that the Bill of Attainder would not be passed in the Lords if More's name remained in it. For this reason they begged the King on their knees to omit his name. This, with some reluctance, he at last did.

Fisher was not so fortunate. Cromwell—and we note the manoeuvring and harsh manner of his approach—had sent the aged prelate "heavy words" and "terrible threats" because of his dealings with the Nun. What Fisher had already declared about the business was far from sufficient. He was advised to write to the King, recognize his offence and crave for pardon. And Cromwell continued to lay it on thickly. Fisher had "tried nothing" of the Nun's "falsehoods"; he should have examined credible witnesses; he should have looked at her book of revelations. He would find it difficult to purge himself, for he had concealed things that tended to the destruction of his Prince. But Fisher did not seem to find it so difficult to justify the part he had played.

He wrote to the King. The Nun, Fisher explained, came to see him three times in all and on the first occasion she came uninvited. She had already visited the King and had told him of one of her revelations which she maintained was of a divine character and which implied that if Henry fulfilled his purpose of marrying Anne Boleyn he would live no longer than seven months. Fisher did not, he maintained, know that the Nun's prophecy was "feigned", and he considered he was on invulnerable ground because she had already been to see the King. He wrote in similar vein to the House of Lords, emphasizing the Maid's valid reputation for sanctity. He wanted to be heard in his own defence before the Bill of Attainder was passed.

The Marchioness of Exeter, another of the Nun's associates, was obviously distressed and apprehensive at finding herself included in the Bill of Attainder and wrote most submissively to the King. She was, in fact, more deeply involved than some of the other victims. The Nun had visited her at her home and she had asked for her prayers for the alleviation of some domestic troubles. She was now the "most sorrowful and heavy creature alive", for she had listened to seditious tales, blasphemies and false prophecies. However, she received the King's pardon.

How considerable was the disillusionment with the Nun which the government succeeded in striking home is clear from what Henry Gold, one of her chief associates, said when he asked Cromwell to intercede for the King's pardon for his brother, John Gold. John had been implicated, said his brother Henry, in the business of "that false and dissembling Nun", as others had been, such as the religious of Syon and the Carthusians of Sheen and the Observants, all of whom "we esteemed virtuous and learned". Henry was executed, but his brother was not.

The inclusion of Thomas Abell in the Attainder is difficult to understand, except on the ground of the government's determination to secure his conviction. He had, it is true, been sent in 1533 to the Tower because of his counsel to Catherine and her household to persist in their refusal to recognize the new title of "Princess Dowager". But he appears to have had no association with the Nun. Hugh Rich, the Observant, had told him, as he had told others, of the Nun's prophecy that Henry would not be king a month after his marriage with Anne Boleyn. Who, indeed, had not heard of that from some source or other? The Attainder said that Abell had taken such firm and constant credit to the feigned revelations and miracles of the Nun that he caused to be printed and set forth in England divers books—there was only one, the *Invicta Veritas*—to the slander of the King and had also "animated" the Lady Catherine obstinately to persist in her wilful opinion against the divorce. That publication and that "animation" were the crux of the business, so far as Abell was concerned. He did not, however, need "feigned revelations and miracles" to convince him of the justice of Catherine's cause.

The government, despite all its efforts, failed to achieve what would have been the greatest coup of all—the implication of Catherine in the Nun's proceedings. Catherine would have nothing to do with any matter which seemed to tend towards violent action against the King. She remained perfectly firm in her personal loyalty to her husband and during the whole duration of this episode her judgement was superbly wise. It seemed, said Chapuys, as if God inspired the Queen on all such occasions to conduct herself well and to avoid all inconveniences and matters which might evoke suspicion. The Nun had been very urgent in her desire to speak with the Queen and to console her in her affliction. Catherine would never see her. And all the time the government did not pause in its attempts to discover whether she had become involved. But for herself, she said, she had no fear, since she had never had any communication with the Nun, though she was apprehensive for her friends, the Marquis and Marchioness of Exeter and "good Bishop Fisher". Cromwell, the chief architect of the case against the Nun, used all possible devices to extract from the Maid an admission that Catherine had had dealings with her. He was entirely unsuccessful. And this was not the only occasion on which he expressed his admiration for Catherine's judgement and his respect for her character. He praised her greatly for her refusal to have anything to do with the Nun, adding that it must be God who had provided her with her sense and wit.

The Nun and four of her close associates were executed in April 1534. Hugh Rich, the Observant, had died in prison.

The government succeeded in its main aims, and its victory was a warning to people of the fate to be expected if any overt opposition to the divorce and the King's marriage seemed to endanger, or could plausibly be argued as endangering, the country's peace. The government's victory was an easy one, and the Attainder, and even the Nun's confession, were secured long after the Nun's major political prophecy was proved to be wrong. All the persons executed, however, were minor figures. The whole episode temporarily rallied, indeed, some of Catherine's friends and supporters, but the net result was favourable to the government, which was encouraged by its success to pursue its revolutionary policy.

CHAPTER 14

The Queen's Bishop

JOHN FISHER remained the Queen's greatest supporter among the bishops throughout the years following the collapse of the Legatine court, and towards the end of his life he was to be her sole friend among them. The frequent attempts of the King and the council to win him over, by one means or another, to their side, was a tacit tribute to Fisher's great reputation. He had grown old in the service of the Church, and after the death of the aged Archbishop Warham in 1532 he was much the most senior of the bishops. No churchman could point to such distinguished attainments of their particular kind: none had such sanctity of living. Did Henry, now in these years of upheaval, remember that Fisher had been a much respected bishop in the time of his father and the friend and confessor of his grandmother, Margaret Beaufort, whose memorable educational designs he had done so much to foster? He, the distinguished humanist, had long been the friend of Erasmus and an associate of those many noted humanists who had once adorned the court of the young Henry. He was the great University Chancellor, the distinguished Court preacher, the ablest of theologians and controversialists, always the valiant defender of orthodox religious beliefs. He had been practically the only member of the bench of bishops—except Richard Fox of Winchester in his later, remorseful days—who gave himself to such conscientious, unremitting toil in his diocese. No one could doubt for a moment the sincerity of his religious views—views which he would express with scholarly balance and tempered vigour; no one was less inclined to compromise principle for mere material gain or through fear. He had been the respected, admired friend of the King; he was still the unswerving friend of Catherine.

Archbishop Warham, probably at the express desire of the King, used the weight of his authority and his long acquaintance with Fisher in attempting to induce him to change his attitude to the divorce, and shortly before Christmas 1530 he summoned the bishop to his house. Fisher found there Stokesley, the new Bishop of London and a strong opponent of Catherine, and Doctors Lee and Fox, all waiting for him. The archbishop pleaded with Fisher to retract what he had written in favour of the Queen and, in an endeavour to convince him, invoked the aid of the other clerics present. But Fisher replied that the matter was so clear that it was unnecessary to bring forward further reasons. Besides, the Pope was the proper judge of the marriage cause: it could properly be argued only before him and certainly not before Fisher himself or Dr Stokesley or anyone else. Fisher would not be drawn into further controversy and he was accused of obstinacy. The Spanish ambassador prudently advised him and other Queen's counsellors to avoid any oral argumentation about the marriage.

Yet a month later the King tried again. He told Fisher "many falsehoods", it was said. The pressure was such as to have been "almost incredible", but it did not succeed. As for "the false-hoods", the Papal Nuncio in England, Pulleo, a Sicilian layman, went to see Fisher and left him completely informed and convinced about the real situation. Full of suspicion, the King next next day sent for Fisher to know what had taken place at the meeting, but the bishop seems to have been able to allay the royal apprehensiveness.

In the spring of 1531 there were attempts on Fisher's life. On his house in Lambeth a shot was fired from the direction of the opposite bank of the Thames. The shot from such a distance seems to have had little potency and did small damage. And then we learn that a cook was suborned to poison the bishop. Fortunately, Fisher did not that day, as usually he did, dine in his parlour, and so, though others were poisoned, he was not. Whether, as has been thought, Anne Boleyn or one of her coterie was responsible for these attempts is problematical, but there is little doubt that, some two years yet from the fulfilment of her ambition, Anne

N

feared at this time the standing and influence of the bishop. There is no one, said Chapuys, of whom she is more afraid than the Bishop of Rochester, the man who, without any sort of fear, had always defended the Queen's cause. In the autumn she tried to make him stay in his diocese and not attend Parliament, lest, so full of consideration she seemed to be, he should catch fever, as he did a year before. But it was useless. The bishop was resolved that, should he die a hundred thousand deaths, he would come up to London and speak more boldly than ever for the Queen.

The Imperial ambassador was in frequent communication with Fisher, communication which was all the more necessary because the bishop could not see the Queen or write to her. Even the ambassador was carefully watched and was obliged to write to Fisher only through a third person, perhaps the indefatigable Marchioness of Exeter. The bishop had recently told Chapuys that when they met in public there must be no attempt at recognition of each other or any attempt to speak. To such a pass had matters come. But it was all necessary "until the present storm had blown away".

Parliament was to meet a little later (in February 1532) and it would continue with increased vigour its anti-papal and anti-clerical attacks. Fisher at this juncture offered the Emperor his unconditional services in the Queen's affairs, but he asked Chapuys not to mention his name when writing to Spain, unless he wrote in cypher.

The bishop was now in danger of imprisonment because of his forthright preaching in the Queen's cause. And when in 1533 the King was bullying Convocation in order to obtain a favourable decision on the marriage issue from the theologians and canon lawyers, he used such language to them that no one dared to open his mouth except Fisher, though a number of other clerics actually voted with Fisher in favour of the validity of Catherine's marriage.

Fisher's mouth must be stopped, so evidently the King felt, and some weeks before the proclamation of the divorce the bishop was placed in the protective custody of Gardiner, Bishop of Winchester. He was deprived of liberty because, such was the reason given out, he was supposed to have said that the Earl of

Rochford had been sent abroad to offer bribes to France and so obtain assistance in getting the Pope's agreement to the proposed marriage to Anne Boleyn or, in any case, assistance in arranging that the Sovereign Pontiff should wink at the marriage when it occurred. But the real cause was Fisher's vigorous defence of Catherine.

Opposition to Henry's plans was being stifled. The Queen was isolated at Ampthill, having been sent there in some haste. Fisher and Thomas Abell were unable to preach for her because they were imprisoned, and John Forest, the Queen's Observant confessor and preacher, was effectively silenced in his convent in the north. Cranmer, almost in concealment at Dunstable, could conveniently carry out his stupendous work. And then, when it was all over and less than a fortnight after Anne Boleyn's coronation on 1 June, Fisher was set free through Cromwell's intercession.

During these anxious years Fisher had dissented, protested, preached and written—all on behalf of the Queen. Often he wrote. His written works were poured forth at intervals in eager response to the books on the King's side. He admitted some years later that he wrote a total of seven or eight treatises, not all of which, however, were printed. "The matter", said Fisher, "was so serious, both on account of the importance of the persons concerned and on account of the injunction given me by the King" (presumably, when Fisher was appointed as one of the Queen's counsellors for the divorce trial), "that I devoted more attention to examining the truth of it—lest I should deceive myself and others—than anything else in my life." Perhaps the best known of the treatises was the second, which was published in Spain. It was, in fact, a revision of the first dissertation which Chapuys had sent to the Emperor. Publication, so it was thought, might annoy Fisher, because of possibly arousing the royal displeasure, but when it was established that the printing had been done without the bishop's knowledge he did not mind very much. It was therefore considered that two further treatises might be published, and the Imperial ambassador sent to Rome to have them printed in time for distribution in England before the opening of Parliament in 1531. A book in favour of the divorce was being rushed through the press at this time by the King's party.

Fisher's reply to the official government book, which incorporated the views of the universities on the marriage was, many years later, in Mary's reign, used by Archdeacon Harpsfield for his *Pretended Divorce of Henry VIII and Catherine*; and perhaps the generally-accepted reliability of this work owes not a little to Fisher's scholarship. He knew certainly, he once wrote to Archbishop Warham, that all the universities in the world could never prove that marriage with a dead brother's wife was against the laws of God and nature.

Inevitably, Fisher's written works invited the government's attention to Thomas Abell's own considerable work on the marriage, the *Invicta Veritas*, and some attempt was made to establish collusion between the two men. Fisher was a few years later asked by the government whether he gave "counsel or consent" to the publication of Abell's book against the King's cause. This was likely, the government added, since most of the book was "gathered out of Rochester's [Fisher's] books". It was natural that Abell should survey for his own work much of the ground covered by Fisher, but he was abundantly qualified to study the matter and to write quite independently; and the fact that the work created something of a *furore* is a measure of its intrinsic merit. Fisher replied tersely to the government's question: he had never counselled Abell or consented to the publishing of his book; "neither had he any book of mine to my knowledge".

In the spring of 1533 Chapuys suggested that the Emperor should make an armed intervention in the affairs of England. He displayed less intelligence than usual. He was, of course, impressed by the great injury being done to the Emperor's aunt, and he says, with truth, what subsequent events were to prove, that as soon as Anne Boleyn had "set her foot firmly in the stirrup" she would do as much harm as possible to Catherine and Princess Mary. For these reasons the Emperor could not "avoid making war upon the kingdom" and it was desirable

that, because Englishmen were being alienated from the ancient
Faith, the Pope should invoke the aid of the secular arm. The
ambassador even spoke of the desirability of bringing Reginald
Pole, Margaret Pole's son, who was then studying at Padua, into
the net, since he and his brother, Lord Montague, as kinsmen of
the King, would have firm pretensions to the English throne in
the event of a revolution. And there was also talk of Reginald's
marrying Princess Mary.

But when Chapuys implied that practically the whole of the
nation would be only too pleased to welcome the Emperor's
well-trained cavalry and infantry to English shores, assuming
that they could once establish a foothold, he naïvely, even pathetically, under-estimated the resilience, tenacity and genius for
improvisation of Englishmen to meet a grave crisis. It was one
thing to appreciate the undoubted affection for the Queen
which almost everywhere existed, and another thing to imagine
that matters would be put right by the employment of foreign
troops. An invasion in the cause of religion would have little
chance of success, for the Church in England had palpably
forfeited much of the respect and sympathy of the people, and
it would not be difficult for the government to divert attention
from religious motives and point to the grave threat to the
country's independence. Charles V showed better sense than his
ambassador, to whose suggestions he remained deaf. Even if complicated international factors had not existed, he was only too
well aware of the extremely hazardous nature of an undertaking
of the kind. Chapuys himself at this time was cognisant of the
King's own view of the probable fate of armed intervention and,
curiously enough, he even represented that view to the Emperor.
"I hear", he said, "that when anyone represents to him [the
King] the many inconveniences arising therefrom and the
dangers of a foreign invasion, he resolutely answers that, if united
and in harmony together, the English shall never be conquered
by a foreign prince." It was the King and Catherine—as we shall
see—who were saying the most sensible things.

It has been necessary to give some idea of the kind of action
that Chapuys was fatuously intriguing to bring about because it

is a prelude to the things which Fisher himself was thinking and saying in the autumn of this same year, 1533. The spiritual arms of the Pope were insufficient: they were very malleable, said Fisher, when moved against these men (the King and his advisers) and he would like strong measures to be taken immediately, but he is afraid that the Emperor will not listen to such a proposal. So writes the ambassador to his master. We can readily assume from all that we know of his character that only the most grave, conscientious motives could have driven Fisher to the view that action of the kind he advocated would alone save the Church and the nation from complete capture by heresy; recent events had apparently urged him to that conviction. Nevertheless, by his talks with Chapuys he was making an incursion in treason.

Catherine herself was adamant in her opposition to any kind of armed intervention to be made by the one person who seemed able to make it—her nephew, the Emperor. She would not hear of it because, she said, of the love she bore to the King. She was confident of her own success—that is, apparently, a decision by the Pope in her favour—since she trusted "to the laws" (of the Church) and to the justice of her cause.

In April 1534 Fisher was summoned to take the Oath of Succession. Like Thomas More, who was also asked to swear, he complained that the oath did not accord with the Act. The Act had not prescribed any form of oath and both Fisher and More were required to swear not only to the succession, but also to the whole effects and contents of the Act, including the preamble. The oath administered thus involved the dispensing power of the Pope. It was refused. When it was proffered a second time and again refused, Fisher and More were sent to the Tower because they had incurred the penalty for misprision of treason.

Several attempts were made while he was in the Tower to induce Fisher to yield, and among others Stokesley of London, Gardiner of Winchester, and Fisher's old colleague, the brilliant Tunstall of Durham, came to him, possibly with little relish, but at the command of the King, to parade their arguments and make their supplications. But it was futile. Fisher made it clear that he would swear to the succession, but would not swear an oath that embraced the preamble to the Act. The implications of this suggested compromise were significant. What Fisher and More—for More took the same course—were now prepared to do was to accept the right of succcession of Anne Boleyn's child, Elizabeth, because that right had been established, much as they disliked it. In other words, they accepted the constitutional position that King and Parliament had definitively and statutorily pronounced upon the succession. It is true that acceptance of the position involved the disinheritance of Princess Mary, but, on the other hand, by refusing to accept the preamble to the Act there was implicit acknowledgment of the validity of Catherine's marriage to Henry and of the right of the Pope to dispense.

It was hardly likely that the King would accept the compromise, nor did he accept it. Before the King's decision Cranmer had tried to help. He wrote to Cromwell recommending acceptance of the modified oaths: if it were the King's pleasure, the oaths "might be suppressed, but [i.e. except] when and where his Highness might take some commodity by the publishing of the same". The King would not budge. If, he said, they were sworn to the succession and not to the preamble, it might be taken as "confirmation of the Bishop of Rome's authority and a reprobation of the King's second marriage".

Fisher remained in the Tower. The many months of his imprisonment were having their grim effect on his frail body, hacked by a painful, perhaps consumptive, cough. Three days before the Christmas of 1534 he wrote, in his needs, to Cromwell. He had neither shirt nor sheet, nor any necessary clothes that were not ragged and rent shamefully, but even this he could endure easily enough, if only he could keep his body warm. As for his diet, God knew how slender it often was, for now in his old age his stomach could only tolerate a few kinds of meat "which if I want I decay forthwith and fall into coughs and diseases of my body, and cannot keep myself in health". His brother, to his great embarrassment, provided for him out of his own purse. The bishop besought Cromwell to have pity on him and to move the King to take him into favour again and release him from this "cold and painful imprisonment". And could he have a priest to hear his confession "against this holy time", and some books "to stir his devotion more effectually"? He wished Cromwell a Merry Christmas.

One event relieved the monotony and distress of Fisher's existence in the Tower, for shortly before his trial he learnt that the Pope had made him a cardinal. The Pope meant well, but the King was consumed with wrath. He is said to have asserted that, if the Red Hat came to England, Fisher should wear it on his shoulders, for head there would be none to set it on.

The bishop was brought to trial on 17 June 1535. The necessary evidence for conviction under the Treason Act had been obtained. The Solicitor-General, Sir Richard Rich, had come to him secretly in the Tower. The King, he said, wanted to know Fisher's real opinion of the royal supremacy. He wanted it to satisfy his own conscience and what Fisher answered would be treated in confidence and never revealed to anyone else. The bishop fell into the trap and gave his view: "He believed directly in his conscience, and knew by his learning, precisely, that the King was not, nor could be, by the law of God, Supreme Head in earth of the Church of England". This was all the evidence that was required. It was used.

The indictment of the bishop was extremely long and full of redundant phrases. The effect may be stated in simple terms: he had maliciously, traitorously and falsely said that the King was not Supreme Head on earth of the Church of England. He had no illusions about the result of the trial. He was found guilty and the sentence was the sentence for treason: he was to be hanged, drawn and quartered, but this was later altered to beheading.

The story of Fisher's last hours is well known. Very early in the morning of 22 June the Lieutenant of the Tower came to him, and finding that he slept, wakened him, saying he had come with a message from the King. His Grace's pleasure was that he should die that day. The bishop thanked the Lieutenant for his words and said he had brought no great news, for he had long looked for that message. "And I most humbly thank the King's Majesty that it pleaseth him to rid me from all this worldly business. . . . But I pray you, Master Lieutenant", said he, "when is mine hour that I must go home?" "Your hour", said the Lieutenant, "must be nine of the clock." "And what hour is it now?" "It is now about five." "Well, then", said the bishop, "let me, by your patience, sleep an hour or two, for I have slept very little this night, and yet to tell the truth, not for any fear of death, I thank God, but by reason of my great infirmity and weakness."

Then at nine o'clock the Lieutenant came. Fisher asked him to reach for his furred tippet to put about his neck. The Lieutenant understood not this care for his health, since he had not much more than an hour to live. He mentioned this. "I think no otherwise", spoke the bishop, "but yet meantime I will keep myself as well as I can till the very time of my execution." He was very willing to die, but he would continue his health as long as he could "by such reasonable ways and means as God Almighty hath provided for me". And then he took a little book in his hand which was a New Testament that was lying by him. He made a sign on his forehead and went out of his prison chamber with the Lieutenant. He was so weak that he could scarcely descend the stairs.

It was ten o'clock by the time he reached the scaffold. The executioner, who was standing ready, knelt before the bishop to ask forgiveness for the deed he was to perform. "I forgive thee", said Fisher, "with all my heart, and I trust thou shalt see me overcome this storm lustily." Then his gown and tippet were taken from him and he stood in his doublet and hose in full sight of a great crowd of people. "There was to be seen a long, lean and slender body, having on it little other substance beside the skin and bones, insomuch as most of the beholders marvelled much to see a living man so far consumed, for he seemed the very image of death." He spoke to the people and displayed, we are told, a countenance so cheerful, a courage so stout and a gravity so reverent, that he seemed to be not only without fear, but also to be glad of death.

Then came the executioner a little towards him and bound a handkerchief about his eyes. The bishop "said a few prayers which were not long but fervent and devout". The executioner then raised high his arms and with one stroke cut the slender neck.

It was 22 June 1535, the day before the eve of St John the Baptist.

CHAPTER 15

Sir Thomas More

FISHER and More were perhaps of all Henry's subjects those whom he was most anxious to convert to the idea of the divorce, but it was More, in particular, for whom he made the most persistent efforts at conversion. Henry's admiration for More had been as boundless as was the admiration of Catherine. "No one conceived a greater affection for More's rare and almost divine virtues and powers of mind, and the King himself was a man of penetrating judgement who chose his servants at this time with the greatest prudence." Yet More was reluctant to go to Court and when there he minimized the value of the favours which Henry showered on him. Fisher once congratulated him on his influence with the King and on the King's great trust in him, but he modestly thought little of all this and spoke rather of his sovereign's appealing qualities: he was "so courteous and kindly to all that everyone who is in any way hopeful finds a ground for imagining that he is in the King's good graces".

Henry valued More's legal and diplomatic gifts highly and in the summer of 1527 he sent him to France in the embassy of Wolsey. The cardinal was to ratify the treaty of England with the French against the Emperor and was hoping to be made the Pope's deputy, for the Sovereign Pontiff was at this time the Emperor's captive. In this way Wolsey optimistically thought he would have the necessary power to resolve the King's Great Matter. On his return from France More went to see the King. "Suddenly", said More, "his Highness, walking in the gallery, broke with me of his Great Matter, and showed me that it was now perceived that his marriage was not only against the positive laws of the Church and the written word of God, but also in such wise against the law of Nature that it could in no wise by the

Church be dispensable." That the marriage was against the law of Nature, was, says More, a new point: the first time he heard of it was when "the King's grace shewed it me himself and laid the bible open before me".

The King consulted More about the marriage twice within the next two years. On the first occasion More was told to discuss the matter with the Bishops of Durham and of Bath and Wells; on the second to confer with Dr Stokesley, the one early convert to the royal cause, who, it was thought, might bring over More to the King's side. At first, said Henry, Stokesley was out of his senses, but had since recovered his reason: he had studied the marriage question and had arrived at a view opposite to that which he formerly held.

More, after a full examination, could not support the King on the divorce and he made his views perfectly clear. He was never to change them. But he was in an invidious position when Henry invited him to be Lord Chancellor after the fall of Wolsey. The Spanish ambassador could tell the Emperor, truthfully enough, that everyone was delighted at the appointment, and that More was an upright and learned man, and a good servant of the Queen. It was precisely because he was so strong a supporter of Catherine that his relations with the King were likely to prove delicate. He could not, however, refuse the appointment, for Henry had promised him liberty of conscience and employment on affairs disparate from the divorce question where conscientious scruples were unlikely to arise. He therefore reluctantly accepted the Chancellorship, but continued as a member of the small group of the Queen's friends and lent the strength of his reputation to her cause.

Nevertheless, More's position was now always precarious. In the autumn of 1530 Chapuys said that the chancellor had spoken so much in the Queen's favour that he had narrowly escaped dismissal. Perhaps that was mere gossip. Yet in the following spring the ambassador again praises all that More is doing for the Queen: he not only acts in the best possible way on behalf of Catherine, but also shows much sympathy with all that concerns the Emperor and his subjects.

But the situation was becoming very difficult. Chapuys, for instance, had on one occasion received a letter for More from the Emperor and wished to deliver it personally. The chancellor thought that such a proceeding would be perilous and he begged the ambassador, for the honour of God, not to visit him. He had, of course, he says, given sufficient proof of his loyalty to the King, yet, considering the times, he ought to abstain from any action that might excite suspicion. The ambassador's visit might, indeed, cause the King to suspect More and deprive him of the liberty of speaking boldly of affairs concerning the Emperor and Catherine. He certainly did not regard those affairs as less important than his own life, not only out of the respect which was due to those two personages, but also because of the welfare, honour and conscience of his master and the well-being of the realm. Would, therefore, Chapuys keep the letter till some more favourable moment, for if he received it now he would have to tell the King? The letter must have related to the marriage question, but we are left in ignorance of its precise nature.

Thomas More resigned the Lord Chancellorship on 16 May 1532, the day after the momentous Submission of the Clergy reached the King. The Submission was the culmination of those ecclesiastical events which he had been watching closely and anxiously during the past year or two. Perhaps, as we are told, he was glad to resign, so that he might devote his life to "spiritual studies, meditations and exercises to heavenward". National events were distressing enough, but More would for a short period find some solace in his Chelsea home where he had been sometimes "for goodly purpose desirous to be solitary and to sequester himself from worldly company". And he would have the consoling company of his united and devoted family, who lived in the exquisite house near the river, with its gardens and orchards and "all other necessaries so handsome".

After his retirement, Cromwell came to him one day with a message from the King and More took the opportunity to give him the elder statesman's advice which has become so famous. It will bear mention once again: "Master Cromwell, you are now entered into the service of a most noble, wise and liberal prince; if you will follow my poor advice, you shall, in your counsel-giving unto his Grace, ever tell him what he ought to do, but never what he is able to do. . . . For if a lion knew his own strength, hard were it for any man to rule him". But Cromwell was hardly likely, as the student of Machiavelli's realistic political philosophy, to take such advice.

And so for the next year or so, while Cromwell advanced steadily in the King's favour, Thomas More spent a quiet, con-genial life away from the worrying affairs of the great world of the Court. He would not meddle with those affairs, especially he would not meddle with the marriage question, but he retained his old opinion of it. Then came the epoch-making event of the divorce. More did not attend Anne Boleyn's coronation which followed soon afterwards. How could he do so, holding such views as he held? He was asked to accept twenty pounds to buy a new gown for the great occasion. Prudently, he kept this sum, but he put in no appearance.

The omission of More's name from the Bill of Attainder relating to the Nun of Kent was made by the King with much unwillingness. Previously, when he had heard that the Bill would probably not pass if More's name remained, Henry had said that he would himself go down to the Lords and compel them to pass it. How little inclined More was to meddle with the divorce question or with the political aspects of the Nun's business is realized from something he told Cromwell at this time. He had never, he said, adopted any attitude concerning the King's new marriage which might cause the King any sort of annoyance. Once again he showed how far removed he was from any injudicious conduct: he was a model of propriety. "I am not he", he said, "which can, or whom it could become, to take upon him the determination or decision of such a weighty matter." To do anything of the kind was past his learning. He was among His Grace's faithful subjects. The King was "in possession of his marriage and this noble woman [Anne Boleyn] really anointed Queen". There would be from him no meddling in the matter.

More's attitude foreshadowed the position he was to assume on the question of the royal succession.

On Low Sunday, 1534, he went to St Paul's to hear the sermon with his son-in-law, William Roper. The sermon over, he visited the home of Dr John Clements, the husband of his adopted daughter, Margaret Gigs. While there one of the royal officers brought a writ citing him to appear before the King's commissioners at the archbishop's palace on 13 April. It was for the purpose of taking the Oath of Succession.

And so Thomas More left Chelsea on this day in spring to travel the short distance by water to Lambeth. It is said that, as he was leaving his home, which he was never to see again, his wife and children, who were in tears, wanted to accompany him to the riverside. This he would not let them do, but, shutting the gate, went on his brief journey with only William Roper as his companion. "Sitting in the boat that was taking him . . . he was silent and sad. . . . But at last he turned a bright and cheerful countenance to his son-in-law, and said: Son Roper, I thank our Lord, the field is won." Roper did not understand these words at the time, but afterwards he knew "it was for that the love he had to God wrought in him so effectually that it conquered all his carnal affections utterly".

More was required, like Fisher, to swear not only to the Succession but also the whole contents of the Act. He refused. As some inducement to make him change his mind he was told that a large number of people had already sworn "without sticking". More blamed no one for that, but he himself would not swear to what was wanted nor would he give any reason for his attitude: if he did so he would only exacerbate the King. His conscience had been fully informed "by long leisure and diligent search". Finally, he told Audley, the Lord Chancellor, that he would swear to the Succession if the oath were so formulated as would accord with his conscience.

The courtesy and considerateness of More's attitude on this vital matter, as on other matters, were combined with a prudence that was informed and influenced by his own unique legal training and practice, but he was always careful not to offend the King.

"Cleverly", however, "like a stag surrounded by baying hounds, he kept his pursuers at bay." First, the King was desperately anxious to win him over to his side; then the council tried "sometimes in common, sometimes separately to seduce him. Nothing could show more clearly the honour and respect that More enjoyed in the eyes of King, Parliament and the people." For his refusal to swear he was committed on 13 April to the custody of the abbot of Westminster and with him he remained four days. Then he was sent to the Tower. For refusing the oath he was guilty of misprision of treason, and the penalty was life imprisonment and the forfeiture of all his property. It was under the Treason Act that next year More, like Fisher, was brought to trial for alleged treason.

In the spring of 1535—on 30 April—began a short series of examinations of More in the Tower. The King was now fortified with the Statute of Treason which had come into operation two months earlier. It was now treason "maliciously" to desire to deprive the King of any of his titles: even to deny them by word of mouth was treason. More at his first examination by Cromwell and other councillors was asked for his view on the Royal Supremacy. He told them he had truthfully declared to the King from time to time his mind on the subject. "And now I have in good faith discharged my mind on all such matters, and neither will dispute the King's titles nor the Pope's, but the King's true, faithful subject I am and will be." Cromwell said that the answer would not satisfy the King.

A few days later Margaret Roper visited her father in the Tower. From a window of More's chamber they watched Dr Richard Reynolds and three of the Carthusian priors going forth to their deaths at Tyburn. All had strongly supported Catherine's cause and had refused to acknowledge the royal supremacy. "Lo!", said More, "dost thou not see, Meg, that these blessed fathers be now as cheerfully going to their deaths as bridegrooms to their marriage?"

On 7 May Cromwell went again to see More, who replied as before to all his solicitations. And then at the beginning of June was sent a deputation consisting of Cromwell, Audley, the new

Lord Chancellor, Cranmer, Suffolk and Wiltshire. Cromwell, the principal spokesman, said that the King was dissatisfied with More's attitude which was doing much harm in the realm. He must be unequivocal and should acknowledge the Supreme Headship. But More would not change. It was hard, he said, that he should now be compelled to declare his mind in the manner required, for he had never done or asserted anything against the statute. As for the oath which was now proffered to him, he had resolved never to swear an oath as long as he lived. More's defence was always in the sense that though he refused the oath, he would never declare the reasons for his refusal. He would not deny that the King was Supreme Head, but he declined to assert that he was.

Thomas More was taken from the Tower on 1 July 1535 for trial at Westminster Hall. He was very weak in body, but it was weakness caused not so much by age as by the suffering he had endured in prison. Yet his countenance showed no anxiety.

The indictment, which was in Latin, was long and intricate in its maze of clauses. More, indeed, spoke of its great length. It was difficult for him to grasp the whole import of the terms as they were read to him. Owing to his bodily weakness he lacked the wit, memory and power of speech to reply to each charge. He met the main charges, however, and the answers were these:

He had never approved of the King's marriage to Anne Boleyn. The King was well aware of his opinion and he had never tried to conceal it. For this error, if error it were, he had already been punished by imprisonment and the total loss of his goods.

It was alleged that he had maliciously and treasonably declined to acknowledge the King's new title of Supreme Head. He had told the King's counsellors that the Supremacy Act was "no concern of his . . . at law he was civilly dead". He could not be compelled to give his view of the law since he did not come within its orbit. There were no words, there was no deed of his, which could ever be construed as disapproval of the statute. In making this answer he violated no law nor was he guilty of a capital

o

offence. He could not be condemned for maintaining silence. "Of secret thoughts God alone is judge."

It was said that there had been correspondence between More and Fisher while they were in the Tower, and so the bishop's "obstinacy" had been stimulated. But More explained that the correspondence was of a quite innocent nature between old and close friends. It concerned their private affairs, though one letter of the bishop's enquired what reply to the King More had given about the Statute of Supremacy. More had answered merely that he had satisfied his own conscience and that Fisher must satisfy his.

Lastly, More told his judges of the opinion of the statute which he had given to the commissioners who came to see him in the Tower. The statute was a "two-edged sword", he had said: if he infringed its provisions he would lose his head; if he obeyed it he would lose his soul. But never, in fact, did he speak against it to any living person.

More's defence was the defence of a great lawyer and advocate. The prosecution on behalf of the Crown had not gone well and it was now that Rich, the Solicitor-General, came forward to fill the gap with his perjured evidence. He falsely alleged that More had uttered fatal words which implied a recognition of the papal supremacy. Yet it is significant that the two persons he called upon for the support of his allegation did not give it: their heads, they said, were concerned with other business at the time. More gave Rich the trouncing he deserved.

The jury after a retirement of only fifteen minutes returned to give a verdict that More had maliciously offended against the Treason Act, and he was therefore sentenced to be hanged, drawn and quartered, a penalty which the King subsequently commuted to beheading. Before, however, sentence was pronounced, More uttered his well-known declaration of faith and his defence of the Pope's Primacy. It was no longer necessary to adopt an attitude of lawyer-like caution and he now spoke with a freedom that was newly-born.

When he saw, said More, from the way the affairs of the realm were going that it would be necessary to enquire into the origin of the Pope's authority, he studied the question for ten

years. "But never could I find in any writing of the doctors whom
the Church approves that a layman ever had been, or ever could
become, head of the spirituality." And then spoke the defender of
Catherine's marriage: "Yet I know full well what has been the
cause of my condemnation: it is that I would never give any
approval to this new marriage".

He had not long to wait for the end. Sir Thomas Pope, "his
singular friend", brought him the decision of the King that
he was to die on 6 July before nine o'clock in the morning. He
thanked Master Pope for this good news. He was obliged to the
King for many blessings showered on him from time to time. But,
"most of all, Master Pope, am I bound to His Highness that it
pleaseth him so shortly to rid me out of the miseries of this
wretched world. And therefore will I not fail earnestly to pray for
His Grace, both here and also in another world."

On the appointed day he was taken from the Tower by the
Lieutenant to the place of execution. The scaffold appeared so
frail as More ascended it that it seemed likely to break. More then
said to the Lieutenant: "I pray you, Master Lieutenant, see me
safe up, and for my coming down let me shift for myself".

He asked all the assembled people to pray for him and to bear
witness that he died in and for the faith of the Catholic Church.
Then, having knelt and said some prayers, he turned cheerfully
to his executioner: "Pluck up thy spirits, man, and be not afraid
to do thine office; my neck is very short; take heed, therefore,
thou strike not awry, for saving of thine honesty".

So did Sir Thomas More, once Lord Chancellor of England,
pass from this world on the Eve of the Translation of St Thomas
of Canterbury, 1535.

There was consternation and great sorrow in every part of
Europe when the news was known. Erasmus, More's old friend,
a little later this same year, recalling all the friends he had lost,
wrote: ". . . and Thomas More, Lord Chancellor of England,
whose soul was more pure than any snow, whose genius was
such as England never had, yea, and never shall see again,
mother of wits though England be".

CHAPTER 16

Catherine Dies: Her Spanish Suite

I

IT WAS only too probable that after her rejection of the oath and of all thought of accommodating herself to the King's will the treatment of Catherine would deteriorate, and so it proved. At Kimbolton Castle, situated in country that was not unpleasant in the height of summer but unhealthy in winter, she was made to feel herself to be more of a prisoner than at any of the residences in which Henry had placed her. She lived her lonely life in one room on the ground floor of the castle from which there was a view of the deer park, of the neighbouring moats and then of the hill beyond. The keeper's lodge still bears her name. It is said that there was once a secret passage which led to Catherine's small oratory whence she escaped from the watchfulness of her guards and spies. In the one bed-sitting room which was now her home she lived with a few English maid-servants who attended to her simple wants and who alone prepared her food in her presence.

Had it not been for the devotion of these women and of the handful of Spanish household officers who had been with her for years, and for the consolation she derived from her religious faith, Catherine would have felt bitterly the desolation of her grim life. Increasingly in her isolation, she looked for sympathy —but, as yet, little more—from Spain, the one strong source whence it could come, and her intermediary with the Emperor was the attentive, ever-resourceful Chapuys. But though in these earlier days she sent somehow or other urgent messages to him to visit her, he never came: either the ambassador could never get an answer to his request for permission to see her or Cromwell said that he was unable to persuade the suspicious King to allow him to do so. In the summer of 1534, however, after excuses and evasions enough on the part of Cromwell, the ambassador determined to go to Kimbolton, and he set out with a posse of sixty horse. But he was not allowed to enter the castle or to speak to Catherine, nor did he himself pass through the village. Nevertheless, Catherine's servants gave him to understand that it would give her great pleasure if some of the men of the ambassador's company presented themselves before the castle walls. Then she with her servants managed to speak to the men from a near balcony "and it seemed to the country people about that the Messiah had come". But it did not console Catherine, who apparently wished to speak to Chapuys on some important business.

She was very poor and even her most urgent wants were not made good. Money was indeed paid to certain people at Kimbolton, but Catherine said that it was not for her nor to be spent by her staff, but was for her guardians and keepers. Her old servants, some of whom had come with her from Spain, had been dismissed, and though she was in duty bound to pay pensions for their maintenance she had no money to give them, not even in charity. As for herself, she had had only two new dresses in two years. Cromwell's answer to all this was that she could have as much money and as many dresses as she wished: she had only to ask. But he could safely talk like this since he well knew that Catherine would never actually beg for her needs to be supplied, nor would she receive anything that was sent to her in the name of "Old Princess Dowager".

She had other trials and anxieties. She was worried at the way in which the fabric of an ancient religious faith was slowly being destroyed and at the great spread of heresy in the land; she was grievously troubled at the ill-health of her daughter, Mary, whom she had not seen for years. In the autumn of 1534 the Princess, who had never been physically strong, was very ill, and the King was obviously perturbed. He allowed his own physician, good Doctor Butts, and Catherine's own physician, faithful Miguel De La Sá, and her apothecary, Juan de Soto, to visit her. Suspicion, as ever, accompanied the King's concession, for he ordered no language to be spoken at the visits but English. Chapuys tried to get Henry to let Mary live with her mother, and Miguel said that, if that were done, he would undertake to cure the Princess's illness. The attempt was unsuccessful. But Mary recovered.

In the early part of the next year, however, there was a recurrence of the illness and again the King seemed to be full of anxiety. Doctor Butts was very sensible and said that Mary's ill-health was caused by "sorrow", by which he seems to have meant the tension of continually living in the inimical atmosphere of Princess Elizabeth's establishment and that, entirely cut off from her mother, she had no sympathetic friends. Even Chapuys could not get permission to visit her.

Catherine strongly renewed her desire that Mary should come to stay with her. She would herself nurse her and she would have the skilful help of her physician and her apothecary. But the King would not allow it: Mary might escape from the realm: Catherine was the cause of Mary's "obstinacy". That—the withstanding of his will—was the one thing that Henry would not forgive.

With great prudence Chapuys did not attempt to dispute with the King, but, finding that Catherine's suggestion which he had sponsored was unacceptable, requested Henry's permission to let Mary be in the care of her old governess, Margaret Pole, whom, said the ambassador, she regarded as her second mother. But Henry now showed that he had greatly changed, or professed to have changed, his opinion of his distinguished kinswoman, the oldest friend of Catherine, in whose choice for the superintendence of his daughter's affairs from an early age he had been so ready to acquiesce, and whom, until he began to discern in her opposition to his wishes, he had always favoured. He told Chapuys that the Countess of Salisbury was a fool, of no experience, and that if his daughter had been under her care during her recent illness she would have died, for the Countess—the person, it is worthy of note, who had always until the last year or two looked after a delicate girl from earliest childhood—would not have known what to do. But perhaps we perceive the kind of influence at work when the King added that Mary's present governess, Lady Anne Shelton, the new Queen's aunt, was "an expert lady even in such female complaints", apparently wishing to imply a contrast to Margaret Pole. Yet when Henry consulted his physicians they were unanimous in the opinion that the Princess's illness proceeded from "distress and sorrow", so that Doctor Butts' early diagnosis was accurate. The trouble would easily be remedied if she were removed to a different environment where she could have agreeable recreation and suitable exercise: to remain where she was would be to court death.

Shortly after this Mary became ill again and Catherine in her loneliness at Kimbolton was distraught with anxiety. But Cromwell at length obtained the King's permission for placing the Princess in some house not far distant, where Catherine's physician and apothecary could conveniently visit her. For this kindness Catherine expressed her gratitude to Cromwell. Henry would not, however, let Mary be with her mother or even to visit her. He would take good care not to allow anything of that kind, for Catherine "being so haughty in spirit might raise a number of men and make war as boldly as her mother, Isabella, had done". So Chapuys said, but the notion of armed intervention in England was as much in his mind as he alleged it was in Henry's. Catherine had firmly all these years set herself against any action of the kind.

Catherine's personal circumstances did not improve. In the spring of 1535 she told the Emperor that she was resigned to bear whatever burden was sent to her. She was "as Job waiting for the day when I must go sue alms for the love of God". And even when Mary's illness was over there was anxiety arising from the ever-present possibility of further attempts to make them both take the oath. There was always the bitter attitude of Anne Boleyn which found expression in much adverse treatment by the King. At times there was petty persecution. In Lent, for example, Catherine wished to keep a Maundy, the centuries' old religious ceremonial of washing the feet of a number of poor people on the day before Good Friday, a ritual that was followed by gifts to them of clothing, food or money. The country people of Kimbolton would have welcomed it. Catherine let the government know that she would keep the Maundy quite secretly in her chamber. The King's reply was that if she held the ceremony she must preside under the title of "Princess Dowager": if it were in the name of Queen she and all her officers present and those who received the Maundy would be guilty of treason.

So Catherine lived in isolation, poverty and constant anxiety. She, who had been England's Queen, who long ago had put into enthusiastic practice the sage advice of Fray Diego to forget Spain and Spanish customs for the sake of England's good, was now made to feel herself a stranger—a Spaniard once again, with a handful of Spaniards around her and a few English women servants, and forced to look towards Spain for sympathy and, at last, for possible help to alleviate what she regarded as a desperate national situation. In one sense—but in most other ways there was a radical difference—she was in these last years much as in those distressing early days in Durham House. There, too, she had been isolated and poor, relying on people who had come with her from Spain. But she was then young, exuberant, full of hope —with life and its fair prospects beckoning to her enchantingly, even if at times there was anxious care.

Her memories were now her sad, almost forgotten friends, wakened into life by the very poignancy of her changed circumstances. Did she sometimes talk to Bishop Jorge or Miguel the physician about far-off Spanish days—about her mother, the great Isabella, with her enlightened views on education and culture, or about Granada which Isabella had captured—Granada with its great palace, its orange groves and palm trees and cool fountains? Did she remember that long slow progress in a mellow autumn which she made across southern England to London immediately after her landing on English soil, when she met all those pleasant simple country people who lined the route to welcome her? And how she had kept their affection through all the vicissitudes of her tragedy? She would meet those country folk often in later days in neighbouring towns and villages when she stayed at the great mansions of the nobles or at great religious houses. London knew her well, too, and perhaps she thought of the Londoners who welcomed her enthusiastically at her first entry to the capital or, much later, in the time of trouble, of the crowd of people who assembled to cheer her on her way to Blackfriars. So great was the concourse on that occasion and so spontaneous and excited the welcome, that the King, hearing of it, ordered none of the common people to be admitted in future near the gallery through which she had passed.

Did she also think, one wonders, of the scintillating English Court in the halcyon days of the reign, when gay pleasures seemed unending—banquets and dancing, music and "masking"? Especially there was dancing—dancing till early morning, with the viols playing their light, merry tunes, and the jewels and the dresses glittering in the light of many torches, and the centre of it all was the handsome King, her husband. And there at Court Catherine found her friends, like Mary, the King's sister, and the Poles and the Exeters and the Burgavennies, Elizabeth Howard and the Willoughbys and the Jerninghams. She would meet men of genius, More and Fisher and Vives, or, going to Syon, seeking tranquillity, she would converse with "Angelical" Richard Reynolds and Richard Whytford, the former to meet a brutal death and the latter to stay on till the end of Syon in 1539, departing then with a small pension, but probably never accepting the Supremacy.

Catherine had been the devoted wife of a one-time devoted husband. There were few consoling resources left to her now. She had lost the love of the King, who had become vindictive, cruel, deplorable. She had never been allowed to see her daughter Mary after the first stage of a lonely existence five years before. None of her old friends was permitted to visit her, not even Chapuys. He, it is true, had not been idle on her behalf and had long been trying, as we have seen, to arrange for armed intervention by the Emperor; but whatever subversive elements may have existed among some powerful figures in England could never be organized because of the attitude of Catherine herself: she must inevitably serve as the focal point for revolt, but she would do nothing to assist, out of the love and allegiance she bore to her husband. Chapuys and any others who thought like him were helpless.

But the terrible events of the spring and summer of the year 1535 were never long absent from her thoughts: the execution of Richard Reynolds and the Carthusians, and of Fisher and More. She thought long before she acted and then in October, only three months before her death, her mind was made up. Matters had already gone far and something, she evidently felt, must be done. The country was in schism and cut off from the head and main current of Catholicism. A violent, remorseless despotism was gaining momentum. She took up her pen and wrote. She wrote two letters: one to the new Pope, Paul III, and the other to her nephew, the Emperor. They were both in the same vein.

She told the Pope of the urgent needs of the kingdom. She thanked Christ that Christendom had now such a Vicar at a time of necessity. She begged him to keep England, the King, "my lord and husband", and their daughter, Mary, specially in mind. If a remedy was not quickly found for those things which His Holiness and all Christendom knew to be so offensive to God and were the scandal of the whole world, there would be no end to the loss of souls and the making of martyrs. Good people, indeed, would be constant and suffer, the lukewarm would perhaps fall away, whilst the rest would just stray like sheep without a shepherd. She wrote, she said, in this way to the Pope in discharge of her conscience, and as one who expected death. She was comforted when she thought of those holy men (they had been her friends) who endured such torments, though it was grief to her that she was unable to imitate their lives.

Less than a month before her death her mind recurred to the same theme. She was forced to write to her nephew again because of what she was daily told would be attempted in Parliament and she "implores him for the remedy"; whilst to Doctor Ortiz, the Emperor's proctor in Rome, she wrote that he should be most diligent in urging a swift remedy.

II

At the beginning of December Catherine was very ill and the King was told. She had violent internal pain accompanied by vomiting, and she was very weak. But in seven days she recovered. Shortly before Christmas she asked Chapuys to urge Cromwell to remove her from Kimbolton. She also asked for payment of the arrears of monies due to her, for she wished to provide things for the Feast and presents for her staff.

It must have been a poor little party at Catherine's last Christmas. She had a few maids who looked after her unexacting needs. There was her small suite of officers, all Spaniards, except one, and all notably her faithful friends. With an increasingly suspicious King and government, the trustworthiness and discretion of those about her were of paramount importance, but there was never any failure.

Foremost among this little company was Jorge de Atheca, her chaplain. He had long been in Catherine's service. A Dominican friar, he had in the earlier years of the reign—as long ago as 1517—been consecrated Bishop of the small see of Llandaff. He had also been made Master of St Catherine's Hospital, a very ancient charitable institution, near St Catherine's Docks in London, which Henry VIII and Queen Catherine had reorganized. For many years he had been Catherine's confessor, though Thomas Abell, because he knew Spanish, had also acted in that capacity.

There was also courageous Francisco Phelippes, now her *maître de salle*. Earlier in this year of 1535 Chapuys told the Emperor that Francisco had, for some undisclosed reason, been removed from Catherine's service and had nothing to live on. It would be well, said the ambassador, if the King would allow him to return to his mistress or retire to Spain, "where he would make some report of affairs here". And so Chapuys put the matter to Cromwell, who replied that the Spaniard could either go back to Catherine's service or go to Spain, in which case he could have money for the journey. As for the "report of affairs" Cromwell made little of it: the Emperor was not so credulous as to believe all that was said, although Phelippes "might, by his report, cause people to murmur over there in accordance with their arrogant disposition". Perhaps, after all, the King had second thoughts, for Francisco returned to Catherine.

Her valued physician, Miguel De La Sá, had taken the place of Doctor Fernando Vitoria when he returned to Spain. Catherine had great confidence in Miguel. She entrusted him with important matters of business and he acted (as had also Fernando) as her secretary, writing letters for her and ensuring that they evaded the constant vigilance of her guards and spies, and reached the safe custody of Chapuys. The apothecary was Juan de Soto, assisted by the one Englishman of Catherine's tiny suite, Philip Grenacre.

Catherine's recovery from her illness of early December was short-lived and Doctor Miguel had soon cause for much greater anxiety. Towards the end of the month she became extremely ill. The physician wrote urgently to Chapuys, who immediately sought an audience of the King. Henry showed little regret and was much more concerned with the implications of Catherine's attitude to him than with her illness. He wished the Emperor would cease to "favour these good ladies" (Catherine and Mary) and get the sentence of the Pope revoked. He believed that Catherine, whom he called "Madame", would not live long. If she died there would be no need for the Emperor to trouble himself about the affairs of England.

After he left the palace, Chapuys was recalled by the King, who told him that Catherine was so dangerously ill that if he went off to see her he would probably not find her alive. The pain and sickness had, indeed, returned. She was very weak and could take little rest. De La Sá tried to persuade her to obtain other medical advice, but she would have no physician except himself. She committed herself to God. Perhaps she already knew that she would soon die.

Again Henry seemed to feel no sorrow, but merely said that her death would remove all the difficulties between him and the Emperor. Chapuys set out at once for Kimbolton, but before leaving he asked that Princess Mary might be allowed to see her mother. Henry refused, but on the ambassador's making some remonstrance he said he would think about it. She never went.

Chapuys arrived at the gates of Kimbolton on New Year's Day, 1536. He stayed four days. Catherine thanked him for the numerous services he had rendered and for the trouble he had taken in coming to see her. She had ardently desired his visit, for she thought it would be so good for her. If, however, it pleased God to take her it would be a consolation to die in his arms. The ambassador sought to make her cheerful, trying to inspire in her a hope of recovery and telling her of the King's offer of some other place than Kimbolton where she might live. He begged her to take heart and get well. She was very grateful and, full of kindly thought, bade him rest a little after the fatigue of his journey. Meanwhile, she thought she would herself try to sleep, for she had not slept more than two hours altogether for the past six days.

She sent for him again a little later and conversed with him for fully two hours. He thought he was troubling her too much and that he ought to leave her, but she did not wish it: it was so great a pleasure and consolation that he was near her. Some part of each day during his short stay at Kimbolton he spent with her. She enquired of him particularly about the health of the Emperor and the state of his affairs.

Her old Spanish friend and former lady-in-waiting, Maria de Salinas, Lady Willoughby d'Eresby, came also. She wrote to Cromwell, as soon as she heard of Catherine's serious illness, asking for a letter either from the King or himself which she could show to the guards at Kimbolton. Tactfully, she spoke in her request not of the "Queen" or of the "Princess Dowager", but of "Her Grace". The letter does not seem to have been forthcoming, or perhaps she would not wait for it.

Maria de Salinas went at once to Kimbolton and arrived at the gates of the castle on the evening of New Year's Day. The guards on duty saw by her countenance that she was greatly dismayed and, indeed, she told them of the grave news of Catherine's illness that she had heard on her journey thither. Perhaps she thought that this might be sufficient and that they would let her enter the castle, but they, nevertheless, demanded to see her passport. She replied that she would deliver to them next morning such authority as would fully satisfy them. Meanwhile, because, so she said, she had suffered an injury through a fall from her horse—and was, perhaps, spattered with mud and wet and cold

—could they not let her rest a little by the fire? What, after this, could they do? She was injured, she was a great lady, the friend of Catherine, the mother of the Duchess of Suffolk, who was the wife of a chief counsellor of the King. She could surely be trusted and she had asked only for a small, reasonable service. And so the guards allowed her to enter.

There may have been still a great number of Chapuys' men about the place and there may have been noise and confusion. At any rate, whatever the circumstances, Maria seems to have watched for her chance of escape and to have quickly taken it when it occurred; and, no longer the injured horsewoman, she fled to the dying Catherine. There, in Catherine's chamber, she remained. "And since that time", writes, almost pathetically, Sir Edmund Bedingfield, the chamberlain at Kimbolton, to Cromwell, "they never saw her, nor any letter of licence to repair thither that was shewed them."

Chapuys with his retinue returned to London, for Catherine seemed for the moment out of danger and she desired him to return. Two days afterwards she was better, and in the evening of the Feast of the Three Kings (6 January), she, without any help, combed and dressed her hair. But on the next day, a little after midnight, she enquired what o'clock it was and whether it was near daybreak. Several times she asked this with no other object but to hear Mass as soon as possible and receive Holy Communion. She now knew that death was near. The members of her suite, her few maidservants and no doubt Maria de Salinas were all there, keeping watch intently. The King's chamberlain and the King's steward were called in at Catherine's request to see her die.

The Bishop of Llandaff offered to say Mass before day dawned, but Catherine would not allow it, giving reasons and also authorities in Latin why it was against ecclesiastical law to do so, so well she knew her religion. But when daybreak came she heard Mass and received Holy Communion with the greatest fervour. She said many prayers and begged all those around her to pray for her soul and for her husband, the King, that God would forgive him for the wrong he had done against her and would, in His goodness, lead him to "the true path" and grant him good counsel.

She called Miguel De La Sá to her side and asked him to write "a little bill" of very modest bequests. And when he had finished the writing she made her signature on it. We know the details. Out of the small amount of gold and silver and other things, which were her property and which she asked the King to let her have, together with certain sums of money due to her, she wished each member of her suite to be paid a year's income in advance. She desired that some person would go on pilgrimage to Our Lady of Walsingham and distribute twenty nobles to the poor on the way. She wished many Masses to be said for her soul. She left a gift to Mistress Mary, the wife of Miguel the physician, and asked that "ornaments" should be made of her gowns for the convent where she would be buried. To her daughter Mary she left her furs and "the collar of gold which I brought out of Spain". And, finally, "to the little maidens" she left ten pounds each.

She wrote sincerely and very tenderly to the King, "My most dear Lord, King, and husband", or perhaps it was Miguel De La Sá who wrote for her and she just signed the letter, which does not seem to have survived. She told the King of the approaching hour of her death. She bade him think of his soul's health, which he ought to prefer before "all worldly matters, and before the care and tendering of your own body, for the which you have cast me into many miseries and yourself into many cares". For her part, she forgave him and devoutly prayed God that He also would forgive him. "Lastly, I make this vow: that mine eyes desire you above all things. Farewell."

At ten o'clock in the morning the bishop anointed her and she followed the office very attentively and made the responses with great devotion. She continued with her prayers for a few hours. Then, early in the afternoon, before the shadows had begun to form and spread across the marshes on that January day, Catherine the Queen died, dying, as she had always lived, with superb fortitude. It was but two o'clock.

They buried her in the great Benedictine abbey of Peterborough. There was little elaboration of ceremony and the honours were those due to a Princess Dowager. The chief mourner was the King's niece, Eleanor, the daughter of her old friend, Mary the French Queen. The second mourner was the daughter of Maria de Salinas.

The provision for the few Spanish members of Catherine's suite raised problems. Cromwell asked Miguel de la Sá to enter the King's service. This was some measure of the worth placed on Miguel's skill, but there were political and other factors to be considered. The physician told Cromwell that to accept such service at once might provoke people to think ill of him. Besides, he was the Emperor's subject and he was not sure how acceptance of the royal offer so soon after Catherine's death would be interpreted. But Cromwell saw no difficulty. He was sure that within three months there would be as much amity between England and Spain as there had ever been, and, increasing his blandishments, he said that the King intended to be munificent. Miguel refused, but he took service with Princess Mary, whom he was allowed to visit whenever necessary and this was a great comfort to her. She trusted no physician but Miguel. He was still in her service in 1539 and so was Juan de Soto, Catherine's apothecary.

Francisco Phelippes, the *maître de salle*, returned to Spain and so did Jorge de Atheca, who longed to leave England, but he experienced some troublesome changes of fortune before he was eventually able to depart.

Although naturally a quiet, timid, anxious soul, the bishop did not lack constancy. He had refused, like the rest of Catherine's suite, to take the Oath of Succession. He had also in his small diocese of Llandaff allowed preachers to deliver papist sermons, and this, so it was alleged, was becoming a matter of embarrassment and scandal to the government. He was therefore commanded in 1535 to deal at once with the situation. In particular, he was to review the appointments of priests allowed to preach and to revoke the commissions of preachers "noted to want judgement". The position, however, did not improve, and at a visitation held later in the year the bishop and his archdeacon were found guilty not only of allowing the ecclesiastical buildings to decay, but also of various faults n the administration of the diocese. The fruits of the bishopric and of the archdeaconry were therefore sequestered into the hands of the Vicar-General, Cromwell. Nor, it was found, had the problem of the preachers received attention: the bishop had failed "to declare to the people the Word of God", and so certain preachers were appointed to do it.

It was clear to de Atheca that after the death of Catherine he would be unable to live the life of a conscientious Catholic in England and, moreover, by refusing to take the oath, he feared he would be treated in the same way as Fisher, More and the Carthusians. He seems to have been refused a passport for Spain and, in consequence, he determined to leave the country secretly and in disguise. Perhaps he did not take sufficient precautions, perhaps he was merely unfortunate; but what clearly emerges is that he was caught trying to escape from England, carrying plate and household stuff which probably belonged to him or had been in Catherine's use at Kimbolton, but which the government claimed as its own. He was charged with concealment and embezzlement, and was examined by the council, with the result that he was imprisoned in the Tower for some seven months.

Eventually, by the good offices of Chapuys, a passport was obtained and Jorge de Atheca returned to Aragon. He died four years later and was buried in the middle of the priory church of Calatayud, where long ago he had taken the Dominican habit. A man of sanctity and engaging simplicity, he served Catherine for many years faithfully and well.

Maria de Salinas lived on. The date of her death is unknown, but she was still living at the beginning of 1547. It is said that she was buried in Queen Catherine's tomb at Peterborough, a fitting end to a close, enduring friendship. But there was irony in future events. Her only surviving child, Catherine, Duchess of Suffolk, who had doubtless been named after the Queen and who had been the second mourner at her funeral, became a notable Protestant and fled from the country in the reign of the Queen's daughter, Mary, returning after the accession of Elizabeth I.

P

Part III

THE LAST DRAMAS

CHAPTER 17

John Forest

SOME of Catherine's remaining prominent friends were almost inevitably involved in her own tragedy. They had given whole-hearted allegiance to her cause, and those who with constancy opposed the royal supremacy, because they held that their opposition followed logically from a maintenance of the Pope's dispensing power, became the government's victims. In the developing drama these victims were almost entirely clerics, like John Forest, the Queen's confessor, Thomas Abell, the Queen's chaplain, Edward Powell, her counsellor, and Master Fetherston, Princess Mary's old schoolmaster. The Queen's death made no difference to the vigilance which the government felt compelled to exercise for the discovery of opposition to its revolutionary policy, a vigilance which increased as the attacks on the surviving bastions of the ancient faith proceeded. But one great friend of the Queen, Margaret Pole, was in a different category from the clerical victims of the government; and though, like all the Poles, her predilections and associations proved her to be a strong adherent of orthodox religious beliefs, her case was complex, for it contained elements that were political. In the end she was to suffer mainly because she was a Pole and because she was the mother of the cardinal in exile—Reginald Pole, who represented in his person all that the King and the council viewed with pronounced detestation.

The government's first victim was John Forest, who suffered some two years after the Queen's death. It is well to perceive the real significance of his fate, for he was not a mere obscure recalcitrant priest who denied the supreme royal claims. Friar Forest was a member of that religious order, the Franciscan Observants, which had caused the King so much trouble in the crisis of the marriage and which had been the first of the orders to be dissolved. He had been known to the King for many years and also to members of the Court, where, since his convent had adjoined the royal palace of Greenwich, individual members of the Order had once moved freely. Learned, devout, diplomatic, administratively able, it was too much to expect that anyone like Forest holding such conservative religious views would be allowed to remain completely unchallenged. Pertinacious attempts would be made to bend the Queen's confessor to the King's will, for his conversion was likely to prove a valuable weapon in the government's armoury; but if those attempts failed then the punishment must meet the offence and the inevitable result would be his complete elimination from the religious and political scene. So, it would seem, the King argued.

In the year, 1534, following Forest's despatch to a convent in the north of England, we find him in prison in London. The reason for his imprisonment is obscure, but he may have been involved in the business of the Nun of Kent, like his fellow Observants, Risby and Rich, though obviously, in any case, to a less extent. While in prison he was found corresponding with Thomas Abell, whom he must have known well. Abell was then in the Tower because of his allegiance to Catherine. He told Forest that at the end of March or the beginning of April 1534 he had been for nearly forty days in the Beauchamp Tower, the least desirable place of imprisonment in the whole of the Tower of London. He was evidently in great distress and it was probable that he was in solitary confinement and in chains. He spoke of possible martyrdom: "our senses shrink", he said, "from the intensity of torments, yet our faith . . . requires us to bear them". Forest endeavoured to give Abell comfort, urging him not to think of present pains, but of a future glory. As for himself, a great combat awaited him, and this seems almost certainly a reference to the inner tension he was already experiencing, because of an impending requirement to swear to the Oath of Succession. Judging by later events that inner conflict must have been very real.

Catherine also wrote to Friar Forest at this time. If he has to suffer martyrdom, she would be left in the deepest sorrow, for of all men he had been her greatest teacher of spiritual things. She urged him to be brave. If his family, she said, was noble (no evidence has ever come to light that he was of high birth), he must "not disgrace it by yielding to the King's wicked request". Was Catherine merely anxious or had she discerned a sign that her old spiritual director might lack constancy at a critical hour? If it were the latter, subsequent events were to support her discernment.

The friar, in his reply, praised Catherine for her strong religious faith: she was not to have any doubt about his own. He would not disgrace his grey hairs, for he had striven for God's glory all the forty-four years that he had passed in the Order of St Francis. He expected martyrdom and sent Catherine his rosary, because he had, he said, only three days to live. But that expectation of immediate death was unrealized. Friar Forest disappointed his distinguished spiritual daughter and subsequently accepted the Supremacy.

There is now silence for some years about Forest's activities and he appears to have been unmolested till the spring of 1538. We then find him living a tranquil life at the convent of the Grey Friars (the Conventual Franciscans) in London, for all the Observants had been suppressed four years previously. But it seems possible that at this time the government had grounds for renewed suspicion of the friar's religious attitude, since the Warden of the convent had been asked by Cromwell to enquire about Forest's particular friends. Lord Mordaunt was mentioned as a visitor to the convent, but he was a genuine penitent of the friar's and revealed nothing incriminating about him. Lest Cromwell should have any doubt about the Warden's own religious attitude it is made plain: "I will be true to my Prince and so will all my brethren". They would all be ready "to change their coats" when commanded. Of course, he said, he could speak only for those who were not Observants, and so by implication he excluded Friar Forest and any other Observant friars who were in his convent.

After this came the visit of one Wafferer, a spurious "penitent" and agent of the government, who had been sent to ensnare him; and Forest, all unsuspecting, told him, under the seal of confession, of his belief in the papal supremacy. He had taken the oath with his "outward man" and his "inward man" had never consented. Forest was not the only one who had tried to salve his conscience in such a way.

It was afterwards asserted that the friar in the confessional had urged men to remain steadfast to the old faith, saying that the King was not Supreme Head and that St Thomas à Becket had died for the rights of the Church. The result was his arrest, an examination by Cranmer at Lambeth and then a formulation of a charge of "heresy". Certain articles were drawn up which related mainly to belief in the Pope's primacy and he abjured them all, subscribing the abjuration with his own hand. He went back to Newgate prison and awaited a summons to Paul's Cross to make a public recantation and receive sentence for his offences. The Cross had long been a famous spot where recantations were made, and here in the middle of the fifteenth century, Reginald Pecock, Bishop of Chichester, was brought, in order to renounce his notorious heterodoxy. Sermons had been preached there since the previous century.

The day arranged for Friar Forest's public appearance was 12 May 1538. Latimer, Bishop of Worcester, was to preach. But when all was ready the friar failed to arrive. The great assembly of people, full of expectancy, was robbed of excitement and Latimer awkwardly deprived of an opportunity to deliver one of his long, famous sermons. But his time would come. All that he could now do was to urge the people to pray for the friar that he might be moved from his obstinacy.

What had happened to cause the anti-climax? It would seem that in his tolerable confinement Forest had had time for reflection, and having had, in addition, an opportunity to converse with those in the prison who remained constant in their religious orthodoxy, "he was as far from his open submission as ever he was . . . and stood obstinately in all his heresies and treasons before conspired". It is known that in Newgate at this time were Laurence Cook, prior of the Carmelites at Doncaster, and William

Horne, a lay-brother of the London Charterhouse. With these Forest seems to have spoken. And some days later Latimer provided an ominous, rather sinister commentary on what had recently occurred. "It is to be feared", he wrote to Cromwell, "that some instilled into him that, though [even if] he had persevered in his abjuration, yet he should have [after all] suffered for treason." This is Latimer's unsupported opinion. It casts doubt on Forest's own spirit of resolution and may be quite unjustified, but in the context of what had occurred it cannot be ignored.

The consequence of Friar Forest's attitude was his condemnation as a relapsed heretic and the due penalty for this was death by burning. His public execution was made into an instrument of government propaganda. It was not only that the well-known confessor of Catherine of Aragon was to die, but also that a spectacular mode of death would be looked upon as a significant stage in the religious revolution.

The government did not spare themselves. They issued a proclamation to the people of London summoning them to Smithfield, where it was arranged that Bishop Latimer should preach. It was Cromwell's pleasure, said Latimer, "that I shall play the fool when Forest shall suffer". This time there would be no failure.

The people came from London and its inner suburbs in their thousands to the place of execution, coming then as people do today to watch a great national show. The contemporary chronicler, Wriothesley, who was possibly an eye-witness, said that more than ten thousand people assembled—a figure which need not indicate arithmetical accuracy, but does suggest the magnitude of the crowd. They must have come from many directions—watermen and bargemen from Thames-side, leaving for the time their tied-up wherries and barges; innkeepers and butchers and tailors; makers of tapestry and weavers and embroiderers; fishermen from the suburbs near the River; booksellers and printers from Paul's and Paternoster Row; sleepy watchmen, their work lately ended; leatherworkers from near-by St Martin's-le-Grand and goldsmiths from Cheap. And there were no doubt important burgesses and rich merchants from the city, with a protective guard of servants, for such a concourse was an attractive opportunity for rogues and petty thieves. Almost certainly some Spanish merchants must have come from the region of Tower Street and from each side of Tower Hill, for from ancient times this part of London had housed merchants from Spain: they would have come to see the end of the noted confessor of Queen Catherine, their countrywoman.

The surging crowds swept on past the Strand, flanked with the majestic palaces of the bishops, along Holborn where, in the exquisite garden of the Bishop of Ely, it was well known that luscious strawberries in due time grew, past the populous district of Cheap, where gaunt black and white dwellings overlooked narrow alleys, and so to Smithfield, which is directly opposite the great hospital of St Bartholomew. To mark the importance of the occasion there was placed near the scene of execution a stand to hold the notables of the City and the chief men of the council—the Mayor of London, Master Gresham, who was in his long gown and wore his chain of office, the sheriffs in their scarlet robes, who were attended by their servants in modest uniforms of tawny, the Dukes of Norfolk and Suffolk, both now growing old in the King's service, the Bishop of London, the Lord Admiral, and most significant of all, Thomas Cromwell, the chief minister of the King and his Vicar-General.

Before the final stage of the drama, a great image called Darvel Gatheren was brought to the gallows in order that it might start the flames which would consume the friar. This proceeding was an impressive piece of government publicity, intended to ridicule, in the eyes of the vast assembly, the attention, superstitious or otherwise, which had been paid to images in the Catholic days that were quickly passing, and it vulgarly marked a stage in the government's iconoclastic campaign. For during all that year of 1538 the campaign proceeded. In February the rood of Boxley had been exhibited and burnt. Latimer in his cathedral of Worcester had already seen that an image of the Blessed Virgin had been stripped of its ornaments and jewels: now, in 1538, he wanted "our great Sibyl" to be burnt at Smithfield "with her sister of Walsingham". There was the "Rood of Grace", which had "certain engines and old wire" that caused the eyes to move. It was probably made generations previously and could hardly have imposed on many people in Tudor times. The image was, however, taken to Paul's Cross, and, after being broken into pieces by the assembled crowd, was burnt. There was also the celebrated "Blood of Hale"—liquid contained in a phial which, it was said, was the Blood of Christ. It was a very old "relic" and perhaps few people had any real belief in it, merely coming to see it, as they came to see other so-called relics, to relieve the monotony of their dull lives. It was to receive the attention of the King's Visitors in the autumn of 1538.

The attack on the images and the relics kept step with the dissolution of the monasteries and prepared the way for the destruction of the great ancient shrines of England, those shrines which were not spurious, but were very valuable, and thus attractive to the government, and for which there existed a genuine devotion. Since this devotion had attained considerable popularity everywhere in the country, it was well that the government should be sure of its ground for attack. After Forest's execution the momentum of the government's campaign increased. In July was destroyed the famous shrine of Walsingham which the King as well as Catherine had once held in great esteem. In September the celebrated shrine of St Swithun at Winchester was demolished and, shortly before, had been pillaged the richest shrine of all, that of St Thomas à Becket, the saint who symbolised in his person all that was antagonistic to the King's supreme claims. "Pilgrimage saints goeth down apace", John Husee had already written to Lord and Lady Lisle, whilst George Rolle had told his lordship that the abbeys "go down as fast as they may and are surrendered to the King. I pray God send you one among them."

"Darvel Gatheren" was a gigantic image of St Derfel, or Derfel the Strong, the patron saint of Llandderfel in North Wales, and Cromwell himself had caused it to be brought to London. Made of wood, it was "like a man in his harness, having a little spear in his hand and a casket of iron about his neck with a ribbon". It was said that eight men could scarcely carry it, whilst three men had as much as they could do to keep it upright. The Welsh held the image in considerable esteem and the parson of the place was loth to let it go. A large paper was put on the gallows where Friar Forest stood and on it was written about Darvel Gatheren some doggerel in great letters, so that those people in the crowd who were literate could read it:

"David Darvel Gatheren,
As saith the Welshmen,
Fetched the outlaws out of Hell.
Now is he come, with spear and shield,
In harness to burn in Smithfield,
For in Wales he may not dwell".

Latimer had asked for a platform to be set up close to the spot where Friar Forest was to suffer: he said he wanted to "content" the people with his eloquence, and also, if possible, to convert the friar. The bishop was no bloodthirsty monster and if, he said, Forest "would yet with heart return to his abjuration, I would wish his pardon, such is my foolishness". The King's councillors present would also have offered the royal pardon if the friar again made an abjuration, but, though Latimer declared to him his errors, "and openly and manifestly by the scripture of God confuted them, and with many and godly exhortations moved him to repentance", it was all unavailing, such was his "frowardness".

Latimer preached for a long time. When he had finished, it was the turn of Friar Forest and he spoke firmly, tersely and very bravely. The relation of what he said comes from a contemporary, hostile source. "If", the friar said, "an angel should come down from Heaven and show him any other thing than that he had believed all his lifetime past, he would not believe him, and that if his body should be cut joint from joint or member from member, burnt, hanged or what pain soever might be done, he would never turn from his old sect of this Bishop of Rome". Then, on this day of May, the 22nd of the month, 1538, he was burnt to death with extreme brutality.

Many years later, in the autumn of 1555, a very old man in a poor Bristol frieze frock, very worn, and wearing a buttoned cap and a kerchief on his head, stood, waiting to die, near the ditch which in those days ran against Balliol College, Oxford. Because he held firmly and valiantly to his Protestant faith they burnt him alive, and he has therefore been rightly accounted a true martyr. He had at one time been Bishop of Worcester, and his name was Hugh Latimer.

CHAPTER 18

Three Priests

O F THE three secular priests, Thomas Abell, Edward
Powell and Richard Fetherston, Queen Catherine's close
associates, it was Abell, her chaplain, who first received
the attention of the government: he had been imprisoned since
the end of 1533. But in 1534 the three priests were all in the
Tower, Fetherston not till the end of the year; and when the
time came to swear to the Act of Succession they steadfastly
refused to take the oath.

Dr Powell, after his return to the cathedral close at Salisbury
from his preaching campaign in Bristol, was carefully watched.
In August 1533 Cromwell wanted to interview him and asked
Richard Hilley, the chancellor of Salisbury, to send him up to
London. Hilley, who had instituted Latimer to the living of West
Kington some two years previously, told the King's minister
that Powell would be with him later in the month: he could not
come at once because his leg was "diseased". He went. We do not
know what happened at the meeting, but a few months later
some incriminating evidence given by his servant came into the
possession of the government. Edward Powell was said to have
spoken strongly in Salisbury against the King's marriage to Anne
Boleyn and also to have written against it. He had called the new
Queen's father a heretic. He had asserted that the French king,
the King's ally, would never prove to be constant. Then, in
January, Richard Arche, a Salisbury priest, desiring to court
favour with those placed about the powerful, wrote to Sir
Edward Baynton, Anne Boleyn's vice-chamberlain. He wanted
Dr Powell and other local clerics to be discharged because of their
opposition to the King's policy: others should be elected to serve
as proctors in ecclesiastical affairs, and if the King's Grace "would

name Dr Benett and me, he may be assured of the diocese of Sarum being on his side in all causes, whereas others, as you know, were directly against His Grace's cause, or absented themselves when they might have advanced it". Richard Arche was duly rewarded for his services and a benefice "requiring residence, besides those which he now enjoys" was conferred on him. And when the desired state of diocesan affairs which he mentions had been brought about, it was to be a useful prelude to an event which took place in 1535, for in that year Nicholas Shaxton, Anne Boleyn's almoner and a noted Reformer, became Bishop of Salisbury.

The persistent vigilance of the government and the local machinations against Powell succeeded. He was thrown into Dorchester Gaol and treated with cruelty. He pleaded poignantly in April 1534 with Sir Thomas Arundel for some relief of his distress. His keeper had not only put him in chains, but had even taken away his bed and tied him up in such a way that he was unable "to lie down on the boards, but [is] hanged in the collar and do lie in the stocks with gyves on my legs". Judging by the laboured, erratic character of his writing, Powell must have been in considerable pain. It was apparently the welcome chink of gold for his keeper that was lacking, and he was likely "to be lamed", he said, "in all my limbs", unless Sir Thomas had compassion on him. We do not know whether this condition was relieved. In June he was committed to the Tower.

Richard Fetherston was at liberty for a longer period than his two priest-colleagues and was actually unmolested till December 1534. In the spring he was able to help his old pupil, Princess Mary.

Mary, who had been compelled after the dissolution of her own establishment to wait on the infant Princess Elizabeth, was now in the charge of Anne Boleyn's aunt, Lady Anne Shelton. Her treatment was extremely unpleasant. She was commanded by her governess to confine herself to her chamber. She was told that the King did not in the least care about her determination not to renounce her title of Princess, since, by the Act of Succession, she had been made a bastard and was thus deprived of all right of

inheritance to the Crown. If Lady Shelton were in the King's
place she would be merciless and would kick her out of doors for
her disobedience. The King had stated, she added, that he would
make her lose her head for not subscribing to the Statute. He
was, indeed, being relentless towards everyone at this time who
withstood his will, and Mary's friends had reason to be
alarmed.

Chapuys, the Imperial ambassador, was the only person who
could help, but with enemies and spies everywhere how could
she get news to him? Yet a way was soon to be found. Mary,
according to the ambassador, asked for leave to speak to someone
about the place who "was formerly her preceptor and physician".
The context of Chapuys' account makes it sufficiently clear that
this person could have been no other than Richard Fetherston,
one of the few people whom she trusted implicitly. Chapuys
did not perhaps know Fetherston well and his addition of
"physician" was probably gratuitous. But, in any case, leave was
not given to Mary to see her old tutor in private (assuming it was
he), and when actually she did meet him she was not alone.

How could the suspicions of the inimical members of the household be rendered innocuous? When, she decided, she should meet
Master Fetherston she would speak to him in Latin, the language
which for years he had taught her. Catherine had begun the
teaching, but it was Fetherston who continued it. "As for your
writing in Latin, I am glad that ye shall change from me to Master
Fetherston, for that shall do you much good", the Queen had
long ago said. And now, talking in Latin, a proceeding which
must have perplexed and defeated the servants about her, Mary
apologised to her schoolmaster for her lack of fluency: she had
been so long, she said, without speaking the language that she
could not say two words of it. But it was at once an exaggeration,
a gesture of modesty and a ruse. She managed to tell him about
the King's grievous threat, and he was so astounded that he knew
not what to reply, except that what she had said "was not good
Latin". But it all found a safe home and Chapuys made the
Emperor fully aware of Mary's dangerous position.

A little later subscriptions to the Oath of Succession were

everywhere being taken and Lord Cobham found that in Kent the commissioners for the oath were very well received. All coming before him had sworn, except Richard Fetherston, who apparently held a benefice of his lordship. Fetherston had been made Archdeacon of Brecknock more than ten years previously, when he had probably just come under Queen Catherine's notice and when, perhaps, he was already in prospect as Princess Mary's schoolmaster. Only three days before Cobham had begun to preside on the Kentish commission the archdeacon had gone into Wales. Prudence seemed to be governing Fetherston's actions. But he did not escape, and in December he was committed to the Tower for refusing the royal demands.

Next year, 1535, when Fisher and More were required to take the Oath, Richard Fetherston and Thomas Abell (and presumably Edward Powell, who was in the Tower like the other priests, though he is not specifically mentioned) were also commanded to do so, otherwise they would be no better treated than the recently-executed Carthusians. A period of six weeks was given them to consider the matter, but they were very unlikely to prove amenable. They replied that they were ready to suffer whatever kind of death the King pleased: they would not change their opinion in six weeks or in six hundred years, if it were possible for them to live so long. In the event, Fisher and More were put to death, but the three priests continued their painful existence in the Tower.

The Imperial ambassador in the early spring of 1536 was enlightening the Emperor's chancellor, Granvelle, about some of the things that were happening in England. He spoke of the King's fickleness and his propensities to "new and strange things": Henry had given orders that certain articles of "this new sect" were not to be preached about, but he later ordered the contrary, especially in regard to the Pope, against whom most offensive sermons were delivered. And to remove any impression that the King had abated his desire for harsh measures, it was said he had determined to execute "three doctors": Dr Richard Fetherston, Dr Thomas Abell, whom Granvelle had known years ago on a well-known occasion at Saragossa, and Dr Nicholas Wilson,

Q

former Court preacher and King's chaplain. It was even feared that the King's anger would affect Princess Mary.

The royal mood passed, but the lot of the prisoners remained distressing. Abell implored Cromwell, piteously, for some alleviation of his lot. Perhaps, because of the marked support he had always given to Catherine's cause, Henry's animus against him was greater than in the case of the others. Abell's letter to Cromwell, written in a clear, exquisite, scholarly hand, survives. He speaks in it of his unjust condemnation. He asserts that since his imprisonment he had never yet been examined about any offence charged against him. On the other hand, Master Barker, his "fellow", and formerly, like him, Queen Catherine's chaplain, who had been sent to prison at the same time, had been examined and delivered. Abell protests his innocence: "all that was put in my condemnation is untrue". This must refer to the particular part of the Act of Attainder of 1534 concerning the Nun of Kent which had accused him "of firm and constant credit to the said false and feigned revelations" of the Nun: it could not have referred to the remaining charges which were too obviously true to be denied—charges which referred to the encouragement which he had given to Catherine in maintaining her recalcitrance and to his writing against the divorce.

Thomas Abell did not ask for much in the way of relief. He had been in close confinement for well over three years and suffered from various diseases. He lived in great poverty and misery. Could he be granted leave to go to church somewhere within the Tower and say Mass there, and also to lie in some house on Tower Green? If his lot were ever improved, the improvement was not maintained.

When some relief later came it did not emanate from the government: it came from two ecclesiastics, Bishop Sampson of Chichester, and Dr Nicholas Wilson. Wilson, conservative in religion, had been imprisoned for opposing the royal supremacy, but he eventually submitted and was released from the Tower in 1537. Well-acquainted with the three priests, he had managed, like Bishop Sampson, to relieve their distress. For this he was faced with the government's wrath, and in explanation he said that his charitable actions were not to be regarded as implying any sympathy with their evil opinion. He ought, nevertheless, to have obtained permission beforehand, and he should have been more diligent in instructing them with a view to their conformity. That they were in an appalling condition and well merited the attention that had been given seems clear from what Richard Hilles later told Bullinger, the Continental Protestant, about Thomas Abell. Abell, he said, was in a most filthy prison and was alleged to be "almost eaten up by vermin".

Sampson and Wilson were both sent to prison for a time because of what they had done, whilst Richard Farmer, a wealthy London citizen, who had also given charitable aid, was imprisoned in the Marshalsea. His offence was construed as praemunire. He lost all his goods, and his wife and children were cast out of doors. Even the prison keeper of Powell and Abell was sent to the Marshalsea for allowing them out on bail.

The end came in 1540. The three priests were attainted of treason because of their refusal to acknowledge the King's supremacy. For this offence they were to be hanged, drawn and quartered, the legal penalty for treason. With them were to suffer three well-known Protestants, Robert Barnes, the former Austin friar, Thomas Garrett, curate of Honey Lane in the city of London, and William Jerome, vicar of Stepney. As heretics they were to be burnt. On 30 July 1540 they were brought to Smithfield with the three priests, one Protestant and one Catholic being tied to the same hurdle. It was "a marvellous strange sight", we are told. "For as these [the priests] died for the Catholic religion, so were there burnt three Protestants . . . so that our new religion, as it disagreed with the Catholics, so did it disagree also from [with] other Protestants."

CHAPTER 19

The Tragedy of Margaret Pole

I

IN 1536, the year in which Catherine of Aragon died, an event occurred which was to have the greatest influence on Princess Mary's life. That event was the execution of Anne Boleyn in May which removed the most considerable obstacle to Mary's reunion with the King. The way was firmly secured shortly afterwards by Henry's marriage to Jane Seymour, who had been one of Queen Catherine's ladies-in-waiting and had always held both the Queen and her daughter in affectionate esteem. An additional factor which must have strongly appealed to Mary was the lack of sympathy which the new royal spouse felt for ideas of the Reform. It is doubtful, moreover, whether Jane Seymour ever regarded Anne Boleyn as the King's lawful wife, and now that Anne was dead and Henry legitimately married, Catholic hopes mounted high, especially the hopes of such undoubted religious conservatives as the Poles and the Exeters. Luther was soon to speak pessimistically, but, as it chanced, inaccurately, of the "alteration of the kingdom", because of the new marriage, and he described Queen Jane as an enemy of the Gospel. On the other hand, Reginald Pole said that she was "full of goodness". All men, he was much later to say, expected at that time "a most glorious change" and he did not despair of Henry's return to the Church. Nor did the new Queen lack courage in attempting to stem the current of religious revolution, for at the time of the Pilgrimage of Grace she went down on her knees before the King and begged him to restore the abbeys. It had no effect. Henry told her to get up and not meddle with his affairs, referring warningly to the fate of Anne Boleyn. It was to be made clear by events in the early summer that there would be no return to the old Faith.

Margaret Pole, like the rest of the strong Catholic element, was doubtless full of the newly-born hopes, and we find her back at Cour with her son, Lord Mon ague, shortly before Princess Mary's reconciliation with her father. They were both helping in preparations for the coming coronation and using their influence with Jane Seymour to secure preferment as ladies-in-waiting for Lady Lisle's daughters. The Countess of Salisbury had probab'y returned to Court at Jane Seymour's request, in order to be at hand to welcome the Princess. There is little doubt that Mary's reunion with her father was by many ardently looked for, and once, when it was supposed that she was with her old governess, who had appeared near the royal palace, a great crowd surged forward to greet her. The King enquired the meaning of so many assembled people and was told that they were waiting to catch sight of his daughter. She was not yet at Court, he said to he crowd, though she would soon come back and that then they would see her.

The return of Mary seems to have been due primarily to the new Queen, who promised Chapuys to do all that she could to promote it. She repeatedly threw herself publicly at the King's feet, requesting him to send for his daughter and declare her as Princess again. This greatly pleased the people when it became known. But the path to reunion was strewn with difficulties, difficulties which were to be expected when two such strong-willed persons were involved as Henry and his daughter. The able intermediary was Cromwell, who pledged his reputation—and nearly lost it—in the business.

Mary herself tried hard. She begged the chief minister to secure the King's favour for her and also leave to write to him: she explained that she could never properly ask for this so long as "that woman" (Anne Boleyn) lived. She obtained it. She then acknowledged to the King all her past offences and begged his forgiveness; she rejoiced at the King's new marriage and asked to be allowed to wait on the Queen. She would rather die than di please her father.

The King did not reply and Mary was beside herself with anxiety. She wrote again. She trusted she had the King's pardon, but begged for some token of reconciliation and for leave to come into his presence. All Mary's writing was in accordance with Cromwell's prudent drafts. How carefully in this delicate business he must have considered them! She wrote again a few days later, assuring the King once more of her repentance. But it was a battle of royal wills. She refused to subscribe to the oath. She could not acknowledge the King as Supreme Head: she could not forsake her mother's cause. The King was extremely angry, and Cromwell, fearful of matters going awry, went about in mortal terror. The Marquis of Exeter, Mary's kinsman, and Fitz-william the Treasurer, both apparently suspected of influencing her, were temporarily excluded from the council.

Henry sent a deputation headed by Norfolk to Mary. Because she was young and inexperienced she was at the mercy of pitiless men. They bullied her relentlessly. They directed against her a rapid fire of obloquy. She must obey the statutes. They told her that since she was so unnatural as to oppose the King's will they could scarcely believe her to be even his bastard. If she were his real daughter they would knock her head so violently against the wall that it would become as soft as a baked apple. She was a traitor and would be punished. They demanded complete sub-mission to the King.

Chapuys, the old valued counsellor of her mother, produced arguments that were at once more reasonable, subtle and per-suasive, and it was these that seemed to have induced her to decide. He said that if the King were adamant or it was found that her life was in danger, it was the Emperor's advice that she should submit: her survival meant everything—the peace of the realm and the redress of the great disorders that prevailed. The Pope would impute no blame to her. She must, for the good that would come of it, dissemble for a time. God regarded more the intention than the act. Her return to Court would set her father on the right road again. Thus Chapuys plausibly advised, but it was counsel he would never have dared to have given Catherine in similar circumstances.

So Mary resolved on complete submission. Her resources of resistance were gone. A document was sent to her and she signed it. She acknowledged the King as her sovereign; she recognized him as Supreme Head of the Church of England and repudiated the authority of the Pope; and she acknowledged the marriage of the King and her mother, "the late Princess Dowager", to have been "by God's law and man's law incestuous and unlawful". She was forced to give her opinion about pilgrimages, purgatory, relics and the like, and she assured Cromwell that she had no opinion about such matters "but such as I shall receive from him that hath my whole heart in keeping".

Chapuys was exultant. He said that Mary had never done a better day's work, for, if she had let this opportunity slip, there was no remedy in the world for her. But she was quickly filled with extreme remorse: she had betrayed her mother and all that her mother had stood for. What, indeed, she had done seems to have haunted her for the remainder of her tragic life. She had failed in honour and constancy at a critical moment. Her conscience would never be at rest until she received secret absolution from the Pope and she besought the Emperor's ambassador at Rome to obtain it.

It was a few weeks before Henry would acknowledge Mary's submission. And then, early one day in July, the King and Queen visited the Princess at the manor of Hackney and stayed with her till the next day after hearing vespers. Henry spoke of his deep regret for having been kept from her so long and perhaps they both felt a little awkward at meeting. He seemed to be full of affection for her and made splendid promises. He gave her a "check" for a thousand crowns and the Queen presented her with a very fine diamond ring. She was not to trouble herself in future about money, the King said, for she could have as much as she wanted merely by asking him for it.

Margaret Pole and the rest of the conservatives in religion, inspirited as they had been by the nature of the Queen's religious sympathies and now by the return of a future, potential Catholic leader, must have watched with interest and approval all the recent events. A few months later we observe the Princess to be in high favour. She is now "the first after the Queen, and sits at table opposite her, a little lower down, after having given the napkin for washing to the King and Queen. And the Marchioness [of Exeter] gives the water." The Countess of Salisbury and her son, Montague, could not have been far away.

II

If the Poles and the rest of the conservative element were now more sanguine of a stay in the prosecution of revolutionary designs and of a possible return to undoubted religious orthodoxy, their hopes seemed likely to be dispersed by the attitude of Reginald Pole, who was still on the Continent after having obtained the King's permission to leave England. Pole's high principles and his punctilious desire to do what he regarded as beneficial both to the King and his country are beyond doubt, but his actions in 1536 were unlikely either to restore troubled waters or prevent future storms. They were, in the event, to place his family and their immediate supporters in an invidious position and to defeat the object which his considerable candour advocated. For a complete understanding of the matter it is necessary to discern the main features of his recent career.

Pole had long received the favour of the King. From an early age his intellectual progress owed a great deal to Henry's benefactions. His mind was brilliant. He had been much influenced by great humanists, like Colet and More, and he was a correspondent of Erasmus. He was liberal in outlook and his predilection was for enlightenment in religion and reasonable reform. Abroad he represented all that was best in current English thought.

It was natural that the King in the furtherance of his Great Matter should seek the support of a relative possessed of considerable talent. Reginald Pole was in Paris when Henry sounded the universities about the validity of his marriage to Catherine, and Pole was asked to obtain the opinion of the University of Paris. This he did with the help of Dr Edward Foxe and the result favoured the King, though, as we have seen, the majority in favour was much less than had at first been represented. Henry expressed his gratitude that Pole acted so strongly in his interests and also his satisfaction in having Pole at last for an advocate.

Reginald was later even offered the Archbishopric of York, but Henry's condition that he must declare himself in favour of the divorce was unacceptable: he had "already sinned in his conscience when, in obedience to the King, he had tried to forward the case at Paris". Yet he did not deny that when he saw that the only way to the King's favour was by supporting the idea of divorce, he was in agreement, *for the sake of his relatives*. Nevertheless, even in a difficult situation, he seems to have remained sanguine. He told Dr Foxe and his own brother (presumably this was Montague) that he hoped he had found a way to satisfy His Grace. Both Foxe and Montague (if it were he) informed the King.

Henry was jubilant. His able kinsman would not after all fail him. He invited Pole to see him and himself welcomed him at the door of his apartment at York Place. Of what the plan of compromise consisted posterity has been left in complete ignorance: we only know that the interview was a most stormy one. Pole said the opposite of what he intended and the King fumed with rage, though he gradually cooled down. Reginald later applied to Henry for permission to resume his studies abroad. It was some seven or eight months before leave was granted, but in January 1532 Henry let him go. He even generously continued the pension he had been paying. Perhaps the King still had hopes of his cousin. Had he found, or thought he had found, some sign that Pole had not yet come to an unalterable decision? On the other hand, he had told Henry that if he remained in England he must speak according to his conscience should the divorce be discussed in public.

Early in 1535 Reginald Pole was commanded to give his opinion not only about the marriage question, but also about the primacy of the Pope. Both Cromwell and Thomas Starkey wrote to him. Starkey was an old friend of Pole's and had stayed in his house at Padua. He had been called into the presence of the King, who explained to him what was wanted. Henry wished to have his cousin's real opinion, "disregarding all affections and leaving all possible dangerous results to the King's wisdom and policy". Reginald Pole was to give his opinion plainly, "without colour or cloak of dissimulation". A great book was not necessary, but merely the cogent reasons in the case clearly set forth. Always, however, with Henry's professed wish for objectiveness there was a desire for something to be said that would please the royal mind and accord with the royal views. And so Starkey, fresh from the presence of majesty, gave Pole the hint. If his learning and judgement, Starkey said, would stretch to the satisfying of the King's mind, his return to England would greatly redound to the King's pleasure, Pole's own comfort and—ominous words —to the profit of his friends. If he could not do this, nevertheless, he should still come, for the King would be able to employ him "in other affairs". Perhaps Pole thought the prospect too good to be true.

Starkey, lest he should himself fail the King, argued earnestly, for Pole's benefit, in favour of the King's case and against the papal authority. What, indeed, was there to quibble about? If Henry had withdrawn himself from the Pope's jurisdiction, the face of England was still Catholic; all, otherwise, was the same— "the laws and ceremonies of the Church, which yet stand in full strength". In other words, there was Catholicism as usual without the Pope. And what of the papal primacy? He told Pole a little later that this was, according to St Jerome, merely a remedy for schism and not a necessity of faith, given, in fact, by the patience of princes and the tacit consent of the people. Christians could obtain salvation without it. It was a view which seems to have been invoked at this time in defence of the royal supremacy.

But Reginald Pole did not come to England and went on writing his book for the King. He was writing it in 1535 and until well into the next year. He did not finish it till May and then he sent it to England. The work, *Pro Ecclesiasticae unitatis defensione*, was a vigorous attack on the royal supremacy and as vigorous a defence of the papal primacy. In writing it Pole was strongly influenced by the epoch-making events that had occurred since he left England some three or four years previously and not least by the executions of 1535, which were still fresh in his mind.

The work caused consternation. Henry's wrath was extreme. That Pole had acted on the royal permission to write plainly was only too evident, but, however potent the argument, the language he employed was violent even for that strongly outspoken, polemical age. In modern times Pole's style of presentation has been notably condemned from an unlikely source. "Too often", it has been said, "in the world's history has solid good been sacrificed to the vainglory of style and the power of penning a caustic sentence, and the work is overflowing with a rhetoric which would have stung many a milder man than Henry Tudor into rebellion, or turned him from purposes of amendment." What was singularly unfortunate about the whole episode was that Pole's family, his mother and his brothers Montague and Geoffrey, had been made into potential hostages to fortune. They were indeed always at hand if Henry wished for some reason or other to turn on them in one of his revengeful moods. In his bluntly-expressed earnestness had Reginald Pole, who knew very well the character of the King, forgotten that?

Pole's work had in fact arrived at an unfortunate moment. It came just before Henry married Jane Seymour. After the marriage had taken place many people saw the possibility of a Catholic reaction. We can understand the embarrassment and anxiety of Margaret Pole and her son and heir, Montague, now both active at Court and in close contact with a sympathetic new Queen. They wrote to Reginald and they both spoke plainly.

But before the Countess of Salisbury wrote she sent a special messenger to her son imploring him to return to England. He could not come and gave his reasons. He reminded his mother of her old promise that she had given him utterly to God and he now requires her to keep her promise. She need not have the least care about him, knowing to what Master she had given him.

Pole had also told the King that he was unable to visit him. There was nothing more he would have liked to do, but that would have been "temerariously" to throw himself away. Ever since His Grace had "cast his love" to Anne Boleyn, all men were traitors who would not accept him as Head of the Church.

Margaret Pole, when she wrote to her son, spoke of his "folly", mentioning a message about his attitude which she had received from the King. The comfort which she had had in Reginald was now turned to sorrow. The King had shown such mercy and pity which it never lay in her power to deserve. She had hoped that her children would do some part of her bounden duty for her. But she now saw Reginald "in His Grace's high indignation . . . there went never the death of thy father or of any child so nigh my heart as this has done". She charged him "to take another way and serve our master [the King], as his duty was", unless he chose to be the "confusion" of his mother. He had spoken of a promise made to God, but she reminded him that this was a promise to serve God and his prince, "who, if you do not serve . . . I know thou cannot please God". The King had brought him up and maintained him in his learning. She prayed daily that he would be made the King's servant.

Like Margaret Pole, Montague reminded his brother of the great debt of gratitude which their family owed to the King, and he was quite explicit about the generous restoration to his mother of the large Salisbury estates. His letter had a distinct ring of sincerity. He told of his interview with the King about Reginald's book and of the sorrow he felt about his brother's "unnatural" attitude to so noble a prince from whom he had "received all things". Their family, which had been "clean trodden underfoot", the King had set up nobly again, and this showed "his charity and his mercy". Montague expressed the hope that the present storms would pass and perhaps the country again be united to Rome. He urged Reginald to "let no scrupulosity . . . embrace his stomach". He could never conceive that laws made by man were of such strength that they might not be undone by man, "for that which seemeth politic at one time, by abusion at another time proveth the contrary".

Thomas Starkey, who had apparently been under a cloud because of his unsuccessful overtures to Reginald Pole, spoke at this time of Pole's obstinacy. He had never laboured, he said, at anything more earnestly than to bring "that man" to his office and duty; he had never thought him to be capable of so corrupt a judgement in the matter of the papal primacy. Reginald's own mother "now repents of having brought him to light". Starkey, who had been her chaplain, probably through his friendship with Reginald, was now holding the benefice of Bosham, which was very close to Margaret Pole's home at Warblington, and he was evidently still in close touch with her. He said that none were more "Christian or loyal than the Poles": he would pledge "his life for their truth".

Events in England at this time affected Reginald Pole profoundly and he was very much moved, in particular, by the letters from his kinsfolk. When he read them he said he almost "succumbed". He began to change his plans. He had been summoned to Rome by the Pope, but to go there would, he said, be against the King's wish. His mother and brother had threatened to "renounce all ties of nature between us". He intended, therefore, to write to the King asking for his forgiveness. But he was persuaded not to do so by influential clerical friends in Italy. His position became increasingly dangerous and he asked the Pope for protection from his enemies. Such protection was very necessary in the months to come.

Reginald Pole had been called to Rome to help with Church reforms. The Pope urged him to take deacon's orders, for he was still a layman, and to accept a cardinal's hat. The prospect of becoming a prince of the Church filled the Englishman with dismay: it might affect the hopes of the conservative element in this country and it would place his family in considerable danger. Margaret Pole and Lord Montague are both alleged to have written to Reginald, urging refusal, and to have shown their letters to the King's council. But Pole at length yielded and he became a cardinal three days before Christmas 1536. At this irrevocable step the King was beside himself with wrath, though he temporarily dissembled it.

On Henry's behalf the council wrote to the new cardinal. His letters, writings and proceedings showed, they said, such an "unseemly and irreverent behaviour as no mortal enemy could in manner have contrived". His purpose appeared, indeed, to be to slander the King and bring him into contempt. There did, however, seem to be a small spark of love left in him and they therefore requested him to go to Flanders "of himself without commission from anyone", in order to hold a discussion with persons

whom the King would send to meet him. But Pole did not fall
into that trap.

While the cardinal was away from Rome, English spies were
everywhere trying to capture him. Henry told his agents in
France that he would be very glad to have Pole trussed up and
conveyed to Calais. Pole himself said he went constantly in fear of
spies: his very track was watched, so that it would be easier for an
army to lie hid than for him to do so. Even in the autumn of
1537 the theme of Reginald Pole still occupies the government's
mind, and Cromwell persevered in trying to effect some change of
heart in the King's errant subject: Henry wanted the conversion of
one whom "he hath from the cradle nourished and brought up in
learning". But later there was a grave, ominous change of tone.
"Pity is", said Cromwell, "that the folly of one brainsick Poole,
or to say better, of one witless fool should be the ruin of so great
a family". The sinister drift of Cromwell's thought, perhaps
reflecting the mind of his master, seems unmistakeable. The
cardinal's kinsfolk would have to live with the utmost circumspection.

In October Queen Jane gave birth to a son, the future Edward
VI. Unfortunately, she died twelve days later. These events
seriously diminished, if they did not demolish, the hopes of the
religious conservatives headed by the Poles and the Exeters. Those
hopes had been focused on the person of Mary. But Henry had,
what for long he had wanted, a male heir. The importance of
Princess Mary was greatly lessened.

III

The Reformation went on apace. "Knaves", the Poles were
soon to say, "ruled about the King", but that was only part of the
story and does not take into account the King's own determination to proceed with his radical acts. There were, of course,
prelates about Henry who were full of Protestant notions like
Archbishop Cranmer, pliable, subtle, scholarly, prominent in the
counsels of the King, and there were others. Cromwell, as the
Supreme Head's Vicar-General, was fulfilling his plan of attack

on the monasteries, and the business would gather momentum in 1538. Soon the great rich abbeys would fall like ripe pears into the King's hands. The Poles and other genuine conservatives were viewing it all with dismay. The revolution taking place was brought home to townsfolk and people in the countryside by the sight of abbeys in ruins and by the wholesale destruction of ancient shrines, roods and images.

Protestant ideas were becoming widespread. Purgatory was often ridiculed and, with the demolishing of the great shrines, pilgrimages would be no more. Sometimes the Lord's Supper, a service of remembrance, which it was said was what Christ really instituted, took the place of the Mass. There were sceptics who scoffed and blasphemed. Many of the friars who had travelled about preaching in pre-Reformation England had been ignorant, superstitious, mercenary. They were now sometimes replaced by laymen intoxicated with a newly-found knowledge derived from the English Bible, men who were sincere and enthusiastic, but heretical, arrogant and often unlearned. They were, however, making converts. There was, for instance, Henry Daunce, a bricklayer of Whitechapel, who "used to preach the word of God" in his own garden, where "he set a tub to a tree, and therein he preached divers Sundays, and other days early in the morning and at six of the clock at night, and had great audience of people, which said person had no learning of his book, neither in English nor other tongue, and yet he declared Scripture as well as he had studied at the universities". The authorities did not, however, order him to cease preaching, "because of the great resort of people that drew to his sermons".

Thus was the Reformation making headway. Henry and his executive minister Cromwell had had fairly free scope and had experienced only one dangerous phase of opposition to all their revolutionary acts, the Pilgrimage of Grace in 1536. But it was necessary to exercise constant vigilance about affairs abroad, because of their repercussions on home policy. In 1538 the signs were ominous. The old jealous rivals, Francis I and the Emperor, were drawing closer together and Henry, in consequence, sought for ways to increase his sense of security. Cromwell looked for allies among the Protestants of Germany and in May an important mission came from the Lutheran Elector of Saxony. It stayed till the autumn. For the greater protection of his own person the King considered a plan for tightening-up the loose discipline of the Yeomen of the Guard and, although this seems to have come to nothing, it is clear that Henry was in some amount of anxiety. He also began looking with suspicion on those religious conservatives in England whose leaders were his kinsmen and represented the White Rose, and who were actually at Court. Moreover, the Poles, in particular, had a relative abroad, the detested cardinal, who was in close touch with the Pope and with representatives of the Emperor. Henry may not have known what was seething in the Poles' minds, but Cromwell was conveniently at hand to suggest means of discovering it, and in August the King struck. He arrested Sir Geoffrey Pole, Margaret Pole's youngest son, and sent him to the Tower.

In arresting Geoffrey Pole the Government were shrewd. Of all the Pole family he was the one member of it who was most voluble and indiscreet in speech, and he was also unstable in character. Perhaps Cromwell did not find it difficult to be convinced that he would betray secrets if he were exhaustively examined. For years Geoffrey seems to have been indulging in dangerous talk with the Imperial ambassador, who may have become rather weary of his importunities. As long ago as November 1534 Chapuys had told the Emperor that Geoffrey Pole would visit him every day had he not pointed out how perilous that would be. He was always telling Chapuys of the ease with which England could be conquered and how people were only waiting for the signal in order to assist the conquest. Long before his arrest Cromwell probably knew more about Geoffrey's intrigues than has ever come to light, and he must have had sufficiently good ground for committing him to the Tower, though what precisely it was seems to have remained a secret.

After two months of detention Geoffrey Pole underwent a severe examination and, almost certainly under threat of torture, he made admissions which betrayed his brother, Lord Montague, and the Marquis of Exeter. There were more long examinations and a further spate of betrayals. A considerable body of evidence relating almost entirely to talk that was to be construed as treasonable was collected, but there were no treasonable acts or conspiracies. The disclosures seem to have been sufficient for the government's purpose.

Other people in close touch with the Poles were examined and much use was made of their statements. It was alleged that Lord Montague had favoured Cardinal Pole and "confirmed" him in his traitorous proceedings—the man who had refused to return to this country at the King's request, who had acknowledged the papal supremacy and written trenchantly in favour of it. Montague had wished to be abroad with the cardinal. It was said that there would be civil war in England and that when it occurred "we shall lack nothing so much as honest men". The King would one day die and then "we shall have jolly stirring". If my Lord of Burgavenny, Montague's father-in-law and a great Nevill, were alive "he were able to make a great number of men in Kent and Sussex". Cardinal Wolsey would have been an honest man if he had had an honest master, a remark which would not have been lost upon the King. Montague had lamented the fall of the abbeys and hoped to see them set up again. He had praised the Marquis of Exeter as a man of good mind and courage. There was frequent communication between the two and "a big fellow in a tawny coat had come to the marquis, though it was not known on what errand". There had been a suspicious burning of letters at Sir Geoffrey Pole's place in Sussex and it was believed that Lord Montague was privy to it.

Exeter had said much the same kind of thing, but Geoffrey Pole's talk had been at once more explicit and more serious. He, too, liked not the proceedings in the realm and wanted a change. He wished to be abroad with his brother, the cardinal, "if he will have me", in order "to show him the world in England waxeth all crooked". God's law was turned upside down, abbeys and churches were overthrown, and they will "cast down parish churches and all at the last". It was alleged that he had corresponded both with his brother Reginald and with Hugh

Holland, a Hampshire yeoman and "an abominable traitor", who was intending to pass to Rome and who was suspected of conveying letters abroad. Geoffrey is said to have told Holland to let the cardinal know that men were sent daily from England to destroy him and that much money would be paid for his head.

The government were not slow in taking action. Montague and Exeter were brought to trial and found guilty, the indictments against them being based on the specific talk which had come to light. They were beheaded with Sir Edward Neville, who had also been brought to trial, on Tower Hill on 9 December 1538. There were others, including Hugh Holland, who were tried and convicted, and they suffered the terrible normal penalty for treason. Geoffrey Pole eventually received a royal pardon for having turned King's evidence. But because he had betrayed his kinsmen he had no peace of mind, and, full of remorse, he tried, while in the Tower, to take his life. He afterwards wandered, distraught in mind, from place to place on the Continent, seeming a mere ghost of a man. In the end he obtained, through the agency of his brother, the cardinal, the Pope's absolution.

Montague left a small boy, his heir, who had with his father been taken into custody. He was never heard of again.

The Marchioness of Exeter, held for some time in the Tower, later received the King's pardon. When Princess Mary ascended the throne, this old friend of her mother and herself became one of her ladies-in-waiting. Her small son, Edward, had also been imprisoned in the Tower, but he was excepted from the King's general pardon and remained a prisoner till the accession of Mary, when he was released and taken into favour.

But it was the destruction of the Poles that mattered to the government. "Blessed be God of England", wrote Latimer about it to Cromwell, "that worketh all, whose instrument you be."

IV

During all this time Margaret Pole did not escape attention from the government. She underwent long and sometimes brutal examinations at her seat at Warblington. Fitzwilliam, lately created Earl of Southampton, and the Bishop of Ely "travailed" with her on 13 November 1538 from morning till almost night-fall, but for all that they could do, "though we used her diversely", she protested her innocence to the end. Either, they said, her sons had not made her privy to their talk, or "else she is the most errant traitress that ever lived". She did, indeed, admit that both Montague and Geoffrey had told her the cardinal had escaped assassination, "and for motherly pity she could not but rejoice". One important statement she made was favourable to the King. When, in 1536, Reginald Pole's writing against Henry had been received, Lord Montague had counselled her to denounce the cardinal to her servants. She called them together and told them "she took her son to be a traitor and for no son, and that she would never take him otherwise".

Having failed entirely to obtain any useful information at Warblington, Fitzwilliam removed her to Cowdray in Sussex, an ancient estate which at one time belonged to the great de Bohun family and which the Earl had acquired ten years previously. Margaret Pole must have known it well. It had an exquisite chapel with an altar-piece of rare beauty, and the parlour had been decorated by Holbein or some of his pupils. But she was not sent to Cowdray to admire its beauties or to enjoy any expansive hospitality from the Fitzwilliams. The gruelling examination begun at Warblington continued. Margaret Pole, Plantagenet with a strong Plantagenet's qualities, was, however, proving to be extremely tough. "We assure your lordship", wrote Fitzwilliam and the Bishop of Ely to Cromwell, "we have dealt with such a one as men have not dealt withal to fore us [before]; we may call her rather a strong and constant man than a woman". In whatever way the two inquisitors examined the Countess, gently or harshly, "she hath showed herself so earnest, vehement and precise that we thought it a waste of time to press her further". In her courage and constancy we are reminded of the attitude of her great friend, Catherine the Queen, at similar times of crisis.

Although nothing useful to the government could be extracted from Margaret Pole at Cowdray, Warblington had meanwhile

RX

been ransacked and two items considered to be of interest were found there. But this evidence was not actually incriminating. Some Bulls "granted by a Bishop of Rome" were discovered in a chamber and a copy of a letter to Lord Montague was found in a chest of one of her gentlewomen. The Bulls were undated and had probably lain forgotten for many years, perhaps long before any signs of the religious troubles. As for the letter, it had, said Margaret Pole, been written by her steward on her behalf after the imprisonment of Geoffrey, but before the imprisonment of Montague. She had evidently caused it to be sent while the clouds were beginning to gather over the whole family. "Son Montague", the letter said, "I send you God's blessing and mine. The greatest gift I can send is to desire God's help for you, for which I perceive there is need. My advice in the case you stand in is to endeavour to serve your prince without disobeying God's commandment."

Margaret Pole continued to be held at Cowdray, but neither Fitzwilliam nor his wife would see her. Then, one day in March 1539, Fitzwilliam visited her. His talk was coarse and offensive, but she answered him becomingly. If he is to be believed, she admitted that her son, Reginald, "were a most unhappy and an ill man to behave so unkindly and traitorously to his sovereign lord and master who had ever been so good and gracious to him". She wished he were in Heaven or that she could bring him into the King's presence. Offender as he was, she hoped His Grace would not impute his heinous offence to her. It does not seem that Margaret Pole's opinion of her son's specific acts had changed significantly since 1536. Or was she being wholly sincere?

A comprehensive Bill of Attainder which included, besides the names of those already executed, the name of Margaret Pole, was finally passed in June 1539. On the third reading of the Bill Cromwell ostentatiously exhibited in the Lords, as incriminating evidence, a coat armour of white silk which had lately been found in the Countess's coffer. On one side of the coat were, according to John Worth, the arms of England and "about the whole arms was made pansies for Pole and marigolds for my Lady Mary".

Between the marigolds and the pansies "a tree was made to rise in the midst", and from it hung a shield, on the one side of which there was purple "in token of the coat of Christ and on the other side . . . all the Passion of Christ". Worth said that "Pole [Reginald] intended to have married my Lady Mary, and betwixt them both should arise the old doctrine of Christ". Catherine of Aragon was, indeed, wont to say that she would not die happy unless she were the means of giving her daughter in marriage to one of Margaret Pole's sons.

It was also the government's intention to connect the Poles with the Pilgrimage of Grace, for the "Passion of Christ" (or the "Five Wounds of Christ") displayed on the shield had been represented on many of the banners of the Pilgrims. In itself the whole emblem was innocuous enough, for such emblems were common in pre-Reformation England; but set against the background of the Poles' offences the discovery of the coat armour was made to look plausibly treasonable and, on the surface, at any rate, it seems to have satisfied Parliament. But it is difficult to resist the view that, when he exhibited it in the Lords, Cromwell must have had his tongue in his cheek.

The Act of Attainder asserted that Margaret Pole had traitorously "confederated" herself with Lord Montague and Reginald Pole, knowing them to be traitors and common enemies of the King; she had traitorously aided, maintained and comforted them, and had committed other treasons. She was condemned to death, not, like her son Montague and the others, after trial, but solely by means of the Act of Attainder. After the Attainder was passed Margaret Pole was sent to the Tower. Some months before this event the King's commissioners had visited the exquisite Salisbury chantry at Christchurch and had "clearly deleted" her arms and badges.

She languished for two years in the grim, fortress prison. She was often in great distress and unable to find warmth in winter. Thomas Philipps, one of her gaolers, petitioned for her relief. He was daily conversant, he said, "with them that are pensive. . . . The Lady Salisbury maketh great moan [complaint] for that she wanteth necessary apparel both for to change and also to keep warm." This seems to have been made good, for payment was made to John Scutt "for certain apparel bought and made for Margaret Pole, late Countess of Salisbury, £11.16.4". It was warmth which she appears most to have needed and we find that the cost of clothing nearly approached the sum for every other necessity.

Perhaps, in these desolate days, she thought of the fate of her own near kinsfolk, once held like her within the forbidding walls of the Tower. Margaret Pole's sorrows had been more than the sorrows of most. Her own father, George, Duke of Clarence, had been lodged in this same place and then put to death for his treasonable intrigues. There had been the long imprisonment and then the judicial murder of her brother, Edward, Earl of Warwick, a year before the present century dawned. He was her only brother: she had had no sister. She had scarcely known her mother, who had died when she was very young. Her son and heir, Montague, and his cousin, the Marquis of Exeter, had died because of the accusations of her youngest son, Geoffrey, now a wandering, forlorn figure, seeking a peace which never came. Reginald the cardinal was an exile, hated by the King, and she, because of that hatred, was a remaining hostage to fortune. Catherine had died poor, completely rejected of the King, and almost forgotten. Mary, their daughter, and Margaret's old favourite charge, outwardly reconciled to her father, she, of course, now never saw. Her world and many of the great figures of it had gone. A year before her death she would have learnt that the last of the abbeys, some of which she had known well in times of fortune, had yielded to the King. In the new world she had no place. And she was very old by the measure of Tudor days. She was nearly seventy.

In April 1541 there was a conspiracy in Yorkshire, the county of lingering, strong Catholic beliefs. About fifty angry desperate men, including six or seven priests and twelve laymen of substance, had resolved to march to Pomfret Fair, to kill the President of the North, the Bishop of Llandaff, to capture the castle where he lived, and, then fortifying themselves, to raise the country against the tyranny of the King. The conspirators seem to have been encouraged by a rumour that the Scots were stirring on the Border.

But the conspiracy was betrayed to the government and the King turned fiercely on the conspirators. Sixty men were executed, including Sir John Neville of Chevet, a member of a minor branch of the great Neville connection, who had been High Sheriff of Yorkshire, and there were at least twenty-five priests among the victims, so the Imperial ambassador said. The King's brutal suppression of this conspiracy was a warning to the orthodox in religion of the fate to be expected by any overt opposition to his government. But Henry's revenge extended beyond the range of the immediate conspirators, for it sought as a victim the Countess of Salisbury, who was put to death on the old charge against her.

The execution of Margaret Pole was one of the most unreasonable and merciless acts of the whole reign. The evidence against her was of the flimsiest and she herself had protested her innocence during the course of long, exacting examinations. She had been condemned without trial. She was old and could not in the course of nature live much longer. Although she was a near kinswoman of the King, she could in no real sense threaten the security of his throne. Her death, indeed, merely helped to fulfil the threat which Henry had made a few years previously that he would exterminate all the Poles. And it is significant that, while he pardoned the Marchioness of Exeter, who was no connection of his by blood, he excepted from the general pardon not only Margaret Pole, but even the entirely innocent sons of Montague and Exeter who were mere children. It is also worthy of note that while Cromwell lived the Countess had not been put to death, notwithstanding the fact that he had been the chief instrument in securing her conviction and the conviction of others. But Cromwell had himself been executed in July 1540, so that whatever restraining influence he had possessed over the King—and he had once been able to prevent Henry from sending Princess Mary to the Tower—was now removed. Margaret Pole had the supreme misfortune to be a Plantagenet and the mother of the detested cardinal.

On 27 May 1541, which was the day after Ascension Day, she was told it was the King's wish that she should die that same day. At first she thought the matter very strange, but understanding that there was no remedy for it, she prepared herself for death. And so this valiant, stately, still handsome woman, the last in direct descent of the great line of the Plantagenets, who had been the greatest friend of a tragic Queen, left her prison chamber for the place of execution. She was to suffer by beheading.

The great river near was alive as ever with much traffic. From distant countries had come large vessels laden with spices, silks, tapestries, carpets, fruits and much else. There were barges flying gay pennants—the trim, colourful barges of the nobles and the great merchants, and there were, in contrast, numerous wherries, moving clumsily on the dark surface of the current. In the gardens outside the Tower there were trees nearly in full leaf, for it was almost at the end of May. Men in the neighbouring city were busy about their trades and the sale of their wares. Life with its struggles, its joys and tragedies, went on still. But for Margaret Pole, Countess of Salisbury, who had known joy but also much grief, it was now an end of earthly things.

She walked the short distance to the space in front of the Tower called Tower Green, where there was no scaffold ready but only a small block. When she arrived there, and after a brief interval, she commended her soul to God, as a Christian should, and asked those present to pray for the King, the Queen and the young Prince Edward. But especially she wished to be commended to Princess Mary, whose godmother she had been. Then, after a short pause, she placed her head on the low block, and by a raw novice, acting for the customary executioner, very unskilfully and brutally the fine head was severed.

Authorities

Chapter 1. The description by the Italian visitor is in *A Relation of England* (Camden Society, 1870). Leland's *Collectanea* (1770), 5, describes Henry VII's consultation with his council and Catherine's meeting with Prince Arthur. B. M. Arundel Manuscripts, 249, and R. W. Chambers, *More* (1938), p. 81, contain Thomas More's description of Catherine and her suite. Henry VII's decision about the non-separation of the Prince and Princess is dealt with in the Calendar of State Papers, Spanish, Supplement I, No. 1. C. A. J. Skeel's *The Council of the Marches of Wales* (1904) is the authoritative work on the Welsh Marches, and T. Wright's *Ludlow Castle* (1862) gives the history of Ludlow. There is a short life of "Father Rhys" in the Dict. of National Biog. and the contemporary description of Prince Arthur's burial is in Leland.

Chapter 2. Catherine's lack of English at this time is referred to in M. A. E. Wood, *Letters of Royal Ladies*, I, p. 138, and Span. Cal., I, 459. The requirement to obey Doña Elvira is mentioned in Span. Cal., I, 394. Catherine's relations with the Spanish ambassador and the Spanish members of her household form the subject of letters in the Span. Cal., I, *passim* (together with Spanish transcripts in the Public Record Office), of Wood, *Letters*, I, and especially of the Spanish work, *Correspondencia de Gomez de Fuensalida* (Madrid, 1907), Introduction. The important question of the surviving virginity of Catherine is mentioned in the Span. Cal., I, 364 (and Spanish transcript).

Chapter 3. "Grave and gentle" is the term used by H. A. L. Fisher, *History of Europe* (1936), p. 509; the other description is by the Venetian ambassador, Venetian Cal., 4, 682. Catherine's summoning of her council is mentioned in Letters and Papers, Henry VIII, 2, p. 256. The visit to Eltham is the subject of one of Erasmus's letters—see F. M. Nichols, *Epistles of Erasmus*, I, p. 457— whilst the description of the Archduke's and Joanna's visit is based on Cotton Manuscripts, Vesp. C. XII, p. 282. The authorities for *Evil May Day* are Hall's *Chronicle* (edition, C. Whibley), p. 155, the Venet. Cal., 2, Stow, *Annales* (1605) and Thomas More, *Works* (1557). See also Fisher, *History*, p. 215 *et seq.* Hall, the inveterate eulogist of the King, does not mention the part played by Catherine. Giustinian's *Despatches*, I, p. 79, and II, p. 225, refer to the Court entertainments.

Chapter 4. Reginald Pole's references to his mother are in the Venet. Cal., 5. Camden in his *Britannia* (1606), p. 200, describes Warblington manor and the Victoria County History (Hampshire), 3, p. 134, the castle ruins. The statement about the survival of aristocratic principles is based on Dr A. R. Myres' erudite *The Household of Edward IV* (1956). The favourable characterization of Margaret

253

Pole is in Letters and Papers, Henry VIII, 3(1), 1204. For the councils, see A. P. Newton, *Reforms in the Household*, p. 238, and A. F. Pollard, *Wolsey. Archaeologia*, XXV, p. 311, contains a good description of Thornbury. The instructions to Margaret Pole for the governance of Mary are in Cotton Vit. C. i, f. 7. For Luis Vives see his *Opera* I (Basle, 1558) and Foster Watson, *Luis Vives* (1922). Catherine's letter to Mary is printed by Ellis, *Original Letters*, First Series, p. 19, and the visits to Worcester are mentioned in the Prior's Journal (ed. E. S. Fegan, 1914).

Chapter 5. A. F. G. Bell, *Luis de León* (1925) gives an account of the progress of humanism in Spain. The association of Vives with both Henry and Catherine is dealt with in his own work, *The City of God* (translation, 1610) and by Henry de Vocht in *Monumenta Humanistica Lovaniensia* (Louvain 1934), p. 10. For Vives' humanistic thought, see Foster Watson, *Vives and the Renaissance Education of Women* (1912), p. 141 and the same writer's *The Spanish Element in Luis Vives* (1913), p. 37. The sketch of More and his household is based on the lives of More by Stapleton, Harpsfield and Roper. I have relied for the description of Syon on G. J. Aungier, *The History and Antiquities of Syon* (1840) and Professor M. D. Knowles, *The Religious Orders in England*, Vols. 2 and 3. The talks which Vives had with Catherine are mentioned in his *Opera Omnia* (1782-1790), vol. 4, p. 40, and 7, p. 208. For the visit to England of Ignatius Loyola, see *Archivum Historicum Societatis Jesu*, Vol. 25 (1956), p. 328. Some of Whytford's devotional works have been considered in H. C. White's *Tudor Books of Private Devotion*, p. 157, etc., and there is a good edition (with full introduction) of *The Imitation of Christ* (1941) by E. J. Klein. The extract from *The Imitation* is from Dom Roger Huddleston's edition (1925). There is in the British Museum a rare copy of *The Pipe or Tun of the Life of Perfection*, on the covers of which have been impressed the arms of Henry and Catherine.

Chapter 6. For the allegation against Catherine, see Span. Cal., 3(2), 586. Henry's egocentricity is emphasized in *Henry VIII, An Essay in Revision* (1962) by Dr G. R. Elton, which is a modern re-appraisal of the King's character. More's statement of the chief cause of his condemnation is in Stapleton's *More*, p. 196. The journey of Francisco Phelippes is mentioned in Ellis, *Original Letters*, First Series, I, p. 276 and in L. & P., 4(2), 3278 and 5, p. 306. For Thomas Abell, see B.M. Add. Manuscripts 28578, f. 6. The Spanish transcript makes Catherine's initial distrust of her chaplain quite clear. Cotton MS Vesp. C. iv, 299, 305, describes the events in Spain. Robert Shorton's career is taken from Venn, *Alumni Cantab.* 4; T. Baker, *Fisher's Funeral Sermon for Margaret Beaufort* (1708); T. E. Bridgett, *Fisher* (1885); R. Fiddes, *Collections*, pp. 213-215, which describe Wolsey's approach to Shorton; Pocock, *Records of the Reformation*, II, p. 609; and the Dict. of Nat. Biog. For Catherine's charitable work, see William Forrest, *The History of Grisild the Second* (1875), p. 46. Wolsey's tribute is in L. & P., 4(2), 4897.

Chapter 7. There are documentary details about Robert Ridley in Jasper G.

Ridley's *Nicholas Ridley* (1957) and *Thomas Cranmer* (1962). Cranmer in Germany is described in the second of the foregoing works and in Letters and Papers, 9, 449. Wolsey's visit to Warham is the subject of State Papers, I, p. 196. The Archbishop's change of attitude is referred to in Venetian Cal., 4, 754, Letters and Papers, 3(2), 1223, and P. Hughes, *Reformation*, I, p. 240. For Bishop Clerk, see the Venetian Cal., 4, and Letters and Papers, 4(3), 5865. The question of Flemish advocates for Catherine is mentioned in Span. Cal., 4(i), 16, and L. & P., 4(3), 568, whilst the attitude of Vives is dealt with in F. Watson's *Luis Vives*, Vives' *Opera*, and Wood, *Letters*, 2. The account of the appearance of Catherine at the Legatine Court is based on Cavendish's *Life of Cardinal Wolsey* (ed. S. W. Singer, 1825), Vol. I, p. 146: see also the latest edition of this work, E.E.T.S., 1963. Fisher's and Ridley's views are in Cavendish, whilst L. & P., 4(3), 5774, calendars a good number of the "depositions".

Chapter 8. Wolsey's fall is described in Pollard's *Wolsey*. The protest of the clergy was found in the State Archives at Vienna—see Friedmann, *Anne Boleyn*, I, 142 and Bridgett, *Fisher*, 210. Elton, *England under the Tudors* (1955) deals with the Reformation *vis-à-vis* the Divorce. The episode of Henry and Anne Boleyn is mentioned in Span. Cal., 4(2), 224, and the visit of the lords to Catherine is the subject of L. & P., 5, 287. Cromwell's expression of esteem is in L. & P., 6, 805. For the reduction of Catherine's household and the proffering of the oath, see L. & P., 6, 1571 and Span. Cal., 5, pp. 154, 169, S.P., 1, 419.

Chapter 9. M. A. E. Wood, *Lives of the Princesses*, 5, Appendix 2 (2), prints in full the papal bull obtained by Mary. For Mary's attitude to the divorce, see *Chronicle of Butley Priory* (ed. A. G. Dickens, 1951), pp. 54, 55, P.R.O. S.P. 1/47, 223, and Venet. Cal., 4, 332, *et alia*. The "mission" of Suffolk to Catherine forms the subject of much of L. & P., 6, 1558. Catherine's letter to Mary is in Arundel Manuscripts 151, f. 195 (B. Mus.).

Chapter 10. For the regular observance of the Rule by the three orders mentioned, see Hughes, *Reformation*, I, p. 66. There is a good description of the Greenwich friary by Alphonsus Bonnar, O.F.M., in Cath. Rec. Society, vol. 39, Appendix 9. For the various activities of the Greenwich Observants see L. & P., 5 & 6, *passim*, and Ellis, *Original Letters*, second series. As regards the deaths of the thirty-one friars, see L. & P., 7(2), 6073, and Knowles, *Religious Orders*, III, p. 210.

Chapter 11. Thomas Abell's appearance before the council is described in Span. Cal., 4(i), 396. Chapuys in his letter says it was "a chaplain of hers (Catherine's)". There can be no doubt that this was Abell. Abell's book was published in 1531, with a fictitious date and place. There is a rare copy in the B.M. For the motion of Temses, see Harpsfield, *Pretended Divorce*, p. 197, where Abell and Temses are both mentioned. The relation of the activities of Ortiz is in Span. Cal., 4(2), 984, and L. & P., 5, 1242. The vivid characterization of Bedyll is by Professor Knowles, *Religious Orders*, III, p. 284.

Chapter 12. The preaching in Bristol is mentioned in S. Seyer's *Memoirs of Bristol*, p. 215. For the visits of Latimer, Hubberden and Powell to Bristol, see L. & P., 6, 247, and A. G. Chester, *Hugh Latimer* (1954). Powell's defence of orthodox religion (the *Propugnaculum*) is mentioned in L. & P., 3, 2652, and in Anthony à Wood's *Athenae*, I, 117. The sermon before Bishop Smith on the text from Genesis 37, 14, is noted in Churton's *Lives of Bishop Smith and Sir R. Sutton* (1800), p. 118. For Powell's "seditious" sermon see SP6/3, f. iii (P.R.O.) and for Hilsey, see L. & P., 6, 433 (iii) and 596. The enquiry at Bristol is the subject of SP1/75, f. 228 (P.R.O.).

Chapter 13. For the Nun's chief prophecies, see L. & P., 6, 1419, and Bridgett, *Fisher*. More's association with her is referred to in Burnet-Pocock, *Reformation* (1865), 5, p. 431, and Fisher's is explained in L. & P., 7(1), 239, 240. For Cromwell's praise of Catherine, see L. & P., 6, 1445. "Proto-martyrs of the Catholic cause" is the description by H. A. L. Fisher, *History*, p. 334.

Chapter 14. The pressure on Fisher is mentioned in L. & P., 5, 62 and Span. Cal., 4(2), 615. His offer of services to the Emperor is stated in L. & P., 5, 707, and Span. Cal., 4(2), 883. For Chapuys' idea of invasion, see L. & P., 6, 1164, and Span. Cal., 4(2), 1058, and for Fisher's view, L. & P., 6, 1249. The bishop's letter to Cromwell is in L. & P., 7, 1563. For Fisher's last hours, see Bridgett's *Fisher* (p. 392), P. Hughes, *Earliest Life of Fisher* (1935) and E. E. Reynolds, *St. John Fisher* (1955), which prints many extracts from contemporary documents.

Chapter 15. More, *Works* (1557), p. 1425, describes the Chancellor's meeting with the King in 1527. For More's activity on behalf of the Queen, see Span. Cal., 4(2), 646. His departure from Chelsea is described in Stapleton's *More* and Roper's *Life*. For the Chancellor's answers to the charges against him, see Stapleton, p. 189. More's clear declaration of faith is in Stapleton, p. 27. The scene of the last hours is drawn from Stapleton's work. The words of Erasmus, which can be regarded as an eloquent epitaph on More, are given in Chambers' *More*, p. 73, citing *Ecclesiastes* (Basle, 1535).

Chapter 16. The chief sources for the account of Catherine's life at Kimbolton are L. & P., Vols. 8, 9 and 10 *passim*, and Span. Cal., Vol. 5, parts 1 and 2. These reveal the persistent activity of Chapuys on her behalf. Photostats of the two original Spanish letters (both dated 10th October) which Catherine wrote in October 1535 have been obtained from Staatsarchiv., Vienna. That to Paul III is calendared in Span. Cal., 5(1), 211, with curious inaccuracy, but the summary in L. & P., 9, 588, is fairly accurate. For Catherine's last bequests see L. & P., 10, 40, and Strype, *Memorials*, 1(1), 372. The terms of the last letter to Henry are in *Pretended Divorce* and Herbert, *Henry VIII*, p. 554. For the history of Atheca shortly before he left for Spain, see L. & P., 10, 429. Cal. Span., 5(2), 17, and SP1/101, ff. 33-4 (P.R.O.).

Chapter 17. Forest's actual correspondence with Abell and Catherine does not survive, but there is an account of it in Bourchier's *Historia Ecclesiastica*

(1582). The sense of it is reliable, but the actual details are questionable. Thomas Bourchier, an Observant friar who returned to Greenwich in Mary's reign, obtained his information from Forest's contemporaries. For a critical assessment and a translation see Morris and Pollen in *Lives of the English Martyrs* (1914). Hall's *Chronicle* 2 (Whibley), p. 280, Wriothesley, *Chronicle* 1, p. 78, and Latimer's *Works*, II (Parker Society, 1845), p. 391, are the chief authorities for the events preceding the execution and the execution itself.

Chapter 18. For Powell, see L. & P., 7(1), 27, and 1026(7), SP1/82, p. 445, and L. & P., 8, 534; for Fetherston, L. & P., 7, 530, and Appendix 21; Ellis, Original Letters, First Series, 2. The requirement to take the oath is mentioned in L. & P., 8, 666. Abell's letter to Cromwell is in SP1/116 (P.R.O.). The episode of Richard Farmer is mentioned in Stow, *Annales* (1631), p. 580. For the attainder of the three priests, see Parl. Roll, 32, Henry VIII, c. 57 (P.R.O.), and for the execution, Harpsfield, *Pretended Divorce*, p. 208.

Chapter 19. There is abundant material about the Poles in Letters and Papers, Henry VIII, vols. 10, 11, 12 and 13 (2), *passim*. The reconciliation of Mary to her father is dealt with in L. & P., 10, 1212, *et alia*, L. & P., 11, No. 7, page 7, and Span. Cal., 5(2), pp. 137-139 and 195. For Reginald Pole the main authorities are L. & P., 4(3), 6252, 8(1), 218, 801 and 12(1), 444. The criticism of Pole's work is by Gasquet, *Henry VIII and the English Monasteries* (1899), p. 178. For Margaret Pole's and her son Montague's letters to Reginald about his book, see L. & P., 11, 157 and 169. Reginald Pole's distress on receiving the correspondence from his kinsfolk is expressed in a letter to Contarini (see L. & P., 11, 654). The letters alleged to have been written by Montague and his mother about the cardinalate are referred to in L. & P., 13(2), 822. For the examination of the Poles and Exeters, their associates and servants, see L. & P., 13(2) *passim*. The interrogations of Margaret Pole form the subject of a letter in Ellis, 2, Series, ii, p. 110, and of material in L. & P., 3(2), 818, and Cotton MS. Cleopatra E. iv, f. 209, L. & P., 14(1), 980, Pye, *Life of Cardinal Pole* (1766), p. 10, and Lords' Journals, I, p. 107, refer to the evidence produced against her. Her execution is briefly described in L. & P., 16, 897, and Span. Cal., 6, 166.

(The short life of Margaret Pole in the Dict. Nat. Biog. is inaccurate in some respects.)

ADDITIONAL NOTE

John Forest, Thomas Abell, Edward Powell, Richard Fetherston and Margaret Pole have been equivalently beatified.

Index